དེང་དུས་བོད་ཀྱི་སྐད་ཡིག

Modern Tibetan Language

Volume I

by

LOSANG THONDEN

LIBRARY OF TIBETAN WORKS & ARCHIVES

First Edition 1980
Second Revised Edition 1984
Reprint: 1991, 1993, 1999, 2001, 2003, 2004
Third Edition 2005
Reprint: 2009, 2010

ISBN: 81-86470-39-5

Published by the Library of Tibetan Works and Archives, Dharamsala, H.P., (India) and printed at Indraprastha Press (CBT), 4 Bahadur Shah Zafar Marg, New Delhi-110002.

Publisher's Note

The Library of Tibetan Works and Archives, founded by His Holliness the Dalai Lama to preserve and foster the growth of the Tibetan language and culture, is proud to publish the present work, *Modern Tibetan Language* by Losang Thonden, Language Research Scholar at the Library.

Six long years of research, backed by strenuous study and discussion with numerous native and foreign language scholars have gone into the production of this work whose depth, intensity and rationality in the presentation of the learning process of the Tibetan language has never been attempted before in any other published textbook.

A comprehensive and up-to-date textbook for teaching of Tibetan through the medium of English, *Modern Tibetan Language* has also been based on experiences gained by Mr. Thonden in his years of teaching Tibetan to the many Indian and foreign students in the Library's Language Courses.

The demand for this book was so great that we had to reprint this revised edition before the second volume of this book could be published.

Gyatsho Tshering
Director
October, 1983

Addendum to the Publisher's Note

This *Modern Tibetan Language* has served as a very useful tool for the students of Tibetan language and has been reprinted eight times since its first publication in 1980.

This third revised edition is composed on computer typesetting and errors in language and typography corrections are incorporated.

Publication Department
LTWA
January, 2006

Author's Note: Second (Revised) Edition

The Primary objective of the "Modern Tibetan Language" textbook is to furher the steadily increasing interest of foreigners in Tibetan culture. It is, however, also intended to assist those Tibetans who do not have access to a first-hand study of their language.

Since Tibetan Buddhism is best learnt through the medium of the Tibetan language, the Library of Tibetan Works and Archives, a center for Tibetan culture, provides language classes. While teaching at the Library I have come to identify some comon problems of non-Tibetan speaking people. I have considered these in my book and have also tried to assimilate other scholars' useful suggestions as well as the opinions of many students.

I have concentrated on the dialect of Lhasa and have followed the rules of grammar and linguistics. Certain aspects of grammar, such as verbs, nouns, and particles are dealt with in greater detail. Colloquial expressions were chosen in relation to usual grammar rules. Other features include word by word translations, phonetics, and complete sentence translations. Exercises are included for students to assess their progress and in this revised edition answers are supplied at the back of the book. Thus with the help of this book students can acquire a sound foundation of the Tibetan language.

It is my hope that this book will contribute to the pioneer work of teaching modern Tibetan language. To assist in the learning of spoken Tibetan, a tape cassette based on this book is also under preparation.

I would like to thank the many Tibetan and foreign scholars for their encouragement and praise of "Modern Tibetan Language" as well as for their invaluable suggestions to improve it. I have incorporated many of these suggestions in this revised edition and the general presentation of the book has also been improved. Special thanks are due to Mr. Gyatsho Tshering, Director of the Library of Tibetan Works and Archives, for editing the English translations. I am also grateful to all the others who extended their kind cooperation and helped me to write this book.

Losang Thonden

CONTENTS

The Phonetic symbols

ä This denotes the modified vowel a

ü " " " " " u

ö " " " " " o

ò " " " " " o

è " " " " " e

: This is placed after vowel to denote a long vowel pronunciation.

This is placed above and after a vowel or suffix letter to denote a falling tone.

_ This is placed below a consonant to denote a low tone.

— This is placed above the consonant to denote a high tone.

; This denotes the partially nasal sound of the suffix letter ན་ (n) and ང་ (ng).

' This sign when placed below a consonant denotes the partial pronunciation of any word.

. The cerebro-retroflex sounds in Tibetan are represented by a '.' below the letter.

Punctuation Marks

– Syllables are separated by a hyphen (–)

, Phrases are punctuated with a comma (,)

/ The oblique used to indicate the end of sentence or phrase.

Abbreviations

adj.	adjective	imp.	imperative
c.	complement	lit.	literary
compl.	"	neg.	negative
col.	colloquial	p.	past

demos.	demonstrative
exist.	existence
expr.	experience
fut.	future
H.	honorific
inf.	infinitive
pl.	plural
pres.	present
s.	singular
v.	verb
vr.	verbializer

1. བོད་ཡིག་ཀ་ཁའི་ངོ་སྤྲོད།

Introduction of Tibetan Alphabet

The alphabet of the Tibetan language comprises thirty consonants and four vowels. The consonants are called གསལ་བྱེད་ (sä: -ch'e:) or ཀཱ་ལི་ (ka-li). The vowels are called དབྱངས་ (ȳang) or ཨཱ་ལི་ (a-li).

1. 1. Thirty consonants with precise pronunciation

1.	ཀ་ (ka)	ཁ་ (k'a)	ག་ (k'a)	ང་ (nga)
2.	ཅ་ (cha)	ཆ་ (ch'a)	ཇ་ (ch'a)	ཉ་ (nya)
3.	ཏ་ (ta)	ཐ་ (t'a)	ད་ (t'a)	ན་ (na)
4.	པ་ (pa)	ཕ་ (p'a)	བ་ (p'a)	མ་ (ma)
5.	ཙ་ (tsa)	ཚ་ (ts'a)	ཛ་ (ts'a)	ཝ་ (wa)
6.	ཞ་ (sha)	ཟ་ (sa)	འ་ (ha)	ཡ་ (ya)
7.	ར་ (ra)	ལ་ (la)	ཤ་ (sha)	ས་ (sa)
8.	ཧ་ (ha)	ཨ་ (a)		

1. 2. བོད་ཡིག་ཀ་མད་སུམ་ཅུ་སྒྲ་དྲག་ཞན་གྱི་དབྱེ་བ།

Tibetan consonants arranged according to their pronunciation

Unaspirated high tone	Aspirated high tone	Aspirated low tone	Unaspirated low tone
ཀ་ (ka)	ཁ་ (k'a)	ག་ (k'a)	ང་ (nga)
ཅ་ (cha)	ཆ་ (ch'a)	ཇ་ (ch'a)	ཉ་ (nya)
ཏ་ (ta)	ཐ་ (t'a)	ད་ (t'a)	ན་ (na)
པ་ (pa)	ཕ་ (p'a)	བ་ (p'a)	མ་ (ma)
ཙ་ (tsa)	ཚ་ (ts'a)	ཛ་ (ts'a)	ཝ་ (wa)
	ཤ་ (sha)	ཞ་ (sha)	ཡ་ (ya)
	ས་ (sa)	ཟ་ (sa)	ར་ (ra)
	ཧ་ (ha)	འ་ (ha)	ལ་ (la)

1. 3. གསལ་བྱེད་སུམ་ཅུའི་དག་ཆ་འབྲི་ཚུལ།

Thirty consonants with transliteration

(Romanization or spelling system)

ཀ་ KA	ཁ་ KHA	ག་ GA	ང་ NGA
ཅ་ CA	ཆ་ CHA	ཇ་ JA	ཉ་ NYA
ཏ་ TA	ཐ་ THA	ད་ DA	ན་ NA
པ་ PA	ཕ་ PHA	བ་ BA	མ་ MA
ཙ་ TSA	ཚ་ TSHA	ཛ་ DZA	ཝ་ WA
ཞ་ ZHA	ཟ་ ZA	འ་ 'A	ཡ་ YA
ར་ RA	ལ་ LA	ཤ་ SHA	ས་ SA
ཧ་ HA	ཨ་ A		

1. 4. དབུ་ཅན་འབྲི་སྟངས་ཀྱི་དཔེ་རིས།

How to draw the U-chän script

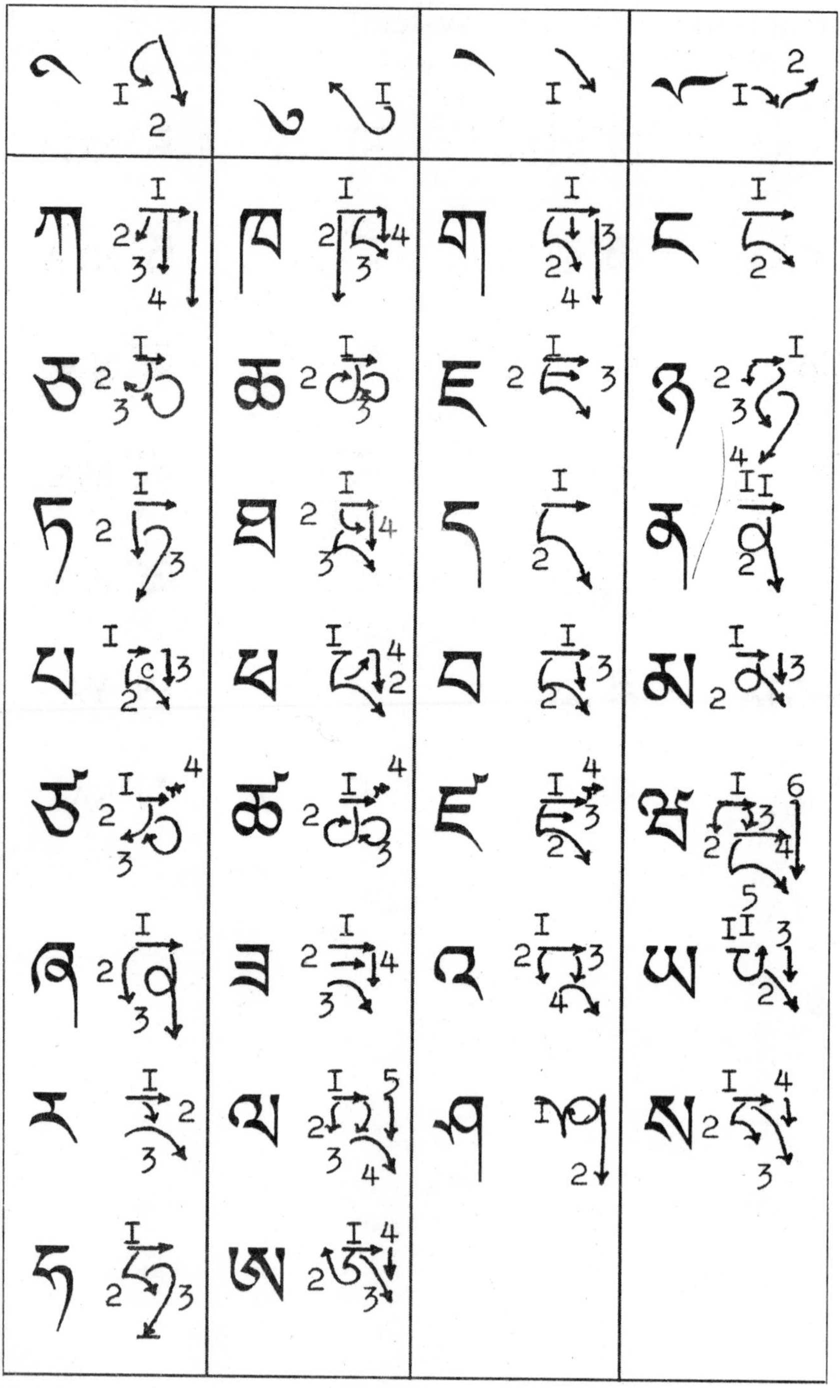

1. 5. ཀློག་སྦྱོང་། = Reading practice

ཀ་	ཙ་	ཏ་	པ་	ཙ
ཁ་	ཆ་	ཐ་	ཕ་	ཚ་
ག་	ཇ་	ད་	བ་	ཛ་
ཝ་	ཞ་	ཟ་	འ་	ཡ་
ཤ་	ས་	ང་	ཉ་	ན་
མ་	ར་	ལ་	ཧ་	ཨ་
ག་	ད་	བ་	མ་	འ་
ག་	ང་	ད་	ན་	བ་
མ་	འ་	ར་	ལ་	ས་
ད་	ས་			

1. 6. དབུ་མེད་ཀྱི་ཀ་དཔེ།

Tibetan alphabet in U-meː script

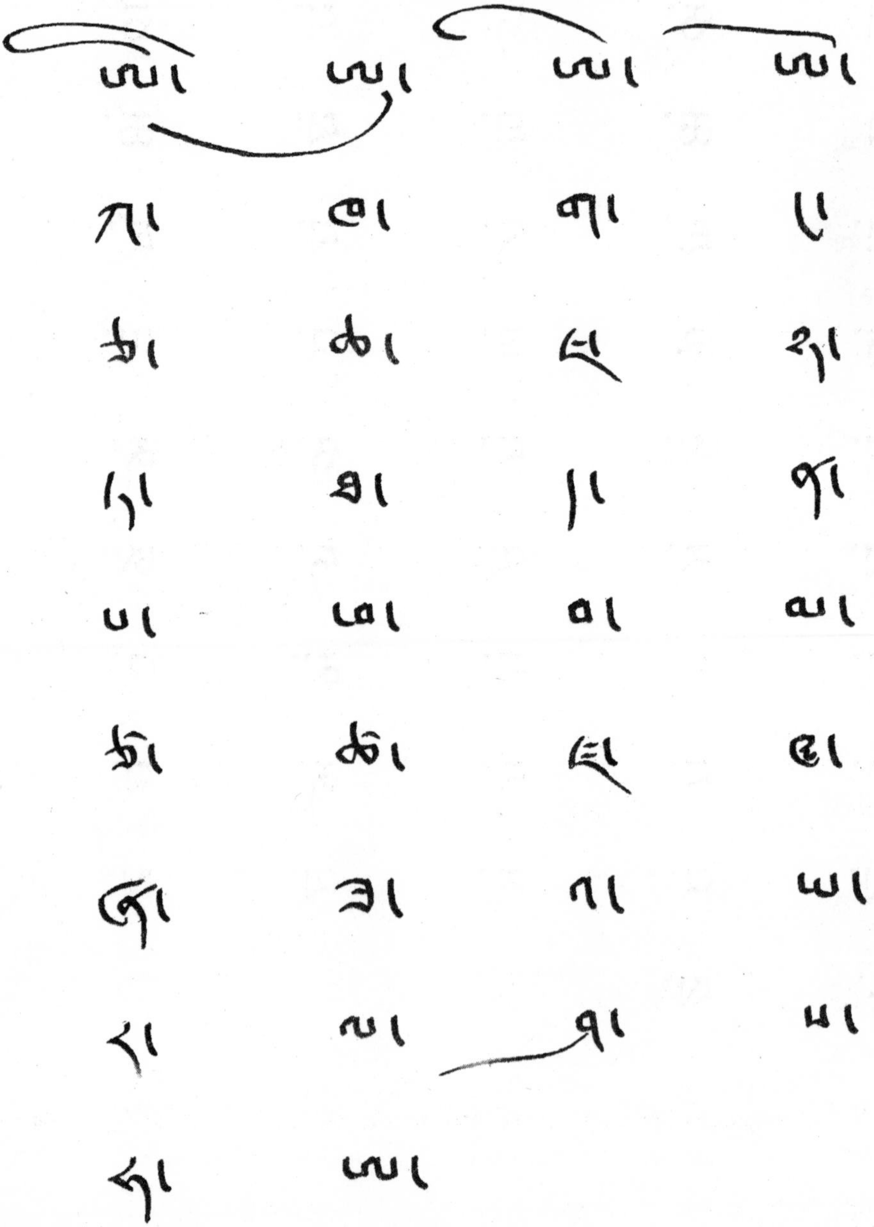

1. 7. མིང་ཚིག་འགའ་ཞིག = Vocabulary

ཀ་ཁ་	(ka-k'a)	=	alphabet
ཀ་བ་*	(ka-wa:)	=	pillar, post
ཀ་ཤ་	(ka-sha)	=	white mushroom
ཁ་བ་*	(k'a-wa:)	=	snow (lit.)
ཁ་ཡ་	(k'a-ya)	=	attention (to another)
ང་	(nga)	=	I
ང་ལ་	(nga-la)	=	to me, at me, for me
ཆ་	(ch'a)	=	a pair, a portion
ཇ་	(<u>ch</u>'a)	=	tea
ཇ་མ་	(<u>ch</u>'a-ma)	=	tea-maker
ཉ་	(nya)	=	fish
ཉ་པ་	(nya-pa)	=	fisherman
ཐ་ན་	(t'a-na)	=	even, at least
ཐ་མ་	(t'a-ma)	=	lowest, last, inferior, worst
པ་ཕ་	(pa-p'a)	=	father
ཨ་མ་	(a-ma)	=	mother
ཕ་མ་	(p'a-ma)	=	parents
བ་ར་	(<u>p</u>'a-ra)	=	cow shed
མ་མ་	(ma-ma)	=	baby sister
ན་ཚ་	(na-ts'a)	=	sickness, illness, pain
ཚྭ་	(ts'a)	=	salt
ཚ་ཁ་	(ts'a-k'a)	=	shooting practice
ཚ་ལ་	(ts'a-la)	=	welding
ཚ་བ་	(ts'a-wa:)	=	heat, fever, temperature
ཡ་	(ya)	=	one of a pair
ལ་	(la)	=	mountain pass

* When བ་ (<u>p</u>'a) is a part of a word, it is always pronounced (wa).

ཤ་	(sha)	=	meat, flesh
ས་	(sa)	=	earth, place, land
ཨ་ར་	(a:–ra)	=	moustache

2. དབྱངས་བཞི། = The four vowels:

The four vowels i, u, e, o are formed by adding 4 signs of vowels 'ི' (k'i-k'u), 'ུ' (shab-kyu), 'ེ' (ḍeng-po) and 'ོ' (na-ro) to the top or the foot of the thirtieth consonant ཨ་ (a).

2.1. དབྱངས་བཞིའི་དཔེ་མཚོན། = Examples of vowels:

ཨི་ ཨུ་ ཨེ་ ཨོ་

How to spell the vowels

ཨ	:	A	k'i-k'u	=	I	:	ཨི་
ཨ	:	A	shab-kyu	=	U	:	ཨུ་
ཨ	:	A	ḍeng-po	=	E	:	ཨེ་
ཨ	:	A	na-ro	=	O	:	ཨོ་

The unwritten vowel ཨ་ (a) is inherent in all the 29 consonants. It is not considered as a distinct vowel which could be joined with the 29 consonants for forming a syllable or word because it already exists in them. Without ཨ་ (a) it is said the consonants would be སྲོག་མེད་ lifeless.

2.2. གསལ་བྱེད་ལ་དབྱངས་སྦྱར་ཏེ་སྦྱོར་ཀློག་བྱ་ཚུལ།

Method of spelling consonants in conjunction with vowels

ཀ	:	ka	k'i-k'u	=	ki	:	ཀི་
ཀ	:	ka	shab-kyu	=	ku	:	ཀུ་

ཀ	:	ka	ḍeng-po	=	ke	:	ཀེ་
ཀ	:	ka	na-ro	=	ko	:	ཀོ་
ཁ	:	k'a	k̲'i-k̲'u	=	k'i	:	ཁི་
ཁ	:	k'a	s̲h̲ab-kyu	=	k'u	:	ཁུ་
ཁ	:	k'a	ḍeng-po	=	k'e	:	ཁེ་
ཁ	:	k'a	na-ro	=	k'o	:	ཁོ་
ག	:	k̲'a	k̲'i-k̲'u	=	k̲'i	:	གི་
ག	:	k̲'a	s̲h̲ab-kyu	=	k̲'u	:	གུ་
ག	:	k̲'a	ḍeng-po	=	k̲'e	:	གེ་
ག	:	k̲'a	na-ro	=	k̲'o	:	གོ་
ང	:	nga	k̲'i-k̲'u	=	ngi	:	ངི་
ང	:	nga	s̲h̲ab-kyu	=	ngu	:	ངུ་
ང	:	nga	ḍeng-po	=	nge	:	ངེ་
ང	:	nga	na-ro	=	ngo	:	ངོ་

2.3. གསལ་བྱེད་སུམ་ཅུ་ལ་དབྱངས་བཞི་སྦྱར་བ།

The four vowels joined with thirty consonants

ཀི་ (ki)	ཀུ་ (ku)	ཀེ་ (ke)	ཀོ་ (ko)
ཁི་ (k'i)	ཁུ་ (k'u)	ཁེ་ (k'e)	ཁོ་ (k'o)
གི་ (k̲'i)	གུ་ (k̲'u)	གེ་ (k̲'e)	གོ་ (k̲'o)
ངི་ (ngi)	ངུ་ (ngu)	ངེ་ (nge)	ངོ་ (ngo)
ཅི་ (chi)	ཅུ་ (chu)	ཅེ་ (che)	ཅོ་ (cho)
ཆི་ (ch'i)	ཆུ་ (ch'u)	ཆེ་ (ch'e)	ཆོ་ (ch'o)
ཇི་ (c̲h̲'i)	ཇུ་ (c̲h̲'u)	ཇེ་ (c̲h̲'e)	ཇོ་ (c̲h̲'o)

ཉི་	(nyi)	ཉུ་	(nyu)	ཉེ་	(nye)	ཉོ་	(nyo)
ཏི་	(ti)	ཏུ་	(tu)	ཏེ་	(te)	ཏོ་	(to)
ཐི་	(t'i)	ཐུ་	(t'u)	ཐེ་	(t'e)	ཐོ་	(t'o)
དི་	(t̲'i)	དུ་	(t̲'u)	དེ་	(t̲'e)	དོ་	(t̲'o)
ནི་	(ni)	ནུ་	(nu)	ནེ་	(ne)	ནོ་	(no)
པི་	(pi)	པུ་	(pu)	པེ་	(pe)	པོ་	(po)
ཕི་	(p'i)	ཕུ་	(p'u)	ཕེ་	(p'e)	ཕོ་	(p'o)
བི་	(p̲'i)	བུ་	(p̲'u)	བེ་	(p̲'e)	བོ་	(p̲'o)
མི་	(mi)	མུ་	(mu)	མེ་	(me)	མོ་	(mo)
ཙི་	(tsi)	ཙུ་	(tsu)	ཙེ་	(tse)	ཙོ་	(tso)
ཚི་	(ts'i)	ཚུ་	(ts'u)	ཚེ་	(ts'e)	ཚོ་	(ts'o)
ཛི་	(t̲s̲'i)	ཛུ་	(t̲s̲'u)	ཛེ་	(t̲s̲'e)	ཛོ་	(t̲s̲'o)
ཝི་	(wi)	ཝུ་	(wu)	ཝེ་	(we)	ཝོ་	(wo)
ཞི་	(s̲h̲i)	ཞུ་	(s̲h̲u)	ཞེ་	(s̲h̲e)	ཞོ་	(s̲h̲o)
ཟི་	(s̲i)	ཟུ་	(s̲u)	ཟེ་	(s̲e)	ཟོ་	(s̲o)
འི་	(h̲i)	འུ་	(h̲u)	འེ་	(h̲e)	འོ་	(h̲o)
ཡི་	(yi)	ཡུ་	(yu)	ཡེ་	(ye)	ཡོ་	(yo)
རི་	(ri)	རུ་	(ru)	རེ་	(re)	རོ་	(ro)
ལི་	(li)	ལུ་	(lu)	ལེ་	(le)	ལོ་	(lo)
ཤི་	(shi)	ཤུ་	(shu)	ཤེ་	(she)	ཤོ་	(sho)
སི་	(si)	སུ་	(su)	སེ་	(se)	སོ་	(so)
ཧི་	(hi)	ཧུ་	(hu)	ཧེ་	(he)	ཧོ་	(ho)
ཨི་	(i)	ཨུ་	(u)	ཨེ་	(e)	ཨོ་	(o)

3. བོད་སྐད་ཀྱི་སྒྲ་གདངས་བརྗོད་ཚུལ་དབྱངས་ཡིག་གི་རེའུ་མིག
The Precise Pronunciation Chart of the Vowels

Short level	Short falling	Long level	Long falling
a	a`	a:	a:`
i	i`	i:	i:`
u	u`	u:	u:`
e	e`	e:	e:`
o	o`	o:	o:`
ò	ò`	ò:	ò:`
è	è`	è:	è:`
ä	ä`	ä:	ä:`
ü	ü`	ü:	ü:`
ö	ö`	ö:	ö:`

3.1. སྒྲ་གདངས་ཀྱི་དཔེ་མཚོན་ཁག
Examples of the phonetic system

(a) Short-level phonetic symbols

Symbols	Tibetan	Phonetic	As in English	Meaning
a	ཨ་མ་	(a-ma)	<u>a</u>rt	mother
i	རི་	(ri)	r<u>e</u>act	mountain

u	དབུ་མ་	(u-ma)	rune	middle
e	མེ་	(me)	maiden	fire
o	མཚོ་	(ts'o)	morality	sea
ò	རོགས་པ་	(ròg-pa)	object	helper
è	ཨ་ཁུ་	(è-k'u)	alone	uncle
ä	གད་མོ་	(k'ä-mo)	telephone	laughter
ü	གུས་པ་	(kü-pa)	as in German ü	I (lit.)
ö	མོས་པ་	(mö-pa)	" " " ö	desire

(b) Short-falling phonetic symbols

Symbols	Tibetan	Phonetic	As in English	Meaning
a`	ཟངས་	(sang`)	sung	copper
i`	བཅིངས་	(ching`)	thing	to bind
u`	བཤུམས་	(shum`)	krumm (German)	to cry (H.)
e`	ཐེངས་	(t'eng)	menge (German)	times
o	འཐོམས་	(t'om)	aplomb	to confuse
ò	ཀྲོག་ཀྲོག་	(tòg-tò:)	?	show-off
è	(It does not exist in Tibetan)			
ä`	སྐད་	(kä`)	?	language, noise
ü`	དབུས་	(ü`)	?	centre, central
ö`	སྤོས་	(pö`)	?	incense

(c) Long-level phonetic symbols

Symbols	Tibetan	Phonetic	As in English	Meaning
a:	ཡར་	(ya:)	yard	up, in
i:	མིའི་	(mi:)	tea	of human

u:	གུར་	(<u>k</u>'u:)	s<u>oo</u>n	tent
e:	མེའི་	(me:)	gay	of fire
o:	རོབ་རོབ་	(r<u>o</u>b-rò:̀)	r<u>o</u>bber	rough, briefly
ò:	ནོར་	(nò:)	n<u>o</u>rmal	wealth
è:		(It does not exist in Tibetan)		
ä:	ངའི་	(ngä:)	<u>ai</u>r	my, mine
ü:	དབུའི་	(ü:)	süß (German)	of head
ö:	ཡོལ་	(yö:)	öse (German)	to pass (for time)

(d) Long-falling phonetic symbols

Symbols	Tibetan	Phonetic	As in English	Meaning
a:̀	ལགས་	(la:̀)	?	a honorific form
i:̀	མིས་	(mi:̀)	?	by human
u:̀	དབུགས་	(u:̀)	?	breathing
e:̀	ཕེབས་	(p'e:̀)	?	to come (H.)
o:̀	ཕོགས་	(p'ò:̀)	?	salary
ò:̀	ཐོག་	(t'ò:̀)	l<u>o</u>st	roof
è:̀		(It does not exist in Tibetan)		
ä:̀	ངས་	(ngä:̀)	?	by me
ü:̀	སུས་	(sü:̀)	?	by whom
ö:̀	བོད་	(<u>p</u>'ö:̀)	?	Tibet

3.2. མིང་ཚིག་འགའ་ཞིག = Vocabulary

ཀི་ཀུ་	(k'i-k'u)	=	name of the first vowel
པུ་གུ་	(pu-k'u)	=	child
ཤོག་གུ་	(shu-k'u)	=	paper
གཞུ་གུ་	(shu-k'u)	=	tail
ཉེ་པོ་	(nye-po)	=	near, close
རྭ་ཅོ་	(ra-cho)	=	horn (lit.)
ཚ་ཁུ་	(ts'a-k'u)	=	salty
ཀུ་ཤུ་	(ku-shu)	=	apple
ས་	(sa)	=	earth
ཆུ་	(ch'u)	=	water
མེ་	(me)	=	fire
དུ་བ་	(t'u-wa)	=	smoke
ཞྭ་མོ་	(sha-mo)	=	hat
ཞི་མི་	(shi-mi)	=	cat
ཞོ་	(sho)	=	curd
ཝ་མོ་	(wa:-mo)	=	fox
ཙི་ཙི་	(tsi-tsi)	=	mouse
ཨུ་སུ་	(u-su)	=	socks
རི་མོ་	(ri-mo)	=	drawing, painting
ཉི་མ་	(nyi-ma)	=	sun
ཉོ་ཆ་	(nyob-ch'a)	=	shopping
ན་ཚ་	(na-ts'a)	=	illness, disease
ནུ་མ་	(nu-ma)	=	breasts

ནེ་ཙོ་	(ne-tso)	=	parrot
བུ་	(p'u)	=	boy, son
བུ་མོ་	(p'u-mo)	=	girl, daughter
ར་མོ་	(ra-mo)	=	she goat
འོ་མ་	(ho-ma)	=	milk
ད་ར་	(t'a:-ra)	=	buttermilk
ཚ་པོ་	(ts'a-po)	=	hot
སོ་སོ་	(so-so)	=	self, different

4. ལེགས་སྦྱར་ཀློག་ཐབས་སུ་དགོས་པའི་ཡི་གེ་ཁག
The Tibetanised Sanskrit Letters

4.1. ལོག་ཡིག་དྲུག = Six reversed letters

ཊ་	ཋ་	ཌ་	ཎ་	ཥ་	ཀྵཿ
ṭa	ṭ'a	ḍa	n̄a	k'a	ky'a

Method of spelling

ཏ	:	ta	lo`	=	ṭa	:	ཊ་
ཐ	:	t'a	lo`	=	ṭ'a	:	ཋ་
ད	:	t̲'a	lo`	=	ḍa	:	ཌ་
ན	:	na	lo`	=	n̄a	:	ཎ་
ཤ	:	sha	lo`	=	k'a	:	ཥ་
ཀྵ	:	ka-sha	lo`	=	ky'a	:	ཀྵཿ

ཨི་དམ་གུ་རུ་རཏྣ་མཎྜལ་ཀཾ་ནི་རྻཱ་ཏ་ཡ་མི།
Idam guru rat-na mandala-kam nir-ya-ta-ya-mi/
I send forth this jewelled Mandala to you precious Gurus.

4.2. མཐུག་པོ་ལྔ་། = Five heavy sounding letters

གྷ་	དྷ་	བྷ་	ཛྷ་	ཌྷ་
g'a	d'a	b'a	z'a	ḍ'a

Method of spelling

ག	:	k'a	ha-ta`	=	g'a	:	གྷ་
ད	:	t'a	ha-ta`	=	d'a	:	དྷ་
བ	:	p'a	ha-ta`	=	b'a	:	བྷ་
ཛ	:	ts'a	ha-ta`	=	z'a	:	ཛྷ་
ཌ	:	ḍa	ha-ta`	=	ḍ'a	:	ཌྷ་

ན་མོ་བུདྡྷ་ཡ། = I take refuge in Buddha

na-mo buddha ya

ན་མོ་དྷརྨ་ཡ། = I take refuge in Dharma

na-mo dharma ya

ན་མོ་སངྒྷ་ཡ། = I take refuge in Sangha

na-mo sangha ya

5. འཕུལ་བརྩེགས་ཀྱིས་སྒྲ་གདངས་བསྒྱུར་བའི་ཡི་གེ་བཅུ།

When superscribed or prefixed the five consonants with a line above their heads are pronounced with a high tone and the five underlined ones are unaspirated and prenasalized with low tone.

ཀ་	ཁ་	ག་	ང་	ཅ་	ཆ་	ཇ་	ཉ་
ཏ་	ཐ་	ད་	ན་	པ་	ཕ་	བ་	མ་
ཙ་	ཚ་	ཛ་	ཝ་	ཞ་	ཟ་	འ་	ཡ་
ར་	ལ་	ཤ་	ས་	ཧ་	ཨ་		

5.1. Examples:

Aspirated	ག་	ཇ་	ད་	བ་	ཛ་
low-soft	k'a	ch'a	t'a	p'a	ts'a
Unaspirated	རྒ་	རྗ་	རྡ་	རྦ་	རྫ་
low-hard	ga	ja	da	ba	za
Prenasalized	འགའ་	འཇའ་	འདའ་	འབའ་	མཛའ་
low-deep	mga	mja	mda	mda	mza
Unaspirated	ང་	ཉ་	ན་	མ་	ཡ་
low-soft	nga	nya	na	ma	ya
Unaspirated	རྔ་	རྙ་	རྣ་	རྨ་	གཡའ་
high-hard	nga	nya	na	ma	ya

6. མགོ་ཅན་གསུམ། (ར་, ལ་, ས་)

Three Superscribed Letters

6.1. ར་མགོ་བཅུ་གཉིས། (ran-go chu-nyi)

ར is superscribed with 12 consonants

རྐ་	རྒ་	རྔ་	རྗ་	རྙ་	རྟ་
ka	ga	n̄ga	ja	n̄ya	ta
rka	rga	rnga	rja	rnya	rta
རྡ་	རྣ་	རྦ་	རྨ་	རྩ་	རྫ་
da	n̄a	ba	m̄a	tsa	dza
rda	rna	rba	rma	rtsa	rdza

Method of spelling

ར	:	ra	ka-ta`	=	ka	:	རྐ་
ར	:	ra	k'a-ta`	=	ga	:	རྒ་
ར	:	ra	nga-ta`	=	n̄ga	:	རྔ་
ར	:	ra	ch'a-ta`	=	ja	:	རྗ་
ར	:	ra	nya-ta`	=	n̄ya	:	རྙ་
ར	:	ra	ta-ta`	=	ta	:	རྟ་
ར	:	ra	t'a-ta`	=	da	:	རྡ་
ར	:	ra	na-ta`	=	n̄a	:	རྣ་

ར	:	ra	p'a-ta`	=	ba	:	རྦ་
ར	:	ra	ma-ta`	=	m̄a	:	རྨ་
ར	:	ra	tsa-ta`	=	tsa	:	རྩ་
ར	:	ra	ts'a-ta`	=	dza	:	རྫ་

6.2. ལ་མགོ་བཅུ། (lan-go chu)

ལ་ is superscribed with 10 consonants

ལྐ་	ལྒ་	ལྔ་	ལྕ་	ལྗ་
ka	ga	n̄ga	cha	ja
lka	lga	lnga	lcha	lja
ལྟ་	ལྡ་	ལྤ་	ལྦ་	ལྷ་
ta	da	pa	ba	lha
lta	lda	lpa	lba	lha

Method of spelling

ལ	:	la	ka-ta`	=	ka	:	ལྐ་
ལ	:	la	k'a-ta`	=	ga	:	ལྒ་
ལ	:	la	nga-ta`	=	n̄ga	:	ལྔ་
ལ	:	la	cha-ta`	=	cha	:	ལྕ་
ལ	:	la	ch'a-ta`	=	ja	:	ལྗ་
ལ	:	la	ta-ta`	=	ta	:	ལྟ་
ལ	:	la	t'a-ta`	=	da	:	ལྡ་
ལ	:	la	pa-ta`	=	pa	:	ལྤ་
ལ	:	la	p'a-ta`	=	ba	:	ལྦ་
ལ	:	la	ha-ta`	=	lha	:	ལྷ་

6.3. ས་མགོ་བཅུ་གཅིག (san-go chuk-chiː)

ས་ is superscribed with 11 consonants

སྐ་	སྒ་	སྔ་	སྙ་	སྟ་	སྡ་
ka	ga	$\overline{\text{ng}}$a	$\overline{\text{ny}}$a	ta	da
ska	sga	snga	snya	sta	sda
སྣ་	སྤ་	སྦ་	སྨ་	སྩ་	
n̄a	pa	ba	$\overline{\text{m}}$a	tsa	
sna	spa	sba	sma	stsa	

Method of spelling

ས	:	sa	ka-ta`	=	ka	:	སྐ་
ས	:	sa	$\underline{\text{k}}$'a-ta`	=	ga	:	སྒ་
ས	:	sa	nga-ta`	=	$\overline{\text{ng}}$a	:	སྔ་
ས	:	sa	nya-ta`	=	$\overline{\text{ny}}$a	:	སྙ་
ས	:	sa	ta-ta`	=	ta	:	སྟ་
ས	:	sa	$\underline{\text{t}}$'a-ta`	=	da	:	སྡ་
ས	:	sa	na-ta`	=	n̄a	:	སྣ་
ས	:	sa	pa-ta`	=	pa	:	སྤ་
ས	:	sa	$\underline{\text{p}}$'a-ta`	=	ba	:	སྦ་
ས	:	sa	ma-ta`	=	$\overline{\text{m}}$a	:	སྨ་
ས	:	sa	tsa-ta`	=	tsa	:	སྩ་

7. འདོགས་ཅན་བཞི།

The Four Subjoined Letters

The subjoined letters ཡ་, ར་, ལ་, ཝ་ and their respective symbolised forms are:

◌ྱ (ya-ta) ◌ྲ (ra-ta) ◌ླ (la-ta) ◌ྭ (wa-sur)

7.1. The subjoined '◌ྱ' (ya-ta)

ཀྱ་	ཁྱ་	གྱ་	པྱ་	ཕྱ་	བྱ་	མྱ་	ཧྱ་
kya	ky'a	<u>ky</u>'a	cha	ch'a	<u>ch</u>'a	nya	hya
kya	khya	gya	pya	phya	bya	mya	hya

Method of spelling

ཀ	:	ka	ya-ta	=	kya	:	ཀྱ་	
ཁ	:	k'a	ya-ta	=	ky'a	:	ཁྱ་	cha
ག	:	<u>k</u>'a	ya-ta	=	<u>ky</u>'a	:	གྱ་	cha
པ	:	pa	ya-ta	=	cha	:	པྱ་	
ཕ	:	p'a	ya-ta	=	ch'a	:	ཕྱ་	~~cha~~
བ	:	<u>p</u>'a	ya-ta	=	<u>ch</u>'a	:	བྱ་	
མ	:	ma	ya-ta	=	nya	:	མྱ་	
ཧ	:	ha	ya-ta	=	hya	:	ཧྱ་	

Note: Pronunciation of པྱ་, ཕྱ་, བྱ་, མྱ་ is the same as of ཅ་, ཆ་, ཇ་, ཉ་ respectively.

More examples of the method of spelling ‘ ྱ ’ (ya-ta) in conjunction with vowels.

ka	ya-ta	=	kya	<u>k</u>'i-<u>k</u>'u	=	kyi	:	ཀྱི་	
k'a	ya-ta	=	ky'a	<u>sh</u>ab-kyu	=	ky'u	:	ཁྱུ་	
<u>k</u>'a	ya-ta	=	<u>ky</u>'a	ḍeng-po	=	<u>ky</u>'e	:	གྱེ་	
pa	ya-ta	=	cha	na-ro	=	cho	:	པྱོ་	
p'a	ya-ta	=	ch'a	<u>k</u>'i-<u>k</u>'u	=	ch'i	:	ཕྱི་	
<u>p</u>'a	ya-ta	=	<u>ch</u>'a	<u>sh</u>ab-kyu	=	<u>ch</u>'u	:	བྱུ་	
ma	ya-ta	=	nya	ḍeng-po	=	nye	:	མྱེ་	
ha	ya-ta	=	hya	na-ro	=	hyo	:	ཧྱོ་	
ha	ya-ta	=	hya	<u>k</u>'i-<u>k</u>'u	=	hyi	:	ཧྱི་	
ma	ya-ta	=	nya	<u>sh</u>ab-kyu	=	nyu	:	མྱུ་	
<u>p</u>'a	ya-ta	=	<u>ch</u>'a	ḍeng-po	=	<u>ch</u>'e	:	བྱེ་	she
p'a	ya-ta	=	ch'a	na-ro	=	ch'o	:	ཕྱོ་	
pa	ya-ta	=	cha	<u>k</u>'i-<u>k</u>'u	=	chi	:	པྱི་	
<u>k</u>'a	ya-ta	=	<u>ky</u>'a	<u>sh</u>ab-kyu	=	<u>ky</u>'u	:	གྱུ་	
k'a	ya-ta	=	ky'a	ḍeng-po	=	ky'e	:	ཁྱེ་	
ka	ya-ta	=	kya	na-ro	=	kyo	:	ཀྱོ་	

7.2. The subjoined ‘ ྲ ’ (ra-ta)

ཀྲ་	ཁྲ་	གྲ་	ཏྲ་	ཐྲ་	དྲ་	ནྲ་
ṭa	ṭ'a	<u>ṭ</u>'a	ṭa	ṭ'a	<u>ṭ</u>'a	na
kra	khra	gra	tra	thra	dra	nra
པྲ་	ཕྲ་	བྲ་	མྲ་	སྲ་	ཧྲ་	
ṭa	ṭ'a	<u>ṭ</u>'a	ma	sa	rha	
pra	phra	bra	mra	sra	hra	

Method of spelling

ཀ	:	ka	ra-ta	=	ṭa	:	ཀྲ་	ta
ཁ	:	k'a	ra-ta	=	ṭ'a	:	ཁྲ་	Tra cha
ག	:	k̲'a	ra-ta	=	ṭ̲'a	:	གྲ་	
ཏ	:	ta	ra-ta	=	ṭa	:	ཏྲ་	
ཐ	:	t'a	ra-ta	=	ṭ'a	:	ཐྲ་	
ད	:	t̲'a	ra-ta	=	ṭ̲'a	:	དྲ་	
ན	:	na	ra-ta	=	na	:	ནྲ་	
པ	:	pa	ra-ta	=	ṭa	:	པྲ་	
ཕ	:	p'a	ra-ta	=	ṭ'a	:	ཕྲ་	
བ	:	p̲'a	ra-ta	=	ṭ̲'a	:	བྲ་	
མ	:	ma	ra-ta	=	ma	:	མྲ་	
ས	:	sa	ra-ta	=	sa	:	སྲ་	
ཧ	:	ha	ra-ta	=	rha	:	ཧྲ་	

More examples of the method of spelling ‘ྲ’ (ra-ta) in conjunction with vowels.

ka	ra-ta	=	ṭa	k̲'i-k̲'u	=	ṭi	:	ཀྲི་
k'a	ra-ta	=	ṭ'a	s̲h̲ab-kyu	=	ṭ'u	:	ཁྲུ་
k̲'a	ra-ta	=	ṭ̲'a	ḍeng-po	=	ṭ̲'e	:	གྲེ་
ta	ra-ta	=	ṭa	k̲'i-k̲'u	=	ṭi	:	ཏྲི་
t'a	ra-ta	=	ṭ'a	s̲h̲ab-kyu	=	ṭ'u	:	ཐྲུ་
t̲'a	ra-ta	=	ṭ̲'a	ḍeng-po	=	ṭ̲'e	:	དྲེ་
pa	ra-ta	=	ṭa	k̲'i-k̲'u	=	ṭi	:	པྲི་
p'a	ra-ta	=	ṭ'a̲	s̲h̲ab-kyu	=	ṭ'u	:	ཕྲུ་
p̲'a	ra-ta	=	ṭ̲'a	ḍeng-po	=	ṭ̲'e	:	བྲེ་

na	ra-ta	=	na	<u>k</u>'i-<u>k</u>'u	=	ni	:	ནྲི་
ma	ra-ta	=	ma	<u>sh</u>ab-kyu	=	mu	:	མྲུ་
sa	ra-ta	=	sa	ḍeng-po	=	se	:	སྲེ་
ha	ra-ta	=	rha	na-ro	=	rho	:	ཧྲོ་

7.3. The subjoined 'ལ' (la-ta)

ཀླ་	གླ་	བླ་	རླ་	སླ་	ཟླ་*
l̄a	l̄a	l̄a	l̄a	l̄a	da
kla	gla	bla	rla	sla	zla

Method of spelling in conjunction with vowels.

ka	la-ta`	=	l̄a	<u>k</u>'i-<u>k</u>'u	=	l̄i	:	ཀླི་
<u>k</u>'a	la-ta`	=	l̄a	<u>sh</u>ab-kyu	=	l̄u	:	གླུ་
<u>p</u>'a	la-ta`	=	l̄a	ḍeng-po	=	l̄e	:	བླེ་
ra	la-ta	=	l̄a	na-ro	=	l̄o	:	རློ་
sa	la-ta	=	l̄a lha	ḍeng-po	=	l̄e	:	སླེ་
<u>s</u>a	la-ta	=	da dha	<u>sh</u>ab-kyu	=	du	:	ཟླུ་

Examples:

ཀླ་ཀློ་	(l̄a-l̄o)	=	barbarian, savage
གློ་བ་	(l̄o-wa:)	=	lungs
བླ་མ་	(l̄a-ma)	=	spiritual teacher, (Guru)
རླུང་	(l̄u;ng)	=	air
སླ་པོ་	(l̄a-po)	=	weak (tea)
ཟླ་བ་	(da-wa:)	=	moon, month

---

* Except 'ཟླ་' which is pronounced as 'da', the other 5 subjoined letters are pronounced 'l̄a'.

7.4. The subjoined ‘ ྭ ’ (wa-sur)

It is generally used with 13 consonants:

ཀྭ་	ཁྭ་	གྭ་	ཉྭ་	དྭ་	ཙྭ་	ཚྭ་
ka	k'a	k̲'a	nya	t̲'a	tsa	ts'a
kwa	khwa	gwa	nywa	dwa	tswa	tshwa

ཞྭ་	ཟྭ་	རྭ་	ལྭ་	ཤྭ་	ཧྭ་
s̲h̲a	s̲a	ra	la	sha	ha
zhwa	zwa	rwa	lwa	shwa	hwa

Examples:

ཀྭ་ཡེ་	(ka-ye)	=	a vocative (lit.)
ཁྭ་ཏ་	(k'a-ta)	=	crow
གྭ་པ་	(k'a-pa)	=	an animal with white face
ཉྭ་	(nya)	=	calf (of leg)
དྭ་ཕྲུག་	(t̲'a-ṭ'u:)	=	orphan
རྩྭ་	(tsa)	=	grass
ཚྭ་	(ts'a)	=	salt
ཞྭ་མོ་	(s̲h̲a-mo)	=	hat
ཟྭ་ཕོ་	(s̲a-p'o)	=	kind of nettle
རྭ་ཅོ་	(ra-cho)	=	horn
ལྭ་བ་	(la-wa:)	=	a white woolen cloth
ཤྭ་བ་	(sha-wa:)	=	deer
ཧྭ་	(ha)	=	edge of clothings (lit.)

7.5. Exercise I དཔོད་བྲིས། = Dictation

ཀ་	རྔ་	ང་	སྙ་	སྟོ་	ཛ་	ལྔ་
རྙ་	ཀྱ་	གྱ་	སྐྱ་	སྤྱ་	སྦྱ་	ཁྲ་
པ་	སྦ་	སྣ་	ལྕ་	ཉ་	བླ་	ཟླ་
ཀྱུ་	ཁྱུ་	སྤྱུ་	ཕོ་	གྲུ་	ཁྲུ་	གུ་
ཆ་	ཐ་	ཏ་	སྒྲུ་	ལྔ་	ལྡ་	སྐེ་
སྙེ་	སྨོ་	ཙེ་	ལྕུ་	སྒྱུ་	བླུ་	ཉོ་
སྤུ་	སྦུ་	སྨོ་	ལྡ་	སྟ་	དེ་	རྟོ་
ཀུ་	ནུ་	སྦྲུ་	སྤྱི་	གུ་	སྦྱི་	བུ་
སྲ་	སྙ་	ཀྲུ་	ཀ་	ཏུ་	སྟ་	ཡ་
ཁེ་	སྨི་	སྦི་	ཁི་	སྙོ་	ཟླུ་	ཕོ་

7.6. མིང་ཚིག་འགའ་ཞིག = Vocabulary

རྒྱུ་མ་	(gyu-ma)	=	intestine
ང་མ་	(n̄ga-ma)	=	yak's tail
རྟ་	(ta)	=	horse
རྡོ་	(do)	=	stone
རྣོ་པོ་	(n̄o-po)	=	sharp
རྨ་	(m̄a)	=	wound, sore
རྨོ་འོ་	(m̄o:)	=	grandmother
རྩ་	(tsa)	=	nerve, pulse
རྩི་	(tsi)	=	varnish
རྫ་མ་	(za-ma)	=	clay pot
ལྔ་	(n̄ga)	=	five
ལྕེ་	(che)	=	tongue
ལྟེ་བ་	(te-wa:)	=	main, navel

ལྷ་	(lha)	=	god
ལྷ་མོ་	(lha-mo)	=	goddess, Tibetan opera
སྐེ་	(ke)	=	neck
སྐུ་ཟླ་	(kun-da)	=	spouse (H.)
སྒ་	(ga)	=	saddle
སྔ་མོ་	(n̄g a-mo)	=	in the past
སྨྱུ་གུ་	(n̄y u-k̲'u)	=	pen
སྟ་རེ་	(ta-re)	=	axe
སྣ་ཁ་	(n̄a-k'a)	=	kind, variety
སྤུ་	(pu)	=	hair
སྤོའོ་	(po:)	=	grandfather
ཁྱི་	(ky'i)	=	dog
ཕྱུ་པ་	(ch'u-pa)	=	Tibetan dress
ཕྱེ་མ་	(ch'e-ma)	=	powder, pulverized substance
བྱ་	(c̲h̲'a)	=	bird
བྱིའུ་	(c̲h̲'iu)	=	small bird
བྱ་ཏེ་	(ch'a-t'e)	=	cock
བྱ་མོ་	(ch'a-mo)	=	hen
སྐྲ་	(ṭa)	=	hair of head
སྒྲ་	(ḍa)	=	sound, pronunciation

8. སྔོན་རྗེས་ཡང་གསུམ་གྱི་ངོ་སྤྲོད།

The Prefix, Suffix & Post-suffix

8.1. སྔོན་འཇུག་ལྔ་། = Five Prefixes

ག་	ད་	བ་	མ་	འ་
k'a	t'a	p'a	ma	ha
ga	da	ba	ma	'a

ག	is used before	ཅ་ཉ་ཏ་ད་ན་ཙ་ཞ་ཟ་ཡ་ཤ་ས་
ད	" " "	ཀ་ག་ང་པ་བ་མ་
བ	" " "	ཀ་ག་ཅ་ཉ་ཏ་ད་ན་ཙ་ཛ་ཞ་ཟ་ཤ་ས་
མ	" " "	ཁ་ག་ང་ཆ་ཇ་ཉ་ཐ་ད་ན་ཚ་ཛ་
འ	" " "	ཁ་ག་ཆ་ཇ་ཐ་ད་ཕ་བ་ཚ་ཛ་

The 5 prefixes should be pronounced as follows

ག	(k'a)	as	k'ao
ད	(t'a)	as	t'ao
བ	(p'a)	as	p'ao
མ	(ma)	as	mao
འ	(ha)	as	hao

Method of spelling of words having prefixes

གཏེ་	k'ao	ta	ḍeng-po	=	te	mean
དགུ་	t'ao	ga	shab-kyu	=	gu	~~ten~~ nine
བཅུ་	p'ao	cha	shab-kyu	=	chu	ten

མཁོ་	mao	k'a	na-ro	=	k'o	necessary
འགོ་	hao	ga	na-ro	=	go	top
གཅུ་	k'ao	cha	shab-kyu	=	chu	turning
དཔེ་	t'ao	pa	ḍeng-po	=	pe	sample
བཀུ་	p'ao	ka	shab-kyu	=	ku	
མགོ་	mao	ga	na-ro	=	go	head
འདི་	hao	da	k'i-k'u	=	di	this
བཞི་	p'ao	sha	k'i-k'u	=	shi	4.
མཆུ་	mao	ch'a	shab-kyu	=	ch'u	lips
འདུ་	hao	da	shab-kyu	=	du	gather
གདུ་	k'ao	da	shab-kyu	=	du	ku bangle
དབུ་	t'ao	w̄a	shab-kyu	=	u	honorific head.

8.2. རྗེས་འཇུག་བཅུ། = Ten Suffixes

ག་	ང་	ད་	ན་	བ་	མ་	འ་	ར་	ལ་	ས་
k'a	nga	t'a	na	p'a	ma	ha	ra	la	sa
ga	nga	da	na	ba	ma	'a	ra	la	sa

Method of spelling of words having suffixes

ཀ	:	ka	k'a	=	ka:	ཀག་
ཀ	:	ka	nga	=	ka;ng	ཀང་
ཀ	:	ka	t'a	=	kä:	ཀད་
ཀ	:	ka	na	=	kä;n	ཀན་

The 10 suffixes are used after any of the 30 consonants:

ཀག་ (ka:)	ཁག་ (k'a:)	གག་ (k'a:)	ངག་ (nga:)
ཀང་ (ka;ng)	ཁང་ (k'a;ng)	གང་ (k'a;ng)	ངང་ (nga;ng)

ཀད་ (kä:)	ཁད་ (k'ä:)	གད་ (k'ä:)	ངད་ (ngä:)
ཀན་ (kä:n)	ཁན་ (k'ä;n)	གན་ (k'ä;n)	ངན་ (ngä;n)
ཀབ་ (kèb)	ཁབ་ (k'èb)	གབ་ (k'èb)	ངབ་ (ngèb)
ཀམ་ (kam)	ཁམ་ (k'am)	གམ་ (k'am)	ངམ་ (ngam)
ཀའ་ (ka)	ཁའ་ (k'a)	གའ་ (k'a)	ངའ་ (nga)
ཀར་ (kar)	ཁར་ (k'ar)	གར་ (k'ar)	ངར་ (ngar)
ཀལ་ (käl)	ཁལ་ (k'äl)	གལ་ (k'äl)	ངལ་ (ngäl)
ཀས་ (kä:)	ཁས་ (k'ä:)	གས་ (k'ä:)	ངས་ (ngä:)

8.3. ཡང་འཇུག་གཉིས། = Two Post-suffixes

ད་ is used after ན་ ར་ ལ་

ས་ " " " ག་ ང་ བ་ མ་

As a rule, in modern Tibetan writing, the Post-suffix 'ད་' is not used. However, in the case of past tense verbs ending with ན་, ར་, ལ་ the Post-suffix 'ད་' is implied to be present, though it is not written.

དཔེར་ན། = For example:

	Traditional		Modern writing			Meaning
ད་	ཕྱིནད་	:	ཕྱིན་	(ch'in)	=	went
	གྱུརད་	:	གྱུར་	(ky'ur)	=	became (lit.)
	རོལད་	:	རོལ་	(röl)	=	enjoyed (")

ས་	ཐབས་	གདངས་	སེམས་	ལེགས་
	t'èb	da;ng	sem	leg
	means	tone	mind	good
	method	melody	heart	nice

8.4. Exercise 2

གཤམ་གསལ་ཚིག་རྣམས་སྦྱོར་ཀློག་རྒྱབ། Spell out the following words

གཤམ་	གསལ་	དཀར་	དབང་	བཅག་	བདག་
མངར་	མཐར་	འདིར་	འཐུང་	རིགས་	གངས་
ཕན་	ཁབ་	སྙམ་	གཟའ་	ཉལ་	ངས་
ལྷགས་	ཚགས་	བབས་	གོམས་	སྟངས་	ཕྱེན་
རེད་	འདུག་	ཡིན་	ཡོད་	ནས་	སྒྲ་
སྤྲ་	ཏྲ་	སྐད་	ཡིག་	ཤེས་	སླ་

9. མིང་གཞི་ངོས་འཛིན་བྱ་ཚུལ།

Root Letter Identification

1	2	3	4
བ	སྒྲུ	བ	ས་

No. 1	is the Prefix	=	སྔོན་འཇུག
No. 2	is the Root letter	=	མིང་གཞི་
No. 3	is the Suffix	=	རྗེས་འཇུག
No. 4	is the Post-Suffix	=	ཡང་འཇུག

Identification of the Root Letter from any given word is done in this way:

9.1. In a word consisting of any number of letters the one combined with a vowel is always the root letter. e.g.

ཁྲོ་ ཚོ་ བསུ་ བདུད་

ཐེབས་ འདེགས་ ཀི་ ཞུགས་

Except the particles འི་, འུ་, འོ་ which are used as part of a word. i.e. ངའི་, ཀའུ་, ལའོ།

9.2. Any superscribed or subjoined letter with or without a vowel is a root letter. e.g.

ཀན་ སྣམ་ ཧན་ ཀླེ་ ཀླུང་ ཟླིང་ བཀྱུད་ དྭངས་ དྭགས་ ཚྭ་

9.3. Any single-letter word with or without a vowel is always a root letter. e.g.

ཁ་ ང་ ཆ་ ཇ་ ཉ་ ར་ ཤ་ ས་ ཕ་ ཡ་ ལ་

9.4. In two-letter words, the first is always the root letter. e.g.

ཁབ་ གང་ ངས་ ཡས་ ཐག་ དག་ མར་ ཕར་ ནང་ བར་ འམ་

9.5. Three-letter words:

(a) If the last letter is a suffix (excluding the suffix 'ས་') the middle letter is always a root letter. e.g.

བཀག་ བཏང་ འབད་ མནན་ འཇབ་ འཇམ་ དཀར་ འདམ་

(b) If the last letter is 'ས་' and the middle letter is a non-affix consonant, then the middle letter is always the root letter. e.g.

བཀས་ མཁས་ བཅས་ གཞས་ གཡས་ བཟས་ བཙས་

(c) If the last letter is 'ས་' and the first two letters are affixes, then <u>the second one</u> is the root letter in the following 9 words only.

གདས་ གནས་ གསས་ དགས་ དམས་ བདས་ མདས་ འགས་ འདས་

And the first one is the root letter in the following 14 words only.

རགས་ ལགས་ནགས་ བགས་ བངས་ གངས་ རངས་
ལངས་ ནངས་ སངས་ བབས་ རབས་ རམས་ ནམས་

9.6. In words consisting of 4 letters, the second letter is always the root letter. e.g.

མངགས་ འཇགས་ བཏགས་ འཕགས་ དམངས་ འབངས་ གདངས་

9.7. Exercise 3

Identify the root letters in the following words

གང་	ལ་	ཡོན་	ཏན་	མཆོག་	མངའ་	བའི། ।
དཀོན་	མཆོག་	དེ་	ལ་	ཕྱག་	འཚལ་	ལོ། ।
གང་	གིས་	སྒྲ་	དབྱངས་	གསུངས་	པ་	ཡི། ।
འཇམ་	པའི་	དབྱངས་	ལ་	ཕྱག་	འཚལ་	ལོ། ।

10. མིང་ཚབ་ཁག

Pronouns

10.1. གང་ཟག་གི་མིང་ཚབ་ = Personal Pronouns

1st person	2nd person	3rd person
ང་ nga I	ཁྱེད་རང་ ky'e-ra;ng you	ཁོང་ k'o;ng he, she
ང་ཚོ་ ngan-ts'o we	ཁྱེད་རང་ཚོ་ ky'e-ra;ng-ts'o you	ཁོང་ཚོ་ k'o;ng-ts'o they

10.2. སྐྱེ་ལ་ཁྱབ་པའི་མིང་ཚབ། = Demonstrative pronouns

When the pronouns become plural, the letter གི་ of ཕ་གི་, ཡ་གི་, མ་གི་ is replaced by ཚོ་ as follows:

འདི་ di this	ཕ་གི་* p'a-<u>k</u>'i that	དེ་** t'e that	ཡ་གི་ ya-<u>k</u>'i that up there	མ་གི་ ma-<u>k</u>'i that down there
འདི་ཚོ་ din-ts'o these	ཕ་ཚོ་ p'an-ts'o those	དེ་ཚོ་ <u>t</u>'e-ts'o those	ཡ་ཚོ་ yan-ts'o those up there	མ་ཚོ་ man-ts'o those down there

* Indicating something seen (e.g. <u>that man over there</u>)

** Indicating something unseen (e.g. <u>that man we talked about</u>)

10.3. Personal pronouns used in writing only

When you make these plural, add 'ཚོ་' after each singular pronoun. After No. 1 & 5 you can put the 'ཅག་' also, in place of 'ཚོ་' as follows:

1st person

No.	Tibetan s.	+ pl.	Pronunciation s. + pl.	Meaning
1.	ངེད་	+ ཚོ་/ཅག	nge: + ts'o/cha:	I + pl. = we
2.	ངོས་	+ ཚོ་	ngö: + ts'o	" + " = "
3.	ཕྲན་	+ ཚོ་	ṭ'ä;n + ts'o	" + " = "
4.	ཁོ་བོ་	+ ཚོ་	k'o: + ts'o	" + " = "
5.	བདག་	+ ཚོ་/ཅག	da: + ts'o/cha:	" + " = "
6.	གུས་	+ ཚོ་	k'ü: + ts'o	" + " = "
7.	གུས་པ་	+ ཚོ་	k'ü-pa + ts'o	" + " = "
8.	གུས་ཕྲན་	+ ཚོ་	k'ü:-ṭ'ä;n + ts'o	" + " = "
9.	གུས་འབངས་	+ ཚོ་	k'ü:-ba;ng + ts'o	" + " = "

(Note: No. 5 to 9 are honorific refering to the object.)

2nd person

No.	Tibetan s.	+ pl.	Pronunciation s. + pl.	Meaning
1.	ཁྱོད་	+ ཚོ་	ky'ö:` + ts'o	you + pl. = you
2.	ཁྱོད་རང་	+ ཚོ་	ky'ö-ra;ng+ts'o	" + " = "
3.	ཉིད་རང་	+	nyi:-ra;ng	(singular only)
4.	ཉིད་	+ ཚོ་	nyi: + ts'o	you + pl = you
5.	ཁྱེད་	+ ཚོ་	ky'e: + ts'o	" + " = "
6.	སྐུ་ཉིད་	+ ཚོ་	ku-nyi: + ts'o	" + " = "

7.	སྐུ་མཆོག་	+ རྣམ་པ་	ku-ch'ò: + n̄am-pa	you + pl = you
8.	མི་མཆོག་	+ རྣམ་པ་	mi-ch'o: + n̄am-pa	" + " = "
9.	མི་རྗེ་	+ རྣམ་པ་	mi-je + n̄am-pa	" + " = "
10.	མི་དབང་	+ རྣམ་པ་	mi-wa;ng + n̄am-pa	" + " = "
11.	མཆོག་སྐུ་	+	ch'o: + ku	(singular only)

(Note: No. 5 to 11 are honorific referring to the object)

3rd person

No.	Tibetan s.	+ pl.	Pronunciation s. + pl.	Meaning
1.	ཁོང་	+ ཚོ་	k'o;ng + ts'o	he/she+pl.= they
2.	ཁོང་	+ རྣམ་ཚོ་	k'o;ng + n̄am-ts'o	" + " = "
3.	ཁོང་	+ རྣམ་པ་	k'o;ng + n̄am-pa	" + " = "
4.	ཁོ་རང་	+ ཚོ་	k'o-ra;ng + ts'o	" + " = "
5.	ཁོ་པ་	+ ཚོ་	k'o-pa + ts'o	" + " = "
6.	ཁོ་མོ་	+ ཚོ་	k'o-mo + ts'o	" + " = "
7.	ཁོ་	+ ཚོ་	k'o + ts'o	" + " = "
8.	མོ་	+	mo	she (singular)

(Note: No. 1 to 3 are honorific refering to the object.)

10.4. Exercise 4

Make the following pronouns plural

ང་	ཁྱེད་རང་	ཁོང་	ལ་གི་	མ་གི་
འདི་	སློབ་ཕྲུག་	ཕ་གི་	ཕྱན་	ཀུན་
ཁོ་པ་	ཁོ་བོ་	ཁོ་མོ་	དེ་	ཀུན་ཕྱན་

11. Linking Verbs with the meaning 'to be'

ཡིན། རེད། ཡིན་པ་རེད།

Unlike the linking verbs in English such as is, was, are, were, etc. these three basic linking verbs do not indicate tense and numbers. The literal translation of these linking verbs is 'IS'. Tenses are shown by the context of the sentence.

ཡིན། is used in the 1st person
རེད། and ཡིན་པ་རེད། are used in the 2nd and 3rd persons

1st person	2nd person	3rd person
ང་ཡིན་ I is/ nga yi;n/ I am	ཁྱེད་རང་རེད། you is/ ky'e-ra;ng re:/ You are	ཁོང་རེད། he/ she is/ k'o;ng re:/ He/She is
ང་ཚོ་ཡིན། we is/ nga;n-ts'o yi;n/ We are	ཁྱེད་རང་ཚོ་རེད། you is/ ky'e-ra;ng-ts'o re:/ You are	ཁོང་ཚོ་རེད། they is/ k'o;ng-ts'o re: They are

Examples:

1. ང་སློབ་ཕྲུག་ཡིན།
   I student is/
   nga l̄ob-ṭ'ù: yi;n/
   I am (a) student.

2. ང་ཚོ་སློབ་ཕྲུག་ཡིན།
   we student is/
   nga;n-ts'o l̄ob-ṭ'ù: yi;n/
   We are students.

3. ཁྱེད་རང་བོད་པ་རེད།
   you Tibetan is/
   ky'e-ra;ng p̲'ö-pa rè:/
   You are (a) Tibetan.

4. ཁྱེད་རང་ཚོ་བོད་པ་རེད།
   you pl. Tibetan is/
   ky'e-ra;ng-ts'o p̲'ö-pa rè:/
   You are Tibetans.

5. ཁོང་ནང་པ་རེད།
   he Buddhist is/
   k'o;ng na;ng-pa rè:/
   She is (a) Buddhist.

6. ཁོང་ཚོ་ནང་པ་རེད།
   they Buddhist is/
   k'o;ng-ts'o na;ng-pa rè:/
   They are Buddhists.

7. ང་དགེ་རྒན་ཡིན།
   I teacher is/
   nga ge-gä;n yi;n/
   I am (a) teacher.

8. ང་ཚོ་དགེ་རྒན་ཡིན།
   we teacher is/
   nga;n-ts'o ge-gä;n yi;n/
   We are teachers.

9. ཁོང་ཨེམ་ཆི་རེད།
   he doctor is/
   k'o;ng äm-ch'i re:̀/
   He is (a) doctor.

10. ཁོང་ཚོ་ཨེམ་ཆི་རེད།
    they doctor is/
    k'o;ng-ts'o äm-ch'i re:̀/
    They are doctors.

11. འདི་སྨྱུ་གུ་རེད།
    this pen is/
    di n̅y̅u-k̲'u re:̀/
    This is (a) pen.

12. འདི་ཚོ་སྨྱུ་གུ་རེད།
    these pen is/
    din-ts'o n̅y̅u-k̲'u re:̀/
    These are pens.

13. ཕ་གི་ཁང་པ་རེད།
    that house is/

p'a-k̲'i k'a;ng-pa re:/
That is (a) house.

14. ཕ་ཚོ་ཁང་པ་རེད།
those house is/
p'an-ts'o k'a;ng-pa re:/
Those are houses.

15. དེ་ཤོག་གུ་རེད།
that paper is/
t̲'e shu-k̲'u re:/
That is (a) paper.

16. དེ་ཚོ་ཤོག་གུ་རེད།
those paper is/
t̲'e-ts'o shu-k̲'u re:/
Those are papers.

17. ཡ་གི་སྤྲིན་པ་རེད།
that up there cloud is/
ya-k̲'i ṭin-pa re:/
That is (a) cloud up there.

18. ཡ་ཚོ་སྤྲིན་པ་རེད།
those up there cloud is/
yan-ts'o ṭin-pa re:/
Those are clouds up there.

19. མ་གི་གཙང་པོ་རེད།
that down there river is/
ma-k̲'i tsa;ng-po re:/
That is (a) river down there.

20. མ་ཚོ་གཙང་པོ་རེད།
those down there river is/
ma;n-ts'o tsa;ng-po re:/
Those are rivers down there.

11.1. The difference of རེད། and ཡིན་པ་རེད།

རེད། is used for definite statements
ཡིན་པ་རེད། is used for indefinite statements (may be)

དཔེར་ན། = For example:

1. ཁོང་སློབ་ཕྲུག་ཞིག་རེད།
she student a is/
k'o;ng l̄ob-ṭ'u: <u>sh</u>ig re:/
She is a student. (definite)

2. ཁོང་སློབ་ཕྲུག་ཞིག་ཡིན་པ་རེད།
she student a is/
k'o;ng l̄ob-ṭ'u: <u>sh</u>ig yi;n-pa re:/
She ~~may~~ be a student. (indefinite)
Wan

11.2. There are three more alternative linking verbs with a slight change in meaning.

ཡིན་གྱི་རེད། (I think)
ཡིན་པ་འདྲ། (I suppose)
ཡིན་པ་བཟོ་འདུག (it seems)

Examples:

1. ཁོང་ཨེམ་ཆི་ཡིན་གྱི་རེད།
she doctor is/

k'o;ng äm-ch'i yi;n-<u>ky</u>'i re:/
I think she is (a) doctor.

2. ཁོང་མི་ཚང་ཡག་པོ་ཞིག་ནས་ཡིན་པ་འདྲ།
she family good a from is/
k'o;ng mi-ts'a;ng yag-po <u>sh</u>ig-nä yi;n-pa-ḍa/
I suppose she is from a good family.

3. ཁོང་དགེ་རྒན་ཞིག་ཡིན་པ་བཟོ་འདུག
she teacher a is/
k'o;ng ge-gä;n <u>sh</u>ig yi;n-<u>s</u>o-du/
It seems she is a teacher.

4. ཁོང་སྐྱེ་དམན་སེམས་བཟང་པོ་ཞིག་ཡིན་པ་བཟོ་འདུག
she woman mind kind a is/
k'o;ng kye-mä;n sem-<u>s</u>a;ng-po <u>sh</u>ig yi;n-<u>s</u>o-du/
It seems she is a kind-hearted woman.

5. འདི་བོད་པའི་ཟ་ཁང་ཡིན་གྱི་རེད།
this Tibetan-of restaurant is/
di <u>p</u>'ö-pä: <u>s</u>a-k'a;ng yi;n-<u>ky</u>'i-re:/
I think this is a Tibetan restaurant.

11.3. Exercise 5

(a) Insert ཡིན། or རེད། appropriately in the following:

1. འདི་སྨྱུ་གུ་ . . . .
2. ཕ་ཚོ་མེ་ཏོག་ . . . .
3. ང་གྲྭ་པ་ . . . .
4. ཁྱེད་རང་ཚོ་སློབ་ཕྲུག་ . . . . . .
5. ང་ཚོ་སློབ་ཕྲུག་ . . . .
8. ང་ཚོ་དགེ་རྒན་ . . . .
9. ཁོང་ཨེམ་ཆི་ . . . .
10. འདི་ཚོ་ངའི་དེབ་ . . . .
11. དེ་ཚོ་གཙང་མ་ . . . .
12. ཕ་གི་བླ་མ་ . . . .

6. ཁོང་མི་སེམས་བཟང་པོ་ཞིག་ . . .
7. ཁྱེད་རང་སྐྱུང་པོ་ . . . .
13. ཡ་གི་མི་ . . . .
14. འདི་ཚོ་རྒྱབ་ཀྱག་ . . . .

(b) Translate the following into English

1. འདི་ང་ཚོའི་རྒན་ལགས་ཀྱི་ཕྱུག་སྟུག་ཡིན་པ་འདྲ།
2. ཕ་གི་བླ་མ་ཞིག་ཡིན་བཟོ་འདུག
3. ཁོང་ཚོ་གསུམ་སྤུན་མཆེད་ཡིན་གྱི་རེད།
4. བུ་མོ་ཕ་ཚོ་མི་ཚང་ཆེན་པོ་ཞིག་གི་ཡིན་པ་འདྲ།

(c) Translate the following into Tibetan

1. This is my hand.
2. These are their children.
3. That is his hat.
4. This is her bag.

12. དགག་སྒྲ་བཞི། མ་ མི་ མིན་ མེད།

Four Negatives

12.1. མིན། and མ། with linking verbs:

Positive ཡིན། becomes negative (མ་ཡིན།)

" རེད། " " (མ་རེད།)

Examples:

	Positive	Negative
1.	ང་བུ་ཡིན།	ང་བུ་མོ་མིན།
	I boy is/	I girl not/
	nga p̲'u yi;n/	nga p̲'u-mo mä;n/
	I am (a) boy.	I am not (a) girl.
2.	ང་ཚོ་སློབ་ཕྲུག་ཡིན།	ང་ཚོ་དགེ་རྒན་མིན།
	we student is/	we teacher not/
	ngan ts'o l̄ob-ṭ'u: yi;n/	ngan ts'o ge-gä;n mä;n/
	We are students.	We are not teachers.
3.	ཁོང་ཨེམ་ཆི་རེད།	ཁོང་ནད་པ་མ་རེད།
	she doctor is/	she patient not-is/
	k'o;ng äm-ch'i re:/	k'o;ng nä-pa ma-re:/
	She is (a) doctor.	She is not (a) patient.

12.2. The interrogative པས་ with linking verbs

Normally in affirmative sentences the linking verb ཡིན། is used in the first person and རེད། in the second and third persons.

However, in the interrogative, the first and second persons change verbs, i.e. རེད། for the first and ཡིན། for the second person and add the interrogative པས།

First person	ང་ ང་ཚོ་	} ཡིན།	becomes རེད་པས།	in question
Second person	ཁྱེད་རང་ ཁྱེད་རང་ཚོ་	} རེད།	becomes ཡིན་པས།	in question
Third person	ཁོང་ ཁོང་ཚོ་	} རེད།	becomes རེད་པས།	in question

Examples:

1. ང་རིག་པ་རྣོ་པོ་རེད་པས། = Am I intelligent?
2. ཁྱེད་རང་བོད་པ་ཡིན་པས། = Are you (a) Tibetan?
3. ཁོང་གྲྭ་པ་རེད་པས། = Is he (a) monk?

12.3. Negative interrogative with linking verbs:

Examples:

1. ང་དྲང་པོ་མ་རེད་པས།
   I honest not is? /
   nga ṯ'ang-po ma re pä/
   Am I not honest?

2. ཁྱེད་རང་བོད་པ་མིན་པས།
   you Tibetan not ? /
   ky'e-ra;ng p̱'ö-pa mä;n pä/
   Aren't you (a) Tibetan?

3. ཁོང་སྐུ་རྐྱང་མ་རེད་པས།
he alone (H.) not is? /
k'o;ng ku-kya;ng ma re pä/
Isn't he alone?

4. ཁོང་ཚོ་འབྲོག་པ་མ་རེད་པས།
they nomad not is? /
k'o;ng-ts'o ḍog-pa ma re pä/
Aren't they nomads?

12.4. A general chart of Linking Verbs and Verbs indicating existence:

Linking Verbs

Person	Affirmative		Interrogative	
	Positive	Negative	Positive	Negative
First	ཡིན་	མིན་	རེད་པས་	མ་རེད་པས་
Second	རེད་	མ་རེད་	ཡིན་པས་	མིན་པས་
Third	རེད་	མ་རེད་	རེད་པས་	མ་རེད་པས་

Verbs indicating Existence and Possession

First	ཡོད་	མེད་	འདུག་གས་	མི་འདུག་གས་
Second	འདུག་	མི་འདུག་	ཡོད་པས་	མེད་པས་
Third	འདུག་	མི་འདུག་	འདུག་གས་	མི་འདུག་གས་

12.5. Yes and No

Linking verbs are also used to denote the sense of 'Yes' and 'No'.

Honorific Yes	Honorific No
ལགས་ཡིན།	ལགས་མིན།
ལགས་རེད།	ལགས་མ་རེད།
ལགས་ཡིན་པ་རེད།	ལགས་མིན་པ་རེད།
ལགས་ཡིན་གྱི་རེད།	ལགས་ཡིན་གྱི་མ་རེད།
ལགས་ཡིན་པ་འདྲ།	ལགས་མིན་པ་འདྲ།
ལགས་ཡིན་བཟོ་འདུག	ལགས་ཡིན་བཟོ་མི་འདུག

1.	ཁྱེད་རང་བཀྲ་ཤིས་ལགས་ཡིན་པས།	ལགས་ཡིན། ང་བཀྲ་ཤིས་ཡིན།
	you Tashi (H.) is ?/	H. yes/ I Tashi is/
	ky'e-ra;ng tashi-la yi;n-pä/	la-yi;n nga Tashi yi;n/
	Are you Tashi?	Yes, I am Tashi.
2.	ཁྱེད་རང་སྐུ་རྐྱང་ཡིན་པས།	ལགས་མིན། ང་གཅིག་པུ་མིན།
	you alone (H.) is ?/	H. no/ I alone not/
	ky'e-ra;ng ku-kya;ng yi;n-pä/	la-mä;n nga chig-pu mä;n/
	Are you alone?	No, I am not alone.

3. ཁྱེད་རང་གཉིས་བུ་སྤུན་ཡིན་པས།
you two brother is ?/
ky'e-ra;ng $\overline{\text{ny}}$i: p'u-pü;n yi;n-pä/
Are you brothers?

4. ལགས་མིན། ང་གཉིས་ཆུང་ཆུང་ནས་གྲོགས་པོ་ཡིན།
H. no/ I two small since friend is/
la-mä;n/ nga-$\overline{\text{ny}}$i chu;ng-ch'ung nä ṭ'og-po yi;n/
No, we have been friends since childhood.

5. ཁྱེད་རང་ཚོ་ཞིང་པ་མིན་པས།
you pl. farmer not ?/
ky'e-ra;ng-ts'o shi;ng-pa mä;n-pä/
Aren't you farmers?

6. ལགས་མིན། ང་ཚོ་འབྲོག་པ་ཡིན།
H. no/ we nomad is/
la-mä;n/ nga;n-ts'o ḍog-pa yi;n/
No, we are nomads.

7. ང་ཚོ་ཧུར་བརྩོན་ཆེན་པོ་མ་རེད་པས།
we diligent not is ?/
nga;n-ts'o hur-tsö;n ch'en-po ma re pä/
Aren't we hard working?

8. ལགས་རེད། ཁྱེད་རང་ཚོ་ཧུར་བརྩོན་ཆེ་ཤོས་ཚོ་རེད།
H.yes/ you pl. diligent most is/
la-re꞉/ ky'e-ra;ng hur-tsö;n ch'e-shö꞉ re꞉/
Yes, you are the most hard working.

9. ཁོང་དགེ་རྒན་ཞིག་མ་རེད་པས།
he teacher a not is ?/
k'o;ng ge-gä;n shig ma re pä/
Isn't he a teacher?

10. ལགས། ཡིན་གྱི་རེད།
H. yes/ I think/
la/ yi;n-ky'i re꞉/
Yes, I think so.

11. ཁོང་སྐྱོ་པོ་མ་རེད་པས།
he poor not is ?/
k'o;ng kyo-po ma re pä/
Isn't he poor?

12. ལགས། ཡིན་གྱི་མ་རེད།
H. no/ I don't think/
la/ yi;n-ky'i-ma-re:/
No, I don't think so.

13. ཁོང་ཁོང་ཚོའི་བློས་འགེལ་ས་མ་རེད་པས།
he their trustee not is ?/
k'o;ng k'o;ng-ts'ö: l̄ö:-kä:-sa ma re pä/
Isn't he the person whom they rely upon?

14. ལགས་རེད། ཁོང་ཁོང་ཚོའི་ལག་པ་གཡས་པ་རེད།
H.yes/ he their hand right is/
la-re:/ k'o;ng k'o;ng-ts'ö: lag-pa yä:-pa re:/
Yes, he is their right hand.

15. ལྷ་ཁང་འདི་རྙིང་པ་རྙིང་པ་ཞིག་མ་རེད་པས།
temple this old old a not is ?/
la-k'a;ng di n̄ying-pa n̄ying-pa shig ma re pä/
Isn't this a very very old temple ?

16. ལགས་འོང་། ཞེ་དྲག་རྙིང་པ་ཞིག་ཡིན་བཟོ་འདུག
H. yes/ very old a seems/
la-ho;ng/ she-t'a: n̄ying-pa shig yi;n-so du/
Yes, it seems to be very old.

17. ཁོང་གཉིས་མཚེ་མ་མ་རེད་པས།
he two twins not is ?/
k'o;ng-n̄yi ts'e-ma ma re pä/
Aren't they twins?

18. ལགས། ཡིན་པ་འདྲ།
H. yes/ I suppose/

la, yi;n-pa-ḍa/

Yes, I suppose so.

19. རྒྱ་གར་ལུང་པ་ཞི་བདེ་ཞེད་པོ་ཅི་མ་རེད་པས།
India country peace very a not is ?/
gya-k̲'a: lu;ng-pa s̲h̲i-de s̲h̲i-po-chi ma re pä/
Isn't India a very peaceful country?

20. ལགས་རེད། ལུང་པ་འདི་ཞི་བདེ་ཆེ་ཤོས་ཤིག་རེད།
H. yes/ country this peace biggest a is/
la-re: lung-pa di s̲h̲i-de ch'e-shö: shig re:/
Yes, this is one of the most peaceful countries.

12.6. Exercise 6

(a) Change the following sentences into negatives:

1.	ང་སློབ་ཕྲུག་ཡིན།	= I am (a) student.
2.	ཁོང་ཡང་སློབ་ཕྲུག་རེད།	= He is also (a) student.
3.	ཁོང་ཚོ་ཚང་མ་དགེ་རྒན་རེད།	= They are all teachers.
4.	འདི་ཚོ་ཁོང་གི་ཕྲུ་གུ་རེད།	= These are his children.
5.	ཕ་གི་ང་ཚོའི་ཁང་པ་རེད།	= That is our house.
6.	ཡ་གི་གནམ་གྲུ་ཡིན་པ་འདྲ།	= I suppose that is an airplane up there.
7.	འདི་གསར་པ་ཡིན་གྱི་རེད།	= I think this is new.
8.	འདི་ཁྱེད་རང་གི་ཡིན་པས།	= Is this yours?
9.	ལགས་ཡིན། འདི་ངའི་ཡིན།	= Yes, this is mine.
10.	ཕ་ཚོ་ཁོང་གི་རེད་པས།	= Are those his?
11.	ལགས་རེད། ཕ་ཚོ་ཁོང་གི་རེད།	= Yes, those are his.
12.	མ་གི་རྟ་ཡིན་པ་འདྲ།	= I suppose that is a horse down there.
13.	མ་གི་དྲེལ་རེད།	= That is a mule down there.
14.	ཤིང་ཏོག་འདི་ཚོ་མངར་མོ་རེད།	= These fruits are sweet.

15. འདི་ཡང་མངར་མོ་རེད། = This is also sweet.
16. འདི་མངར་མོ་མངར་ཀྲུང་རེད། = This is very sweet.
17. ཕ་ཚོ་སྐྱུར་མོ་རེད། = Those are sour.
18. འདི་སྐྱུར་མོ་སྐྱུར་ཀྲུང་རེད། = This is very sour.
19. སྤྱན་དམར་པོ་དམར་ཀྲུང་རེད། = (His) eyes are very red.
20. འདི་ཞེ་དྲག་ལས་སླ་པོ་རེད། = This is very easy.

13. Verbs 'to be' Indicating Existence

ཡོད། འདུག ཡོད་པ་རེད། ཡོག་རེད།

These three basic verbs indicate existence but not tense or number.

ཡོད། is used in the first person
འདུག & ཡོག་རེད། are used in the second and third person.
འདུག expresses a definite and ཡོག་རེད། a general statement.

Examples:

1. ང་འདིར་ཡོད།
I here exist./
nga dä: yö:/
I am here.

2. ཁྱེད་རང་ཕ་གིར་འདུག
you there exist./
ky'e-ra;ng p'a-k'ä: du/
You are there.

3. ཁོང་འདི་པར་གཅིག་ལ་འདུག
he around-here somewhere exist./
k'o;ng di-pa: chi-la du/
He is somewhere around here.

4. ཁོང་ཕ་གིར་ཡོག་རེད།
he there exist./
k'o;ng p'a-k'ä: yò: re:/
He is there.

5. ང་གསོལ་སྟོན་ལ་ཡོད།
I banquet to exist./
nga sö:-tö;n la yöː /
I was at the banquet.

6. ཁོང་ཡང་གསོལ་སྟོན་ལ་འདུག
he also banquet to exist./
k'o;ng ya;ng sö:-tö;n la du/
He was also at the banquet.
(A definite statement: e.g. I saw him at the banquet.)

7. ཁོང་ཚོ་ཡང་གསོལ་སྟོན་ལ་ཡོག་རེད།
they also banquet to exist./
k'o;ng-ts'o ya;ng sö:-tö;n la yòː reː/
They were also at the banquet.
(A general statement: e.g. but I didn't see them.)

8. བོད་ལ་གཡག་མང་པོ་ཡོག་རེད།
Tibet to yak many exist./
p'öː la ȳaː ma;ng-po yò reː/
There are many yaks in Tibet.
(general statement)

9. རྒྱ་གར་ལ་ཚ་བ་ཆེན་པོ་འདུག
India to heat great exist./
gya-k̲'a: la ts'a-wa: ch'en-po du/
It is very hot in India.
(definite statement: e.g. my own experience)

ཡོག་རེད། is used instead of ཡོད་པ་རེད། in colloquial.

13.1. Alternative Verbs indicating existence

There are four alternative verbs indicating existence with a slight change in meaning.

ཡོད་པ་ཡིན་པ་རེད། / ཡོག་ཡིན་པ་རེད།	(may be)
ཡོད་པ་ཡིན་གྱི་རེད། / ཡོད་ཀྱི་རེད།	(think)
ཡོད་པ་ཡིན་པ་འདྲ། / ཡོད་པ་འདྲ།	(suppose)
ཡོད་པའི་བཟོ་འདུག / ཡོད་བཟོ་འདུག	(seems)

Examples:

1. ཁོང་ད་ལྟ་འཛིན་གྲྭར་ཡོད་པ་ཡིན་པ་རེད།
   he just-now class-to exist. may be/
   k'o;ng t̲'a;n-ta zin-t̲'a: yö-pa yin-pa re`:/
   He might be in class just now.

2. ཨཱ་ལས། ཁོང་འདིར་ཡོག་ཡིན་པ་རེད།
   Oh! I see/ he here exist. may be/
   a:-lä:/ k'o;ng dä: yò: yi;n-pa-re`:/
   Oh I see! So he is here.

3. དེ་རིང་གླིང་ཀར་མི་མང་པོ་ཡོད་པ་འདྲ།
   today park-to people many exist. suppose/
   t̲'e-ri;ng līng-k̲'a: mi ma;ng-po yö-pa-ḍa/
   I suppose, there are many people at the picnic today.

4. ཁོང་ཚོར་གླ་ཆ་ཡག་པོ་ཡོད་པ་ཡིན་གྱི་རེད།
   they-to wage good exist. think/
   k'o;ng-ts'o: la-ch'a yag-po yö-pa yi;n-k̲y̲'i-re`:/
   I think they get good wages.

5. ཁོང་ལ་བུ་ལོན་ཞེ་དྲག་ཡོད་བཟོ་འདུག
he to debt very exist. seems/
k'o;ng-la p̲'u-lö;n s̲h̲e-ṯ'a: yö:-s̲o-du/
He seems to be in heavy debt.

13.2. The Possessive Case

These verbs expressing existence also indicate possession.

In sentences expressing possession the Dative is used after the pronoun. The most common Dative in the spoken language is ལ་.

Examples:

1. ངར་དེབ་ཡག་པོ་ཞིག་ཡོད།
I-to book good a exist./
nga: ṯ'eb yag-po chi yöˋ:/
I have a good book.

2. ཁྱེད་རང་ལ་ཕྱག་སྨྱུག་ཡག་པོ་ཞིག་འདུག
you to pen(H.) good a exist.
ky'e-ra;ng la ch'a:-n̅y̅uˋ: yag-po chi du/
You have a good pen.

3. ཁོང་ལ་ཁྱི་ཡག་པོ་ཞིག་ཡོག་རེད།
she to dog good a exist./
k'o;ng-la k'yi yag-po chi yò reˋ:/
She has a good dog.

4. ཁོང་ཚོར་ཨ་ཡོའོ་སྙིང་རྗེ་པོ་དེ་འདྲས་མང་པོ་ཡོད་པ་འདྲ།
they-to puppy beautiful such many exist./
k'o;ng-ts'ò: a-yò: nyi;ng-je-po ṯ'en-däˋ: ma;ng-po yö-pa-ḍa/
I suppose they have many beautiful puppies.

5. ཁང་པ་འདི་ལ་ཁང་མིག་བཅུ་ཡོག་རེད།
house this to room ten exist./
k'a;ng-pa di la k'a;ng-mi:̀ chu yò re:̀/
This house has ten rooms.

6. ཁང་མིག་རེ་ལ་སྒེའུ་ཁུང་གཉིས་གཉིས་ཡོག་རེད།
room each to window two-two exist./
k'a;ng-mi:̀ re la ge-k'u;ng n̄ȳi:-n̄ȳi yò re:̀/
Each room has two windows.

13.3. Negative མེད། and མི། with verbs indicating existence.

Positive ཡོད། becomes negative མེད།
" ཡོད། " " མི་འདུག

Examples:

1. ང་འདིར་ཡོད།
I here exist./
nga dä: yö:̀/
I am here.

ང་ཕ་གིར་མེད།
I there not-exist./
nga p'a-k̲'ä: mä:̀/
I was not there.

2. ཁྱེད་རང་འདིར་འདུག
you here exist./
ky'e-ra;ng dä: du/
You are here.

ཁྱེད་རང་ཕ་གིར་མི་འདུག
you there not-exist./
ky'e-ra;ng p'a-k̲'ä: min du/
You were not there.

3. ཁོང་ཡ་གིར་འདུག
he up there exist./
k'o;ng ya-k̲'ä: du/
He is up there.

ཁོང་ཡ་གིར་མི་འདུག
he up there not exist./
k'o;ng ya-k̲'ä: min du/
He is not up there.

13.4. Negatives in Possessive Case

1. ངར་དུག་སློག་རྙིང་པ་ཁྱོན་ནས་མེད།
   I-to clothing old any not-exist./
   nga: t̲'ug-lò: n̅y̅i;ng-pa ky'ö;n-nä mä:/
   I do not have any old clothings.

2. དེང་སང་ཁྱེད་རང་ལ་དགེ་རྒན་མི་འདུག
   these-days you to teacher not exist./
   t̲'eng-sa;ng ky'e-ra;ng la ge-gä;n min du/
   You do not have (a) tutor these days.

3. དེང་སང་ཁོང་ལ་དམིགས་བསལ་ལས་ཀ་ཡོག་མ་རེད།
   these-days he to particular work not exist./
   t̲'eng-sa;ng k'o;ng la m̅ig-sä: lä:-ka yò: ma re:/
   He doesn't have any particular work thesedays.

4. འདི་ཛ་རམ་ས་ལར་ཡོག་མ་རེད།
   this Dharamsala-to not-exist./
   di da-ram-sa-la: yò: ma re:/
   This is not available in Dharamsala.

5. ཕྲུ་གུ་འདིར་ཕ་མ་ཡོད་ཀྱི་མ་རེད།
   child this-to parents not-exist think/
   pu-k̲'u dä: p'a-ma yö-kyi ma re:/
   (I) think this child has no parents.

6. བོད་ལ་ཚ་བ་ཡོག་མ་རེད།
   Tibet to heat not-exist./
   p̲'ö: la ts'a-wa: yò: ma re:/
   It is not hot in Tibet.

Addition of པ་ at the end converts the following affirmative sentences into questions

7. ངར་ཁག་ཡོག་མ་རེད་པ།*
I-to blame not-exist. ?/
nga: k'a: yò: ma-re-pa:/
I am not to be blamed, am I?

8. ཁྱེད་རང་ཚོར་ཁང་མིག་འཐྲོལ་པ་མེད་པ།*
you pl.-to room extra not-exist. ?/
ky'e-ra;ng-ts'ò: k'a;ng-mi: t'ö:-pa mä-pa:/
You don't have extra rooms, do you?

9. ཁོང་ལ་དེང་སང་ལས་ཀ་ཡོག་མ་རེད་པ།*
he to these-days work not-exist./
k'o;ng la t̲'eng-sa;ng lä:-ka yò: ma-re-pa:/
These days he doesn't have work, does he?

10. པུ་གུ་འདིར་ཕ་མ་སྤུན་མཆེད་སུ་གང་ཡོག་མ་རེད་པ།*
child this-to parents relative nobody not-exist. ?/
pu-k̲'u dä: p'a-ma pün-ch'e: su-k̲'a;ng yò: ma-re-pa:/
This child has neither parents nor relatives, does he?

13.5. The interrogative particle པས། with verbs indicating existence:

1. ཁྱེད་རང་ད་རངས་འཛིན་གྲྭར་ཡོད་པས།
you this morning class-to exist. ?/
ky'e-ra;ng t̲'a-ra;ng zin-t̲'a: yö-pä/
Were you in the class this morning?

---

* The above construction is applicable to all.

2. ཁྱེད་རང་ད་གིན་གཟིམ་ཤག་ལ་ཡོད་པས།
you little-while-ago house(H.) to exist. ?/
ky'e-ra;ng t'a-k'i;n sim-sha: la yö-pä/
Were you at home a little while ago?

3. དེ་དུས་ང་ཁོང་མཉམ་དུ་འདུག་གས།*
at-that-time I he with exist. ?/
t'e-t'ü: nga k'o;ng nyam-t'u du-k'ä:/
Was I with him at that time?

4. ཁ་ས་ཁོང་དཔེ་མཛོད་ཁང་ལ་འདུག་གས།*
yesterday he library to exist. ?/
k'ä:-sa k'o;ng pe;n-zö:-k'a;ng la du-k'ä/
Was he in the library yesterday?

13.6. The Interrogative Particle པས། in Possessive Case:

1. ཁྱེད་རང་ལ་ཕྱག་དངུལ་ལྡང་ངེས་ཡོད་པས།
you to money(H.) enough exist. ?/
ky'e-ra;ng la ch'a:-ngü: da;ng-nge: yö-pä/
Do you have enough money?

2. ཁྱེད་རང་ལ་འདི་པར་ཞལ་འཚོར་ཡོད་པས།
you to around-here acquaintance exist. ?/
ky'e-ra;ng la di-pa shä;n-ts'ò: yö-pä/
Do you have any acquaintances around here?

3. ངར་ཁང་མིག་གཉིས་ལྷག་འདུག་གས།
I-to room two more-than/left exist. ?/
nga: k'a;ng-mi: nyi: la: du-k'ä/
Do I have more than two rooms?/ Are there two rooms left for me?

* གས། is also used in the place of པས། when the verb ends with ག་ (suffix).

4. ཁང་མིག་འདིར་ཆུ་ཁང་གསང་སྤྱོད་ཆབས་སྦྲགས་འདུག་གས།
room this-to bath-room attached exist. ?/
k'a;ng-mi⁝ dä: ch'u-k'a;ng-sa;ng-chö⁝ ch'èb-ḍa⁝ du-k̲'ä⁝/
Does this room have a bathroom attached to it?

5. ཁོང་ཚོར་སྣུམ་འཁོར་གསར་པ་ཞིག་འདུག་གས།
they-to car new a exist. ?/
k'o;ng-ts'ò: n̄um-k'or sa:-pa s̲h̲ig du-k'ä/
Do they have a new car?

13.7. Negative Interrogatives with Verbs Indicating Existence:

1. ཁྱེད་རང་ཚོགས་འདུ་ཉི་མ་དང་པོར་མེད་པས།
you meeting day first-to not-exist. ?/
ky'e-ra;ng ts'ò;n-du nyi-ma t̲'a;ng-pò: mä:-pä/
Were you not at the meeting on the first day?

2. ཁྱེད་རང་གི་སྐུ་ཟླ་འདིར་མེད་པས།
your spouse(H.) here not-exist. ?/
ky'e-ra;ng k̲'i ku;n-da dä: mä:-pä/
Isn't your wife/husband here?

3. ང་ཚོ་མིང་གཞུང་འདིའི་ནང་ལ་མི་འདུག་གས།
we list this-of into not-exist. ?/
nga;n-ts'o mi;ng-s̲h̲u;ng di: na;ng-la mi;n-du-k̲'ä⁝/
Aren't we on this list?

4. ཁོང་ཚོ་ཐོག་ཀར་མི་འདུག་གས།
they upstairs not-exist. ?/
k'o;ng-ts'o t'ò:-ka: mi;n-du-k̲'ä/
Aren't they upstairs?

5. ཁྱེད་རང་གི་ཇོ་ལགས་ཤོད་ལ་མི་འདུག་གས།
your elder-brother(H.) downstairs not-exist. ?/
ky'e-ra;ng k'i ch'o-la: shö:-la min-du k'ä/
Isn't your brother downstairs?

13.8. Negative Interrogative in Possessive Case:

1. ཁྱེད་རང་ལ་དགོངས་ཚུལ་ཁྱོན་ནས་མེད་པས།
you to objection not-at-all not-exist. ?/
ky'e-ra;ng la go;ng-ts'ü: ky'ö;n-nä mä-pä/
Don't you have any objection?

2. ཁྱེད་རང་ལ་ཨ་བ་མེད་པས།
you to child(H.) not-exist. ?/
ky'e-ra;ng la a-wa: mä-pä/
Don't you have children?

3. ང་ཚོར་པུ་གུ་མི་འདུག་གས།
we-to child not exist. ?/
nga;n-ts'ò: pu-k'u mi;n-du-k'ä/
Don't we have children?

4. ཁོང་ཚོར་དངུལ་ཡོག་མ་རེད་པས།
they-to money not-exist. ?/
k'o;ng-ts'ò: nyü: yò: ma-re-pä/
Don't they have money?

5. ཁོང་ལ་པུ་གུ་མ་འབྱར་ཞིག་ཡོག་མ་རེད་པས།
she to child-infant a not-exist. ?/
k'o;ng la pu-k'u ma:-ja: chi yò: ma-re-pä/
Doesn't she have an infant?

6. ཁྱེད་རང་ལ་དུས་ཚོད་འཕྲོལ་པ་མེད་པས།
you to time extra not-exist. ?/
ky'e-ra;ng la t̲'ü:-ts'ö: t'ö:-pa mä-pä/
Don't you have spare time?

7. ཁྱེད་རང་ལ་དགོངས་འཆར་གང་ཡང་མེད་པས།
you to suggestion any no-exist. ?/
ky'e-ra;ng la go;ng-ch'a: k̲'a;ng-ya;ng mä-pä/
Don't you have any suggestions?

13.9. Use of 'YES' and 'NO' in verbs indicating existence

Honorific Yes		Honorific No
ལགས་ཡོད།		ལགས་མེད།
ལགས་འདུག		ལགས་མི་འདུག
ལགས་ཡོག་རེད།		ལགས་ཡོག་མ་རེད།
ལགས་ཡོད་པ་ཡིན་གྱི་རེད། /	ལགས་ཡོད་ཀྱི་རེད།	ལགས་མེད་པ་ཡིན་གྱི་རེད།
ལགས་ཡོད་པ་ཡིན་པ་འདྲ། /	ལགས་ཡོད་པ་འདྲ།	ལགས་མེད་པ་འདྲ།
ལགས་ཡོད་པའི་བཟོ་འདུག /	ལགས་ཡོད་བཟོ་འདུག	ལགས་ཡོད་བཟོ་མི་འདུག
ལགས་ཡོད་པ་ཡིན་པ་རེད། /	ལགས་ཡོག་ཡིན་པ་རེད།	ལགས་མེད་པ་ཡིན་པ་རེད།

Examples:

1. དེང་སང་ཁྱེད་རང་འདིར་ཡོད་པས།
these-days you here exist. ?/
t̲'e;ng-sa;ng ky'e-ra;ng dä: yö-pä/
Are you here these days?

2. ལགས། ང་འདིར་ཡོད།
H. I here exist./

la, nga dä: yö`:/

Yes, I am here.

3. ཨེམ་ཆི་ལགས་དེང་སང་འདིར་ཡོག་རེད་པས།

doctor(H.) these-days here exist. ?/

äm-ch'i-la`: t̲'e;ng-sa;ng dä: yò-re-pä/

Is the doctor here these days?

4. ལགས། འདིར་ཡོག་མ་རེད།

H. here not-exist./

la, dä: yò-ma-re`:/

No, (he) is not here.

5. ཁྱེད་རང་ལ་ཡབ་ཡུམ་ཡོད་པས།

you to parents(H.) exist. ?/

ky'e-ra;ng la yèb-yum yö-pä/

Do you have parents?

6. ལགས་ཡོད། ཡིན་ནའང་ཁོང་རྣམ་ཚོ་འདིར་མེད།

H. yes/ but they(H.) here not-exist./

la-yö`:/ yi;n-nä: k'o-na-ts'o dä:-mä`:/

Yes, but they are not here.

7. ཁྱེད་རང་ལ་སྐུ་མཆེད་ཡབ་གཅིག་ཡུམ་གཅིག་ཡོད་པས།

you to relative same-parents exist. ?/

ky'e-ra;ng la kum-ch'e`: yèb-chi`:-yum-chi`: yö-pä/

Do you have brothers and sisters of the same parents?

8. ལགས་ཡོད། ངར་ཨ་ལྕག་ལགས་གཅིག་དང་ཇོ་ལགས་གཅིག་ཡོད།

H. yes/ I-to elder-sister H. one & elder-brother one exist./

la-yö`: nga: a-cha`:-la`: chig t̲'a;ng c̲h̲'o-la`: chig yö`:/

Yes, I have an elder brother and an elder sister.

9. འདིའི་བརྒྱུད་ལ་སྐྲ་བཞར་མཁན་འདུག་གས།
around-here hair-cutter exist. ?/
di:- gyü:-la ṭa-sha:-k'ä;n du-k'ä:/
Is there a barber around here?

10. ལགས། ཁྱོན་ནས་ཡོད་བཟོ་མི་འདུག
H./ not-at-all not -exist. (seems)/
la, ky'ö;n-nä yö-so-min-du/
No, there seems to be none.

11. བུ་མོ་འདིར་ལྟ་རྟོགས་བྱེད་མཁན་མི་འདུག་གས།
girl this-to supervision-do-er not-exist. ?
p'u-mo dä: ta-tò: ch'e-k'ä;n min-du-k'ä/
Isn't there anybody looking after this girl?

12. ལགས། སུ་གང་མི་འདུག
H. no-one not-exist./
la, su-k'a;ng min-du/
No, there is no one.

13. འདི་པར་བོད་པའི་ཟ་ཁང་ཡོག་རེད་པས།
around-here Tibetan-of restaurant exist. ?/
di-pa p'ö-pä: sa-k'a;ng yò-re-pä/
Are there any Tibetan restaurants around here?

14. ལགས། ཁ་ཤས་ཤིག་ཡོད་པ་འདྲ།
H. few a exist. (suppose)/
la, k'a-shä: chi yö-pa-da/
I suppose there are a few.

13.10. Detailed Notes on Interrogative Particles:

གམ། ངམ། དམ། ནམ། བམ། མམ། འམ། རམ། ལམ། སམ། ཏམ།
are used in literary and པས། ངས། གས། in colloquial forms.

པས།* is used for past tenses.
ངས། is used also for past tenses but only after a verb ending with ང་.
གས། is used for future tenses only.

The interrogative particles of the literary form (except the particle ཏམ།) are used in accordance with the corresponding end-letter of the verb.

ཏམ། is used after a verb ending with Post-Suffix ད་.

(a) Examples of interrogative particles used with verbs:

Literary	Colloquial	Meaning
(བཀའ་) བཅག་གམ།	བཅག་གས།	Will (you) break (the order)?
(ཡི་གེ་) གཏང་ངམ།	གཏང་གས།	Will (you) send (the letter)?
(ཡི་གེ་) བཏང་ངམ།	བཏང་ངས་/པས།	Did (you) send (the letter)?
(ཤིང་) གཅད་དམ།	གཅད་གས།	Will (you) chop (the wood)?
(གཞས་) ཉན་ནམ།	ཉན་གས།	Will (you) listen (to a song)?
(ཤིང་) བཏབ་བམ།	བཏབ་པས།	Did (you) plant (the plants)?
(འགྲོ་) བརྩམ་མམ།	བརྩམ་གས།	Shall (we) start?
(ཆུ་) བཏོར་རམ།	བཏོར་པས།	Did (you) sprinkle (the water)?
(ཉལ་ས་) བཅའ་འམ།	བཅའ་གས།	Will (you) make (the bed)?
ཕུལ་ལམ།	ཕུལ་པས།	Did (you) give?
བལྟས་སམ།	བལྟས་པས།	Did (you) watch?
བལྟ་འམ།	བལྟ་གས།	Will (you) watch?
ཕྱིནད་ཏམ།	ཕྱིན་པས།	Did (you) go?

* པས་ used immediately after a verb indicates past tense. However, when པས། is used after a complementary particle of the main verb, it can show all the three tenses. (see page 98)

(b) Interrogative particles used with nouns:

Literary	Colloquial	Meaning
འདི་ཕྱག་གམ།	འདི་ཕྱག་རེད་པས།	Is this (a) hand (H.)?
འདི་ཚང་ངམ།	འདི་ཚང་རེད་པས།	Is this (a) nest?
འདི་སྐད་དམ།	འདི་སྐད་རེད་པས།	Is this (a) voice?
འདི་སྤྱན་ནམ།	འདི་སྤྱན་རེད་པས།	Is this (an) eye (H.)?
འདི་ཁབ་བམ།	འདི་ཁབ་རེད་པས།	Is this (a) needle?
འདི་སྒམ་མམ།	འདི་སྒམ་རེད་པས།	Is this (a) box?
ཕ་གི་འཇའ་འམ།	ཕ་གི་འཇའ་རེད་པས།	Is this (a) rainbow?
འདི་དཔར་རམ།	འདི་དཔར་རེད་པས།	Is this (a) photo?
འདི་བལ་ལམ།	འདི་བལ་རེད་པས།	Is this wool?
འདི་ལྕགས་སམ།	འདི་ལྕགས་རེད་པས།	Is this (an) iron?
འདི་རྟ་འམ།	འདི་རྟ་རེད་པས།	Is this (a) horse?

13.11. Exercise 7

(a) Insert ཡོད། འདུག ཡོད་པ་རེད། appropriately in the following sentences.

ང་སློབ་གྲྭར་ ....
ཁོང་ཚོ་ཕ་གིར་ ....
བོད་ལ་རི་མཐོ་པོ་མང་པོ་ ....
ཁྱེད་རང་ཚོ་གསོལ་སྟོན་ལ་ ....
ཁོང་ཚོ་བོད་ལ་ ....
བོད་ལ་གཡག་མང་པོ་ ....
དེ་རིང་ཁྲོམ་ལ་མི་མང་པོ་ ....
ང་ཚོར་དངུལ་མང་པོ་ ....

འདི་སྙིང་རྗེ་པོ་ ....
ང་ཚོ་འདིར་ ....
འདི་ཡག་པོ་ ....
རི་འདི་མཐོ་པོ་ ....
ཁོང་ཡ་གིར་ ....
ང་རྒྱ་གར་ལ་ ....
རི་ལ་སེམས་ཅན་ ....
ཁོང་ལ་བུ་གཉིས་ ....

(b) Make the following sentences into negatives.

ང་ནང་ལ་འདུག་གས།
ཁྱེད་རང་ཕ་གིར་ཡོད་པས།
ཁོང་ཕྱི་རྒྱལ་ལ་འདུག་གས།
ཁོང་བོད་ལ་ཡོག་རེད་པས།

ངར་ཁྲི་གཉིས་འདུག་གས།
ཁྱེད་རང་ལ་དེབ་ལྷང་ཁྲ་ཡོད་པས།
ཁོང་ལ་ལས་ཀ་འདུག་གས།
ཁོང་ཚོར་ཕྲུག་ལས་འདུག་གས།

(c) Translate the following into Tibetan.

1. Does he have clothes?
2. Was he in the market?
3. Is she her relative?
4. Do they have children?
5. Is she up there?

14. ལ་དོན་བདུན།

Seven Dative-Locatives

There are seven Dative-locatives which have the function of TO, AT, IN & FOR. Their use is as follows:

སུ་	used after word ending at ས་	
དུ་	" " " " "	ང་ད་ན་མ་ར་ལ་
ཏུ་	" " " " "	ག་བ་ & ད་དྲག་*
ར་ / རུ	" " " " "	འ་ & མཐའ་མེད་**
ལ་ / ན་	" " all the suffixes	

སུ་ དུ་ ཏུ་ རུ་ ན་ are literary

ལ་ & ར་ are colloquial

14.1. Examples of Combination:

(a) Dative-locatives used with nouns

Literary	Colloquial	Meaning
ཐུགས་སུ་/ ན་	ཐུགས་ལ་	in the mind(H.)
དཔེ་མཛོད་ཁང་དུ་	དཔེ་མཛོད་ཁང་ལ་	to the library
བོད་དུ་	བོད་ལ་	to Tibet
སྤྱན་དུ་	སྤྱན་ལ་	in the eyes
ཤར་དུ་	ཤར་ལ་	to the east

* Name of the Post-suffix ད་

** Words without suffix

ཞལ་དུ་	ཞལ་ལ་	into the mouth(H.)
ཕྱག་ཏུ་	ཕྱག་ལ་	into the hand(H.)
རྒྱབ་ཏུ་	རྒྱབ་ལ་	on the back
ཀུན་ཏུ་(ཁྱབ་)	ཀུན་ལ་(ཁྱབ་)	(spread out) all over
མཐའ་རུ་/མཐར་***	མཐའ་ལ་	at the end (shortened)
ས་རུ་	ས་ལ་	to the ground
སར་****	ས་ལ་	" " " (shortened)

(b) Dative-locatives used with verbs:

In colloquial when the Dative-locative is used with the verbs, ག་ is usually used instead of ལ་.

Literary	Colloquial	Meaning
འདེབས་སུ་འགྲོ་	འདེབས་ག་འགྲོ་	go to plant
ཟ་རུ་འགྲོ་	ཟ་ག་འགྲོ་	go to eat
ཟར་འགྲོ་	ཟ་ག་འགྲོ་	" " " (shortened)
མཇལ་དུ་འགྲོ་	མཇལ་ག་འགྲོ་	go to see/meet (H.)
ཀློག་ཏུ་འགྲོ་	ཀློག་ག་འགྲོ་	go to read
ཉོ་རུ་འགྲོ་	ཉོ་ག་འགྲོ་	go to buy

14.2. Examples of complete sentences:

1. དམག་མི་མང་ཆེ་བ་ས་མཚམས་ས་ཁུལ་ཁག་ལ་ཡོད་རེད།
army majority border areas to exist./
m̄a:-mi ma;ng-ch'e-wa sa-ts'am sa-k'ü: k'a꞉ la yò꞉-re꞉/
The majority of the army is at the border areas.

*** When ར་ is used after a word ending in འ་, e.g. 'མཐའ་' the suffix འ་ is replaced by ར་, thus forming མཐར་.

**** When ར་ is used with a མཐའ་མེད་ word, e.g. 'ས་' (ground), ར་ can simply be added after ས་ without the stop sign (.) ཚེག་, thus forming སར་ (to the ground).

2. ང་ཚོའི་དངུལ་ཕལ་ཆེ་བ་དངུལ་ཁང་ལ་ཡོད།

our money most bank to exist./

nga;n-ts'ö: $\overline{\text{ny}}$ü: p'ä:-ch'e-wa $\overline{\text{ny}}$ü:-k'a;ng la yö̀:/

Most of our money is in the bank.

3. བོད་ལ་སེམས་ཅན་སྤུ་གནག་འཕོན་ཆེན་པོ་ཡོག་རེད།

Tibet to animal yaks large-number exist./

<u>p</u>'ö̀:-la sem-chä;n pu-nà: p'ö;n-ch'en-po yò-rè:/

There is a large number of yaks in Tibet.

4. ང་ལོ་ལྟར་རྒྱ་གར་ལ་ཚོང་རྒྱག་ག་ཡོང་གི་ཡོད།

I every-year India to business-da-to come pres. c./

nga lo-ta: gya-k'a: la ts'o;ng-gya:-<u>k</u>'a yo;ng-<u>k</u>'i-yö̀:/

Every year I come to India to do business.

5. ང་མེ་ཏོག་བཏབ་ག་འགྲོ་གི་ཡིན།*

I flower plant to go fut. c./

nga me-tò: tab-<u>k</u>'a: ḍo-<u>k</u>'i-yi;n/

I am going to plant flowers.

6. ང་ཁ་ལག་ཟ་ག་འགྲོ་གི་ཡིན།*

I food eat to go fut. c./

nga k'a-là: <u>s</u>a-<u>k</u>'à: ḍo-k'i-yi;n/

I am going to eat food.

7. ང་ཤ་ཉོ་ག་འགྲོ་གི་ཡིན།

I meat buy to go fut. c./

nga sha nyo-<u>k</u>'a ḍo-<u>k</u>'i-yi;n/

I am going to buy meat.

8. ང་ཡི་གེ་ཀློག་ག་འགྲོ་གི་ཡིན།

I letter read to go fut. c./

---

* གི་ཡིན། is future verb complement (see page 95)

nga yi-k̲'e l̄o:-k̲'a ḍo-k̲'i-yi;n/
I am going to read letters.

9. ང་རྩེད་མོ་རྩེད་ཀ་འགྲོ་གི་ཡིན།
I game play to go fut. c./
nga tse-mo-tse-k̲'a ḍo-k̲'i-yi;n/
I am going to play.

10. ང་ཉོ་ཆ་རྒྱག་ཀ་འགྲོ་གི་ཡིན།
I shopping do go fut. c./
nga nyob-ch'a gya-k̲'a ḍo-k̲'i-yi;n/
I am going for shopping.

11. ང་གསར་འགྱུར་ཉན་ཀ་འགྲོ་གི་ཡིན།
I news listen to go fut. c./
nga sa;ng-gyu: nyä;n-k̲'a ḍo-k̲'i-yi;n/
I am going to listen the news.

14.3. Exercise 8

(a) In the following, fill in each of the blanks with the appropriate Dative-locatives ལ་དོན།

1. ང་རྒྱ་གར་......................བསྡད་པ་ཡིན། = I lived in India.
2. ཁོང་བླ་མ་མཇལ་..............འགྲོ་བ་རེད། = He goes to visit a lama.
3. རས་..........................བྲིས་དགོས་རེད། = Should draw it on cloth.
4. འདི་ཁ་...................................ཆུགས། = Put it into the mouth.
5. འདི་......................................བཞུགས། = Sit here. (H.)
6. གནས་བསྐོར་...............................འགྲོ། = go on pilgrimage
7. ཉན་.......................................འགྲོ། = go to listen
8. སྐད་ཆ་ཤོད་...............................འགྲོ། = go to talk
9. རྟ་བཞོན་..................................འགྲོ། = go horse riding
10. ཆུ་འཐུང་..................................འགྲོ། = go to drink water

(b) Change the following ལ་ Datives into literary forms.

1. ལག་པ་ལ་ལེན། = to take into one's hand
2. ཕྱག་ལ་བཞེས། = " " " " " H.
3. དཔེ་མཛོད་ཁང་ལ་ཕྱིན། = went to the library
4. བོད་ལ་ཕྱིན། = went to Tibet

15. ཨི་ལྡན་ལྔ།

Five Genitives

There are five genitives in Tibetan. They are also used as instrumentive by adding the instrumental particle ས་ immediately after the genitive forms (except the genitive འི་).

འི་* is replaced by instrumental particle ས་

An identical grammatical rule is followed for both the genitives and instrumentives.

གི་ & གིས་	used	after	words	ending	at		ག་ང་
ཀྱི་ & ཀྱིས་	”	”	”	”	”		ད་བ་ས་
གྱི་ & གྱིས་	”	”	”	”	”		ན་མ་ར་ལ་
ཡི་ & ཡིས་	”	”	”	”	”		འ་ & མཐའ་མེད་
འི་ & ས་	”	”	”	”	”		འ་ & མཐའ་མེད་

15.1. Examples with གི་ & གིས་, ཀྱི་ & ཀྱིས་, གྱི་ & གྱིས་.

	Genitives	Instrumentives
1.	གཡག་གི་རྔ་མ་	གཡག་གིས་ཟས།
	yak of tail/	yak by ate/
	ya: k'i nga-ma/	ya: k'i sä:
	Tail of a yak	A yak ate/ Eaten by a yak

* see note on page 76

2.	ཁོང་གི་ཕྱག་ he of hand(H.)/ K'o;ng k'i ch'a⁝/ His hand	ཁོང་གིས་བརྡབས། he by clapped/ K'o;ng k'i⁝ dèb/ He clapped
3.	དགེ་རྒན་གྱི་ལས་ཀ་ teacher of work/ ge-gä;n k'i lä:-ka/ Teacher's work	དགེ་རྒན་གྱིས་བྱས། teacher by did/ ge-gä;n k'i⁝ ch'ä⁝/ Done by the teacher
4.	སྐད་ཀྱི་གདངས་ voice of tone/ kä⁝ ki da;ng/ Tone of a voice	སྐད་ཀྱིས་རྒྱངས། noise by filled/ kä⁝ ki gya;ng/ Filled with noise
5.	དོམ་གྱི་ཤ་ bear of meat/ t'om k'i sha/ Bear's meat	དོམ་གྱིས་ཟས། bear by ate/ t'om k'i sä⁝/ Eaten by the bear
6.	རྒྱལ་ཁབ་ཀྱི་རྩ་ཁྲིམས་ nation of constitution/ gy'ä:-k'èb kyi tsa-ṭ'im/ Constitution of a nation	རྒྱལ་ཁབ་ཀྱིས་བསྲུངས། nation by respected/ gy'ä:-k'èb kyi su;ng/ Respected by a nation
7.	འཁོར་གྱི་གཙོ་བོ་ subjects of chief/ k'or ky'i tso:/ Chief of the subjects	འཁོར་གྱིས་བསྐོར། subjects by surrounded/ k'or ky-i kor/ Surrounded by subjects
8.	དངུལ་གྱི་ཁྲི་ silver of throne/ ngü: k'i ṭ'i/ Throne of silver	དངུལ་གྱིས་བཟོས། silver by made/ ngü: ki sö⁝/ Made of silver

9. ལས་ཀྱི་འབྲས་བུ་
kar-ma of result/
lä: kyi ḍä:-p̲'u/
Result of karma

ལས་ཀྱིས་སྨིན།
kar-ma by ripened/
lä: kyi m̄i;n/
Ripened by karma

15.2. Examples with ཡི་, ཡིས་ & འི་, ས་ after suffix

Both ཡི་ and འི་ are used after a word ending with suffix འ་, e.g. མཁའ།

If the genitive འི་ is chosen, the vowel 'i' can simply be added on the top of the letter འ་, thus forming མཁའི་.

1. ནམ་མཁའི་མདོག
sky of colour/
nam-k'ä: dò:/
Colour of the sky

ནམ་མཁའ་ཡི་མདོག
sky of colour/
nam-k'ä: yi dò:/
Colour of the sky

In the case of **Instrumentive**, if the འི་ is chosen, the ending letter འ་ of the word མཁའ་ is replaced by the instrumental particle ས་, thus forming མཁས་.

2. ནམ་མཁས་ཁྱབ།
sky by covered/
nam-k'ä: ky'èb/
Covered by the sky

ནམ་མཁའ་ཡིས་ཁྱབ།
sky by covered/
nam-k'a yi: ky'èb/
Covered by the sky

15.3. Examples with ཡི་, ཡིས་ & འི་, ས་ after མཐའ་མེད།

མཐའ་མེད་ means a word without any suffixes such as ང་ (I). In this case, if the genitive འི་ is chosen, the stop sign (.) ཚེག་ is omitted and the འི་ is added to the མཐའ་མེད་ word, thus forming ངའི་ (my, mine).

1. ངའི་ལས་ཀ་
I-of work/

ང་ཡི་ལས་ཀ་
I of work/

ngä lä:-ka/	nga yi lä:-ka/
My work	My work

In the case of **Instrumentive,** the instrumental particle ས་ is simply added to the མཐའ་མེད་ word ང་, thus forming ངས་ (by me).

2.	ངས་བྱེད།	ང་ཡིས་བྱེད།
	I-by do/	I by do/
	ngäˋ: <u>ch</u>'eˋ:/	nga yiˋ: <u>ch</u>'eˋ:/
	I do	I do
3.	རྟས་དབྱུགས།	རྟ་ཡིས་དབྱུགས།
	horse-by throw/	horse by throw/
	täˋ: ȳuˋ:/	ta yiˋ: ȳuˋ:/
	Thrown by horse	Thrown by horse

15.4. Further examples of the genitive used in the sentence

1. ཕ་ཚོ་ཁྱེད་རང་ཚོའི་ས་ཆ་རེད།
   those your land is/
   p'a;n-ts'o ky'e-ra;ng-ts'ö: sa-ch'a reˋ:/
   Those are your estates.

2. ཁྱི་འདི་མི་ཡ་གིའི་རེད།
   dog this man that up there-of is/
   ky'i di mi ya-<u>k</u>'i: reˋ:/
   This dog belongs to the man up there.

3. ཞིང་ཁ་མ་གི་ངའི་རེད།
   field that down there my is/
   <u>shi</u>;ng-k'a ma-<u>k</u>'i ngä: reˋ:/
   The field down there is mine.

4. དཔར་ཆས་འདི་བུ་མོ་ཕ་གིའི་རེད།
camera this girl that-of is/
par-ch'äˋ: di p'u-mo p'a-k'i: reˋ:/
This camera belongs to that girl.

5. འདི་ཁྱེད་རང་གི་བཞུགས་ས་རེད།
this your stay-place is/
di ky'e-ra;ng-k'i shu:-sa reˋ:/
This is your house (abode).

6. ཡ་ཚོ་ཁོང་ཚོའི་གཡག་ཡིན་པ་འདྲ།
those up there their yak might be/
ya;n-ts'o k'o;ng-ts'ö: ȳaˋ: yi;n-pa-ḍa/
Those yaks up there might be theirs.

7. ཁོང་ངའི་གྲོགས་པོའི་བུ་རྒན་པ་རེད།
he my friend-of son elder is/
k'o;ng ngä: ṯ'òˋ:-pö: p'u gä;n-pa reˋ:/
He is the elder son of my friend.

8. བུ་འདི་ཁོང་གི་སྐུ་ཟླའི་སྐུ་མཆེད་རེད།
boy this his spouse-of relative(H.) is/
p'u di k'o;ng k'i ku;n-dä: kum-ch'eˋ: reˋ:/
This boy is his wife's brother.

9. ཁོང་ངའི་ཨ་ཞང་*ལགས་ཀྱི་བུ་མོ་རེད།
she my uncle(H.) of daughter is/
k'o;ng-ngä: a-sha;ng laˋ: ki p'u-mo reˋ:/
She is my uncle's daughter.

---

* ཨ་ཞང་ལགས། mother's brother, ཨ་ཁུ་ལགས། father's brother

10. ཁོང་ཚེ་རིང་གི་གྲོགས་མོ་རེད།

she Tsering of friend is/

k'o;ng Tsering <u>k</u>'i ṭ'ò:-mo re̖:/

She is Tsering's friend.

11. འདི་ང་ཚོའི་ལུང་པའི་སྐད་རེད།

this our country-of language is/

di nga;n-ts'ö: lu;ng-pä: kä̖: re̖:/

This is our native language.

12. འདི་བོད་པའི་ལུགས་སྲོལ་རེད།

this Tibetan-of custom is/

di <u>p</u>'ö:-pä: lug-sö: re̖:/

This is Tibetan custom.

13. ལ་མོའི་རྒྱབ་ཀྱི་ཆུ་དེ་དུག་ཆུ་ཡིན་པ་འདྲ།

pass-of behind of water that poison-water might be/

la-mö: gyèb ki ch'u <u>t</u>'e <u>t</u>'ug-ch'u yi;n-pa-ḍa/

The water behind the pass might be poisonous.

14. འདི་རྒྱལ་པོའི་བཙུན་མོའི་མགུལ་རྒྱན་རེད།

this king-of consort-of necklace is/

di gyä:-pö: tsü;n-mö: gü:-gyä;n re̖:/

This is the queen's necklace.

15. འདི་གཞུང་གི་སྨན་ཁང་ཞིག་རེད།

this government of hospital a is/

di <u>sh</u>u;ng <u>k</u>'i mā;n-k'a;ng chi re̖:/

This is a government hospital.

15.5. Importance of ཡི་ and འི།

The use of ཡི་ and འི་ becomes important in metrical compositions for the structure of the rhythm.

Example 1: (Lord Buddha's word)

དགེ་སློང་དག་དང་མཁས་རྣམས་ཀྱིས། །
བསྲེག་བཅད་བདར་བའི་གསེར་བཞིན་དུ། །
ལེགས་པར་བརྟག་ལ་ང་ཡི་བཀའ། །
བླང་བར་བྱ་ཡི་གུས་ཕྱིར་མིན། །

bhikshu-pl. and expert all by/
burn cut rub-of gold like/
nicely examine having my order/
practise-to do imp. respect for not/

ge-lo;ng t'a:-t'a;ng   k'ä:-n̄am kyi:/
seg-chä: dar-wä: ser-shi;n t'u/
leg-par ta:-la   nga-yi ka/
l̄a;ng-war ch'a-yi   k'ü:-ch'ir mi;n/

Bhikshus and learned ones,
Just as gold is burnt, cut and rubbed,
Examine well (or carefully) my speech
And then accept (it), not otherwise, for respect's sake.

Example 2: Invocation to Manjushri (God of wisdom)

བརྩེ་ལྡན་ཁྱོད་ཀྱི་མཁྱེན་རབ་འོད་ཟེར་གྱིས། །
བདག་བློའི་གཏི་མུག་མུན་པ་རབ་བསལ་ནས། །
བཀའ་དང་བསྟན་བཅོས་གཞུང་ལུགས་རྟོགས་པ་ཡི། །
བློ་གྲོས་སྤོབས་པའི་སྣང་བ་སྩལ་དུ་གསོལ། །

compassionate you of wisdom brilliance by/
my mind-of ignorance darkness illuminate and/
Buddha's words and commentaries doctrine understanding of/
wisdom courage-of enlighten imp. c./

tse-dä;n	ky'ö̀:-kyi	ky'en-rèb	ö:-ser	ky'ì:/
dag-l̄ö:	ti-mug	mü;n-pa	rèb-sä:	nä̀:/
ka-ṯ'a;ng	tä;n-chö̀:	shu;ng-lù:	tòg-pa	yi/
l̄o-ṯ̣'ö̀:	pob-pä:	n̄a;ng-wa:	tsä:-ṯu	söl/

With the brilliance of your wisdom, O compassionate one,
Illuminate the darkness enclosing my mind
Enlighten my intelligence and wisdom
So that I may gain insight into Buddha's words and the texts that explain them.

Example 3: From Sixth Dalai Lama's (ts'ang-ȳa;ng gya-ts'o) love song.

ཤར་ཕྱོགས་རི་བོའི་རྩེ་ནས།
དཀར་གསལ་ཟླ་བ་ཤར་བྱུང་།
མ་སྐྱེས་ཨ་མའི་ཞལ་རས།
ཡིད་ལ་འཁོར་འཁོར་བྱས་བྱུང་།

east direction mountain-of top from/
white bright moon rise compl./
unborn mother-of face/
mind to revolving did compl./

shar-ch'ò:	ri-wö:	tse-nä/
kar-sä:	da-wa:	shar-ch'u;ng/

ma-kyeˋ:	a-mä:	shä:-räˋ:/
yiˋ:-la	k'ò:-k'ò:	<u>ch</u>'äˋ:-<u>ch</u>'u;ng/

From the top of the eastern mountain,
a white and bright moon is rising.
The face of my unborn mother (beloved),
vividly comes to my mind.

15.6. Exercise 9

(a) Fill in the blanks with appropriate ཨི་ལྡན། (genitives):

1. ཁོང............................ཕྲུག
2. ང་ཚོ............................ནང་
3. གཡག............................ཤ་
4. གནམ............................སྐར་མ་
5. དཔར............................ཤྲིང་ཤོག
6. དཔར་ཆས............................གོང་ཚད་
7. བོད............................ས་ཆ་
8. མིག............................གཟི་མ་
9. ནམ་མཁའ............................སྤྲིན་པ་
10. རྒྱལ་ཁབ............................མི་མང་
11. བལ............................རྟོད་ཐུང་
12. ཆོས............................དོན་དག

(b) Translate the following into Tibetan

my hat, his house, their books, our son, her children, size of photo, woollen socks, your hand, your pen.

(c) Make new sentences with the following

1. ཆུའི་སྒྲ་
2. ཤིང་གི་ཡལ་ག་
3. ངའི་ལུང་པ་
4. གཞས་ཀྱི་ཚིག་
5. ཁྱེད་རང་གི་བུ་
6. སྟག་གི་མཆེ་བ་
7. སྒམ་གྱི་ལྡེ་མིག
8. བོད་པའི་ཞལ་ལག
9. ལུང་པའི་ཁྲིམས་
10. མིའི་རང་བཞིན་
11. རྒྱ་མཚོའི་ཐ་རླབས་
12. ཞལ་ལག་གི་བྲོ་བ་
13. ང་ཚོའི་སྐད་
14. ཆོས་ཀྱི་དོན་དག་
15. ཁོང་གི་ཕྲུག་

16. དུས་གསུམ་བྱ་ཚིག་ཁ་སྐོང་།
Verb Complement in Three Tenses

In colloquial Tibetan the following verb complements need to be used after the main verb to indicate the tense.

Tense	1st person verb-complement	2nd & 3rd person verb-complement
ད་ལྟ་བ། (present)	གི་ཡོད།	གི་འདུག
མ་འོངས་པ། (future)	གི་ཡིན།	གི་རེད།
འདས་པ། (past)	པ་ཡིན།	པ་རེད།

1st person

1. ང་ཡོང་གི་ཡོད།
   I come pres. c./
   nga yo;ng-k'i yö:/
   I am coming. or I come.

2. ང་ཡོང་གི་ཡིན།
   I come fut. compl./
   nga yo;ng-k'i yi;n/
   I will come.

3. ང་ཡོང་པ་ཡིན།
   I come past. compl./
   nga yo;ng-pa yi;n/
   I came.

2nd person

1. ཁྱེད་རང་ཡོང་གི་འདུག
   you come pres. compl./
   ky'e-ra;ng yo;ng k'i du:/
   You are coming. or You come.

2. ཁྱེད་རང་ཡོང་གི་རེད།
   you come fut. compl./
   ky'e-ra;ng yo;ng k'i re:/
   You will come.

3. ཁྱེད་རང་ཡོང་པ་རེད།
   you come past compl./
   ky'e-ra;ng yo;ng pa re:/
   You came.

3rd person

1. ཁོང་ཡོང་གི་འདུག
   he come pres. compl./
   k'o;ng yo;ng k'i du:/
   He/She is coming. or He/She comes.

2. ཁོང་ཡོང་གི་རེད།
   he come fut. compl./
   k'o;ng yo;ng k'i re:/
   He/She will come.

3. ཁོང་ཡོང་པ་*རེད།
   he come past compl./
   k'o;ng yo;ng pa re:/
   He/She came.

Examples:

1. ང་ཁྲོམ་ལ་འགྲོ་གི་**ཡིན།
   I market to go fut. compl./
   nga ṭ'om-la ḍo k'i yi;n/
   I will go to the market.

2. ང་སློབ་གྲྭར་འགྲོ་གི་ཡོད།
   I school to go pres. compl./
   nga l̄ab-ṯ'a: ḍo k'i yö:/
   I am going to school.

3. ང་ཚོ་རྒྱ་གར་ལ་ཕྱིན་པ་ཡིན།
   we India to went past compl./
   nga;n-ts'o gya-k'a: la ch'i;n-pa yi;n/
   We went to India.

4. ཁྱེད་རང་འདིར་བཞུགས་ཀྱི་རེད།
   you here stay (H.) fut. compl./
   ky'e-ra;ng dä: shu:-ki re:/
   You will stay here.

5. ཁྱེད་རང་འདིར་བཞུགས་ཀྱི་འདུག
   you here stay pres. compl./

---

* པ་ is commonly used after all the suffixes. However, according to the grammar rule, བ་ is used after a verb ending at ང་ འ་ ར་ ལ་.

** གི་ is commonly used after a མཐའ་མེད་ verb in conversation though grammatically it is incorrect.

ky'e-ra;ng dä: <u>sh</u>u: ki du꞉/

You are staying here.

6. ཁྱེད་རང་འདིར་བཞུགས་པ་རེད།

you here stay past compl./

ky'e-ra;ng dä: <u>sh</u>u: pa re꞉/

You stayed/lived here.

7. ཁོང་ཕྱག་ལས་ལ་ཐེག་གི་རེད།

she work (H.) to go (H.) fut compl./

k'o;ng ch'a:-lä꞉ la t'ä: <u>k</u>i re꞉/

She will go to work.

8. ཁོང་ཕྱག་ལས་ལ་ཐེག་གི་འདུག

she work (H.) to go pres. compl./

k'o;ng ch'a:-lä꞉ la t'ä: <u>k</u>'i du꞉/

She is going to work.

9. ཁོང་ཕྱག་ལས་ལ་ཐེག་པ་རེད།

she work to go past compl./

k'o;ng ch'a:-lä꞉ la t'ä꞉ pa re꞉/

She went to work.

[For གི་, ཀྱི་, གྱི་, refer to verb compl. (see genitive rules page 68)]

16.1. Interrogative particles པས་/ གས་

པས་ is used in the past & future tense

གས་ is used in the present tense

1. ང་ཚོ་ལས་ཀ་བྱེད་ཀྱི་རེད་པས།

we work-do fut. c. ?/

nga;n-ts'o lä:-ka ch'e-ki re pä/
Will we work?

2. ང་ཚོ་ལས་ཀ་བྱེད་ཀྱི་འདུག་གས།
we work-do pres. c. ?/
nga;n-ts'o lä:-ka ch'e ki du k'ä:/
Are we working?

3. ང་ཚོས་ལས་ཀ་བྱས་པ་རེད་པས།
we work-do past c. ?/
nga;n-ts'ö: lä:-ka ch'ä: pa re pä:/
Did we work?

4. ཁྱེད་རང་ཞལ་ལག་མཆོད་ཀྱི་ཡིན་པས།
you food(H.) eat(H.) fut. c. ?/
ky'e-ra;ng shä:-la: ch'ö: ki yi;n pä:/
Will you eat food?

5. ཁྱེད་རང་གསོལ་ཇ་མཆོད་ཀྱི་ཡོད་པས།
you tea (H.) drink (H.) pres. c. ?/
ky'e-ra;ng sö:-ch'a ch'ö: ki yö pä/
Are you having tea?

6. ཁྱེད་རང་ཞལ་ལག་མཆོད་པ་ཡིན་པས།
you food (H.) eat (H.) past c. ?/
ky'e-ra;ng shä:-la: ch'ö: pa yi;n pä/
Have you had (your) food?

7. ཁོང་འདིར་ཕེབས་ཀྱི་རེད་པས།
she here come fut. c. ?/
k'o;ng dä: p'e:-ki re pä/
Will she come here?

8. ཁོང་འདིར་ཕེབས་ཀྱི་འདུག་གས།
she here come pres. c. ?/
k'o;ng dä: p'e:-ki du k'ä:/
Is she coming here?

9. ཁོང་འདིར་ཕེབས་པ་རེད་པས།
she here come past c. ?/
k'o;ng dä: p'e: pa re pä/
Did she come here?

16.2. Negative Interrogatives

1. ངས་སློབ་སྦྱོང་བྱེད་ཀྱི་མ་རེད་པས།
I-by study-do neg. fut. c. ?/
ngä: l̄ob-jo;ng ch'e-ki ma-re-pä/
Won't I study?

2. ང་སློབ་སྦྱོང་བྱེད་ཀྱི་མི་འདུག་གས།
I study-do neg. pres. c. ?/
nga l̄ob-jo;ng ch'i-ki mi-du-k'ä/
Am I not studying?

3. ངས་སློབ་སྦྱོང་མ་བྱས་པ་རེད་པས།
I-by study not did past c. ?/
ngä: l̄ob-jo;ng ma-ch'ä-pa re-pä/
Have I not studied?

4. ཁྱེད་རང་སློབ་སྦྱོང་གནང་གི་མིན་པས།
you study-do (H.) neg. fut. c. ?/
ky'e-ra;ng l̄ob-jo;ng n̄a;ng-k'i mi;n-pä/
Won't you study?

5. ཁྱེད་རང་སློབ་སྦྱོང་གནང་གི་མེད་པས།
you study-do neg. pres. c. ?/
ky'e-ra;ng l̄ob-jo;ng n̄a;ng-k̲'i mä;n-pä/
Aren't you studying?

6. ཁྱེད་རང་སློབ་སྦྱོང་མ་གནང་པས།
you study not do past c ?/
ky'e-ra;ng l̄ob-jo;ng ma-n̄a;ng pä/
Didn't you study?

7. ཁོང་འཛིན་གྲྭར་ཕེབས་ཀྱི་མ་རེད་པས།
she class-to come(H.) neg. fut. c. ?/
k'o;ng zin-t'a: p'e:-ki ma-re pä/
Won't she come to the class?

8. ཁོང་འཛིན་གྲྭར་ཕེབས་ཀྱི་མི་འདུག་གས།
she class-to come neg. pres. c. ?/
k'o;ng zin-ṯ'a: p'e:-ki mi;n-du k̲'ä/
Isn't she coming to the class?

9. ཁོང་འཛིན་གྲྭར་མ་ཕེབས་པ་རེད་པས།
she class-to not come past c. ?/
k'o;ng zin-ṯ'a: ma-p'e-pa re-pä/
Didn't she come to the class?

10. ལགས་མ་རེད། ཁོང་འཛིན་གྲྭར་ཕེབས་སོང་།
H.no/ she class-to come past c. ?/
la ma-rè:/ k'o;ng zin-ṯ'a: p'è:-so;ng/
No, she came to the class.

ཁོང་ཕེབས་སོང་། = She came (I saw).
ཁོང་ཕེབས་ཤག = She came (I heard).

16.3. ཕལ་སྐད་དུ་བྱ་ཚིག་ཁ་སྐོང་བསྡུངས་པ། Shortened verb-complements in colloquial language:

In some commonly shortened verb-complements in colloquial, the interrogative particle ཀས། is used to indicate future tense in the first person plural and second persons.

	Usual forms		Shortened forms
1.	ང་ཚོ་ཕེབས་ཀྱི་ཡིན་པས།	=	ང་ཚོ་ཕེབས་ཀས།
	we come fut. c. ?/		come fut. c. ?/
	nga;n-ts'o p'e:-ki yi;n-pä/		p'e:-k'ä/
	Shall we go?	=	Shall we go?
2.	ཁྱེད་རང་ཕེབས་ཀྱི་ཡིན་པས།	=	ཁྱེད་རང་ཕེབས་ཀས།
	you come fut. c. ?/		come fut. c. ?/
	ky'e-ra;ng p'e:-ki yi;n-pä/		p'e:-k'ä/
	Will you come?	=	Will you come?

པས། is used to indicate past tense in the second person.

1.	ཁྱེད་རང་ཕེབས་པ་ཡིན་པས།	=	ཁྱེད་རང་ཕེབས་པས།
	you come past c. ?/		come past c. ?/
	ky'e-ra;ng p'e:-pa yi;n-pä/		p'e:-pä/
	Did you come?	=	Did you come?

ཀྱིས།/ གྱིས།/ གིས། is used to indicate present in third person.

1.	ཁོང་ཕེབས་ཀྱི་འདུག	=	ཁོང་ཕེབས་ཀྱིས།
	he come pres. c./		pres. c./
	k'o;ng p'e:-ki du:/		k'o;ng p'e:-ki:/
	He is coming.	=	He is coming.

Usual forms		Shortened forms

ཀྱིས། / གིས། / གྱིས། is also used to indicate present tense in the 1st person when the verb is unintentional.

	Usual forms		Shortened forms
1.	ངས་འདི་འདྲས་བསམ་གྱི་འདུག	=	ངས་འདི་འདྲས་བསམ་གྱིས།
	I-by like-this think pres. c./		pres. c./
	ngä꞉ di;n-ḍä꞉ sam-k'i du꞉/		sam-k'i꞉/
	I think like this.	=	I think like this.
2.	ང་འཁྱག་གི་འདུག	=	ང་འཁྱག་གིས།
	I feel-cold pres. c./		pres. c./
	nga ky'a:-k'i du꞉/		ky'a:-k'i꞉/
	I feel cold.	=	I feel cold.

ག་ is used to indicate future tense in the first person, but the verb is used in the past tense e.g.

1. ང་ཚོ་ཁྲོམ་ལ་ཕྱིན་ག
   we market to went fut. c. ?/
   nga;n-ts'o ṭ'om-la ch'i;n-k'a/
   Shall we go to the market?

2. ང་ཁྲོམ་ལ་ཕྱིན་ག
   I market to went fut. c. ?/
   nga ṭ'om-la ch'i;n-k'a/
   Shall I go to the market?

3. ངས་ཞལ་ལག་བཟོས་ག
   I-by food (H.) made fut. c. ?/
   ngä꞉ shä:-la꞉ sö꞉-k'a/
   Shall I make food?

4. ཁོང་ལ་ཕྱག་རོགས་ཞུས་ག
   he to help (H) did fut. c. ?/
   k'o;ng la ch'a:-rò꞉ shü꞉-k'a/
   Shall (I) help him?

5. འདི་ངས་ཀློག་ག
   this I-by read fut. c. ?/
   di ngä꞉ lò꞉-k'a/
   Shall I read this?

16.4. Exercise 10

(a) Write down the proper verb-complement for each sentence:

1. ང་ཚོ་ཁྲིམ་ལ་འགྲོ་ ....
2. ཁོང་སློབ་གྲྭར་ཕྱིན་ ....
3. ང་ཚོ་ལས་ཁུངས་ལ་ཕྱིན་ ....
4. ཁྱེད་རང་ཞལ་ལག་མཆོད་ ....
5. ང་ཡི་གེ་འབྲི་ ....
6. ཁོང་གིས་ཕྱག་བྲིས་གནང་ ....
7. ཁོང་སློབ་སྦྱོང་བྱེད་ ....
8. ཁྱེད་རང་ལས་ཀ་བྱེད་ ....
9. ངས་སྐད་ཆ་བཤད་ ....
10. ང་ཚོས་སློབ་སྦྱོང་བྱས་ ....
11. ཁོང་གིས་བསམ་བློ་བཏང་ ....
12. ཁྱེད་རང་གིས་དགོངས་པ་བཞེས་ ....

(b) Translate the following into Tibetan.

1. I am going.
2. She is coming.
3. They came.
4. You did (it).
5. We will come.
6. They will give it to you.
7. They gave it to me.
8. I won't do that.
9. Here she comes.
10. She is having tea.
11. I am eating the food.
12. Did you come?
13. Will you work here?
14. Does she come?
15. Do they go to school?
16. Are they coming?
17. Shall I come?
18. Did you go to the class?
19. Isn't she coming here?

17. Adjectives & Demonstrative Pronouns

17.1. Adj. & Demos. Pronouns follow the noun

ཁང་པ་འདི་	(k'a;ng-pa di)	=	this house
ཁང་པ་ཕ་གི་	(k'a;ng-pa p'a-k̲'i)	=	that house
ཁང་པ་འདི་ཚོ་	(k'a;ng-pa di-ts'o)	=	these houses
ཁང་པ་ཕ་ཚོ་	(k'a;ng-pa p'a-ts'o)	=	those houses
ཁང་པ་ཡ་གི་	(k'a;ng-pa ya-k'i)	=	that house up there
ཁང་པ་མ་གི་	(k'a;ng-pa ma-k'i)	=	that house down there
ཁང་པ་གསར་པ་	(k'a;ng-pa sa:-pa)	=	new house
ཁང་པ་རྙིང་པ་	(k'a;ng-pa nying-pa)	=	old house

17.2. Adj. & Demos. pronouns conform to the following cases:

(a) In the genitive:

ཁང་པ་འདིའི་	(k'a;ng-pa di:)	=	of this house
ཁང་པ་ཕ་གིའི་	(k'a;ng-pa p'a-k̲'i:)	=	of that house
ཁང་པ་འདི་ཚོའི་	(k'a;ng-pa di-ts'ö:)	=	of these houses
ཁང་པ་ཕ་ཚོའི་	(k'a;ng-pa p'a-ts'ö:)	=	of those house
ཁང་པ་ཡ་གིའི་	(k'a;ng-pa ya-k̲'i:)	=	of that house up there
ཁང་པ་མ་གིའི་	(k'a;ng-pa ma-k̲'i:)	=	of that house down there
ཁང་པ་གསར་པའི་	(k'a;ng-pa sa:-pä:)	=	of the new house
ཁང་པ་རྙིང་པའི་	(k'a;ng-pa n̅y̅i;ng-pä)	=	of the old house

(b) In the Dative-locative

ཁང་པ་འདིར་	(k'a;ng-pa dä:)	=	to this house
ཁང་པ་ཕ་གིར་	(k'a;ng-pa p'a-k'ä:)	=	to that house
ཁང་པ་འདི་ཚོར་	(k'a;ng-pa di-ts'ò:)	=	to these houses
ཁང་པ་ཕ་ཚོར་	(k'a;ng-pa p'a-ts'ò:)	=	to those house
ཁང་པ་ཡ་ཚོར་	(k'a;ng-pa yan-ts'ò:)	=	to those houses up there
ཁང་པ་མ་ཚོར་	(k'a;ng-pa ma-ts'ò:)	=	to those houses down there
ཁང་པ་གསར་པར་	(k'a;ng-pa sa:-pa:)	=	to the new house
ཁང་པ་རྙིང་པར་	(k'a;ng-pa nyi;ng-pa:)	=	to the old house

(c) In the Instrumentive or Agentive:

ཁང་པ་འདིས་	(k'a;ng-pa di:̀)	=	by this house
ཁང་པ་ཕ་གིས་	(k'a;ng-pa p'a-k'i:̀)	=	by that house
ཁང་པ་འདི་ཚོས་	(k'a;ng-pa di-ts'ö:̀)	=	by these houses
ཁང་པ་ཕ་ཚོས་	(k'a;ng-pa p'an-ts'ö:̀)	=	by those house
ཁང་པ་ཡ་ཚོས་	(k'a;ng-pa yan-ts'ö:̀)	=	by those houses up there
ཁང་པ་མ་ཚོས་	(k'a;ng-pa man-ts'ö:̀)	=	by those houses down there
ཁང་པ་གསར་པས་	(k'a;ng-pa sa:-pä:̀)	=	by the new house
ཁང་པ་རྙིང་པས་	(k'a;ng-pa nyi;ng-pä:̀)	=	by the old house

If there is more than one attribute to the noun only the last one conforms to the above mentioned rules. e.g.

ཁང་པ་གསར་པ་ཕ་གིའི་ཐོག

house new that-of roof

k'a;ng-pa sa:-pa p'a-k'i: t'ò:̀/

The roof of that new house

ཁང་པ་གསར་པ་སྙིང་རྗེ་པོའི་ཐོག

house new beautiful-of roof

k'a;ng-pa sa:-pa n̄yi;ng-je-pö: t'ò`/

The roof of the beautiful, new house

ཁང་པ་གསར་པ་སྙིང་རྗེ་པོ་ཕ་གིའི་ཐོག།

house new beautiful that-of roof/

k'a;ng-pa sa:-pa n̄yi;ng-je-po p'a-k'i: t'ò`/

The roof of that beautiful, new house

17.3. Examples in complete sentences

1. ཁང་པ་ཕ་གི་སུའི་རེད།

   house that whose is/

   k'a;ng-pa p'a-k'i sü: re`/

   Whose house is this?

2. ཕ་གི་ངའི་ཨ་ཞང་ལགས་ཀྱི་གཟིམ་ཤག་རེད།

   that my uncle (H.) of house (H.) is/

   p'a-k'i ngä: a-sha;ng-la` ki sim-sha` re`/

   That is my uncle's house.

3. ཁོང་ཚོ་ཁང་པ་ཐོག་ས་གསུམ་ཐོག་ཕ་གིར་བཞུགས་ཀྱི་ཡོག་རེད།

   they house 3 storeyed there live (H.) pres.c./

   k'o;ng-ts'o k'a;ng-pa t'ò:-sa-sum-t'ò` p'a-k'ä: shu:-ki yò-re`/

   They are living in that 3 storeyed house.

4. ཁང་པ་ཕ་གིའི་བདག་པོ་སྐུ་ཞབས་སྐུ་འབུམ་ལགས་རེད།

   house that-of owner Mr. Kubum (H.) is/

   k'a;ng-pa p'a-k'i: dag-po ku-shab kubum-la` re`/

   The owner of that house is Mr. Kubum.

5. ཁང་པ་ཕ་གིས་རྒྱབ་ཀྱི་ཡུལ་ལྗོངས་ཐད་དེ་སྒྲིབ་ཀྱི་འདུག

   house that-by behind of scenery completely hide pres. c./

k'a;ng-pa p'a-k̲'ì: gyab-ki yü:-jo;ng bä̀:-t̲'e ḍib-ki du/

That house completely hides the scenery behind it.

6. ཁང་པ་ཕ་གིས་རྙོག་ཁྲ་བཟོས་པ་རེད།

house that by trouble made past c./

k'a;ng-pa p'a-k̲'ì: n̅y̅òg-ṭ'a s̲ö̀:-pa-rè:/

That house caused trouble.

7. ཁང་པ་ཕ་གིས་ཁོང་ཚོ་བུ་ལོན་ནང་ལ་བཅུག་པ་རེད།

house that by they debt into put p.c./

k'a;ng-pa p'a-k̲'ì: k'o;ng-ts'o p̲'u-lö;n na;ng-la chù:-pa-rè:/

That house put them in debt.

18. Prepositions

18.1. The Tibetan prepositions are always accompanied by one of the Datives ལ་དོན།

The Dative ལ་ is commonly used in the colloquial language.

སྟེང་ལ་	(ga;ng-la)	=	on
འོག་ལ་	(h̲ò:-la)	=	under, beneath
ཐོད་ལ་	(t'ö:-la)	=	above
གཤམ་ལ་	(sham-la)	=	below
ཐོག་ཀ་ལ་	(t'ò:-k̀a-la)	=	upstairs
ཤོད་ལ་	(shö:-la)	=	downstairs
འགྲིས་ལ་	(ṭ'i:-la)	=	near, beside
རྒྱང་ལ་	(gya;ng-la)	=	far away, in the distance
ཟུར་ལ་	(s̲u:-la)	=	at the corner (outer)
ཁུག་ལ་	(k'u:-la)	=	in the corner (inner)
བཙིགས་ཟུར་ལ་	(tsig-su:-la)	=	at the corner *of a wall*
བཙིགས་ཁུག་ལ་	(tsi:-k'u:-la)	=	in the corner *of a wall*
ཐོག་ལ་	(t'ò:-la)	=	on the ceiling
ཐོག་ཀའི་སྟེང་ལ་	(t'ò:-kä:-ga;ng-la)	=	on the roof
རྩེ་ལ་	(tse-la)	=	on the peak of, on top of
འདབས་ལ་	(dab-la)	=	at the foot of
ནང་ལ་	(na;ng-la)	=	in, inside, at home
ཕྱི་ལ་	(ch'i-la)	=	outside
ཁ་ལ་	(k'a-la)	=	on the surface
གཏིང་ལ་	(ti;ng-la)	=	at the bottom

རྒྱབ་ལ་	(gyab-la)	=	behind, on the back
མདུན་ལ་	(dü;n-la)	=	in front of
བར་ལ་	(p̲'ar-la)	=	in between
བར་དབྱག་ལ་	(pa:-ra:-la)	=	" "
གསེང་ལ་	(se;ng-la)	=	" "
ཕར་ཕྱོགས་ལ་	(p'a-ch'ò:-la)	=	on the other side
ཚུར་ཕྱོགས་ལ་	(ts'u-ch'ò:-la)	=	on this side
དཀྱིལ་ལ་	(kyi:-la)	=	in the middle, among
མཐའ་ལ་	(t'a-la)	=	at the edge/end
ཟུར་ལ་	(s̲u:-la)	=	" " " "
རྒྱབ་ངོས་ལ་	(gyab-ngò-la)	=	at the back
མདུན་ངོས་ལ་	(dü;n-ngò-la)	=	at the front
འགོ་ལ་	(go-la)	=	in the beginning
གཞུག་ལ་	(s̲h̲u:-la)	=	later, afterwards, after
མཇུག་ལ་	(ju:-la)	=	later, afterwards, after
རྗེས་ལ་	(je:-la)	=	" " "
དངོས་སུ་	(ngö:-su)	=	openly, directly, positively
ཤུགས་ལ་	(shug-la)	=	behind (implication)
གཞུང་ལ་	(s̲h̲u;ng-la)	=	in length, or lengthwise
འཕྲེད་ལ་	(ṭ'e:-la)	=	crosswise
ཞེང་ལ་	(s̲h̲e;ng-la)	=	breadthwise
དཔངས་ལ་	(pa;ng-la)	=	height
འཁོར་རྒྱ་ལ་	(k'òr-gya-la)	=	in circumference

18.2. Examples:

1. ང་ཚོའི་ཁང་པ་དཔེ་མཛོད་ཁང་གི་འཁྲིས་ལ་ཡོད།
   our house library of near to exist./
   nga;n-ts'ö: k'a;ng-pa pe;n-zö:-k'a;ng k̲'i ṭ'i:-la yö:/
   Our house is near the library.

2. ཤིང་ནགས་དཀྱིལ་ལ་གཅན་གཟན་མང་པོ་ཡོད་རེད།
forest middle to beasts many exists./
shi;ng-naː kyi:-la chä;n-s̲ä;n ma;ng-po yòː reː/
There are many beasts in the forest.

3. གྲོང་གསེབ་དེ་རི་གཉིས་ཀྱི་བར་དབྲག་ལ་ཆགས་ཡོད་རེད།
village that hill two of between to situated exist./
t̲'o;ng-seb t̲'e ri n̄ȳi:-ki pa:ra:-la ch'aː yòː reː/
The village is situated between two hills.

4. ཁོང་ལ་དངོས་སུ་སྐྱོན་བརྗོད་བྱས་པ་རེད།
he to real to criticise past c./
k'o;ng-la n̄ḡöː-su kyö;n-jöː c̲h̲'äː-pa-reː/
He was openly criticised.

5. སྐད་ཆ་འདིའི་ཤུགས་ལ་གོ་རྒྱུ་ཡོད་རེད།
talk this-of behind to indirect-meaning exist./
kä-ch'a di: shug-la k̲'o-gyu yòː-reː/
There is an indirect meaning behind this talk.

forest outside no beasts many exists.

There are many beasts in the forest.

village that hill two in between to situated exist.

The village is situated between two hills.

... behind ... there ...

19. མིང་ཚིག་གསར་པ། = New Vocabulary

སྨྱུ་གུ་	(n̄ȳu-k'u)	=	pen
སྣག་ཚ་	(n̄āg-ts'a)	=	ink
དེབ་	(t̲'eb)	=	book
འབྲི་དེབ་	(ḍi-t̲'eb)	=	exercise book
སློབ་དེབ་	(l̄ob-t̲'eb)	=	text book
ནག་པང་	(nag-pa;ng)	=	black-board
ས་སྨྱུག་	(sa-n̄ȳù:)	=	chalk
ཕྱིས་རས་	(ch'i-rä̀:)	=	duster
ཀུབ་བཀྱག་	(kub-kyà:)	=	chair
མདུན་ཅོག་	(dü;n-chò:)	=	desk
སྒོ་	(go)	=	door
སྒེའུ་ཁུང་	(gi-k'u;ng)	=	window
རླུང་འགྲོ་	(l̄u;ng-ḍo)	=	ventilation
ཡོལ་ལ་	(yö:-la)	=	curtain
ཡོལ་བ་	(yöl-wa:)	=	curtain (lit.)
ཁྲ་ཡོལ་	(ṭ'a-yö:)	=	window curtain
སྒོ་ཡོལ་	(go-yö:)	=	door curtain
ཐོག་	(t'ò:)	=	ceiling, roof
བཙིགས་པ་	(tsig-pa)	=	wall
ས་མཐིལ་	(sa-t'i:)	=	floor, ground
ཐོག་ཀ་	(t'ò:-ka)	=	upstairs, roof
ཐོག་ས་	(t'ò:-sa)	=	storey, floor
བང་ཁྲི་	(p̲'a;ng-ṭ'i)	=	shelf
ཅོག་ཙེ་	(chog-tse)	=	table (small)

གློག་	(l̄ò:)	=	electricity, light
རྒྱ་ཅོག་	(gya-chò:)	=	table
ཚ་གློག་	(ts'a-l̄ò:)	=	heater
གྲང་གློག་	(ṯa;ng-l̄ò:)	=	air-conditioning
གློག་སྐུད་	(l̄ò:-kü:)	=	electric wire
གློག་བཞུ་	(l̄ò:-shu)	=	flash light/torch
གློག་ཐབ་	(l̄òg-t'èb)	=	electric stove
གློག་གི་ཤེལ་ཏོག་	(l̄ò:-k̲'i sher-tò:)	=	bulb
འཁྱག་སྒམ་	(ky'a:-gam)	=	refrigerator
མེ་ཏོག་	(me-tò:)	=	flower
རྩ་བ་	(tsa-wa:)	=	root
ཀང་	(ka;ng)	=	stalk
འདབ་མ་	(dab-ma)	=	petal
སོན་	(sö;n)	=	seed
ཤིང་	(shi;ng)	=	tree, wood
ཤིང་སྡོང་	(shi;ng-do;ng)	=	tree
སྡོང་པོ་	(do;ng-po)	=	trunk
ཀུ་ཤུའི་སྡོང་པོ་	(ku-shü: do;ng-po)	=	apple tree
ཤིང་སྣ་	(shi;ng-n̄a)	=	kinds of trees
ཤིང་ཏོག་	(shi;ng-tò:)	=	fruit
ལོ་མ་	(lo-ma)	=	leaf
ཡལ་ག་	(yä:-k̲'a)	=	branch

20. རྒྱན་སྡུད་གསུམ་ནི། ཀྱང་། ཡང་། འང་།
Conjunctive Particles:

These particles express the meaning of 'though', 'also', 'too', 'even', 'ever' and 'any'.

The grammatical rules for use are:

ཀྱང་	used after words ending at	ག་ད་བ་ས་ & ད་དྲག
ཡང་	" " " " "	ང་ན་མ་ར་ལ་
འང་	" " " " "	འ་ & མཐའ་མེད་
ན་ཡང་	" "	all the suffixes (only with verbs)
ནའང་	" "	" " " " " "

20.1. Method of Combination

Combined with verbs

བཞག་ཀྱང་	(sha:-kya;ng)	=	though (he) placed
བཅད་ཀྱང་	(chä:-kya;ng)	=	though (he) cut
འགྲིབ་ཀྱང་	(ḍib-kya;ng)	=	though (it) blocks
བྱས་ཀྱང་	(ch'ä:-kya;ng)	=	though (he) did
བསྟན་ཀྱང་	(tä;n-kya;ng)	=	though (he) showed
བསམས་ཀྱང་	(sam-kya;ng)	=	though (he) thought
བཏང་ཡང་	(ta;ng-ya;ng)	=	though (he) sent
ཉན་ཡང་	(nya;n-ya;ng)	=	though (he) listens
འགོར་ཡང་	(gor-ya;ng)	=	though (it) takes time
འབུལ་ཡང་	(bül-ya;ng)	=	though (he) gives (H.)

དགའ་ཡང་	(ga-ya;ng)	=	though (he) pleased
དགའང་	(ga-ha;ng)	=	" " "
གོ་ཡང་	(k'o-ya;ng)	=	though (he) hears
གོའང་	(k'o-ha;ng)	=	" " "
བྱས་ན་ཡང་	(ch'ä-na-ya;ng)	=	though (he) did
བྱས་ནའང་	(ch'ä-na-ha;ng)	=	though (he) did

Combined with nouns

སྟག་ཀྱང་	(taː-kya;ng)	=	the tigers too
བང་མཛོད་ཀྱང་	(p'a;ng-zöː-kya;ng)	=	the treasury too
རྒྱལ་ཁབ་ཀྱང་	(gyä:-k'èb-kya;ng)	=	the country also
གྱོན་ཆས་ཀྱང་	(ky'ö;n-ch'äː-kya;ng)	=	the costumes also
དགེ་རྒན་ཡང་	(ge-gä;n-ya;ng)	=	the teachers too
ཆང་ཡང་	(ch'a;ng-ya;ng)	=	the Tibetan beer too
སྤྱན་ཡང་	(chä;n-ya;ng)	=	the eyes(H.) also
སྒམ་ཡང་	(gam-ya;ng)	=	the box also
ཟློས་གར་ཡང་	(dö:-k'ar ya;ng)	=	the drama also
བལ་ཡང་	(p'äl-ya;ng)	=	the wool also
མདའ་ཡང་	(da-ya;ng)	=	the arrow also
མདའང་	(da-ha;ng)	=	" " "
ཕྲུ་གུ་ཡང་	(ṭ'u-k'u ya;ng)	=	the children also
ཕྲུ་གུའང་	(ṭ'u-k'u-ha;ng)	=	" " "

Examples:

1. བོད་ལ་སྟག་ཀྱང་མང་པོ་ཡོད་པ་རེད།

   Tibet to tiger even many exist./

   p'öː la taː kya;ng ma;ng-po yö-pa-reː/

   In Tibet, there are many tigers too.

2. ཁྱིམ་མཚེས་རྒྱལ་ཁབ་ཚོ་ཡང་ཞི་བདེར་འཁོད་པ་རེད།
neighbouring countries even peace to settled past c./
ky'im-ts'eː gyä-k'èb ts'o yaṇg <u>sh</u>i-der k'öː pa reː/
The neighbouring countries are also in peace.

3. དགེ་རྒན་ཚོ་ཡང་འགྲོ་དགོས་བྱུང་བ་རེད།
teachers even go have past c./
ge-gäṇ ts'o yaṇg ḍo-gòː <u>ch</u>'uṇg-pa-reː/
The teachers also had to go.

4. ང་བོད་པའི་ཆང་ལའང་དགའ་པོ་ཡོད།
I Tibetan-of beer-to-even like pres. c./
nga <u>p</u>'ö:-pä: ch'aṇg-la-haṇg ga-po yöː/
I like Tibetan beer too.

5. ང་ཡང་དགའ་པོ་ཡོད།
I even like pres. c./
nga yaṇg ga-po yöː/
I also like (it).

6. ཐེངས་གཅིག་གྲྭ་པ་ཚོ་ཡང་འགྲོ་དགོས་བྱུང་བ་རེད།
once monks even go have past c./
t'eng chig <u>ṭ</u>'a-pa ts'o-yaṇg ḍo-go <u>ch</u>'uṇg-pa-reː/
The monks also had to go once.

7. ཁོང་ཚོས་ཕྲུ་གུ་ལ་ཡང་ལས་ཀ་བསྐུལ་བ་རེད།
they-by child to even work persuade past c./
k'oṇg-ts'öː ṭ'u-<u>k</u>'u la-yaṇg lä:-ka kü:-wa-reː/
They made even children work.

8. བུ་མོ་དེ་སྙིང་རྗེ་པོ་ཡང་ཞེ་དྲག་འདུག
girl that beautiful even very exist./

p'u-mo t'e nyi;ng-je-po ya;ng she-t'a: du:/
That girl is very beautiful too.

9. ཁོང་གྲྭ་པ་ཡིན་ན་ཡང་ཆང་རག་འཐུང་གི་ཡོག་རེད།
he monk is if-even alcohol drink pres. c./
k'o;ng t'a-pa yi;n-na-ya;ng ch'a;ng-ra: t'u;ng-k'i-yò:-re:/
Though he is a monk, he takes alcohol.

10. ཁོང་སྐྱོ་པོ་ཡིན་ནའང་དྲང་པོ་ཞེ་དྲག་ཡོག་རེད།
he poor is if-even honest very exist./
k'o;ng kyo-po yi;n-nä: t'a;ng-po she-t'a: yò: re:/
Though he is poor, he is very honest.

11. ཁོང་ཚོས་ཁོང་བཀག་ཀྱང་མ་འཁོག་པ་རེད།
they-by he stop even not stop past c./
k'o;ng-ts'ö: k'o;ng ka:-kya;ng ma-k'ò:-pa re:/
Though they tried to stop him they could not.

12. ང་ཚོས་ཤིང་འདི་གཅོད་ཐབས་བྱས་ཀྱང་མ་ཆོད་པ་རེད།
we-by tree this cut try did even not cut past c./
nga;n-ts'ö: shi;ng di chö: t'ab ch'ä:-kya;ng ma-ch'ö:-pa re:/
Though we tried to cut this tree we could not.

20.2. In spoken language ཡང་ & འང་ are pronounced as follows:

ཡང་	(ya;ng)	as	(yä:)
ལ་ཡང་	(la-ya;ng)	as	(lä:)
ན་	(na-ya;ng)	as	(nä:)

Examples:

1. ང་ཡང་ཕ་གིར་ཡོད།
I even there exist./

2. ཁྱེད་རང་ཡང་ཕ་གིར་འདུག
you even there exist./

nga yä: p'a-k'ä: yöː/
I was also there.

kyʼe-ra;ng yä: p'a-k'ä: duː/
You were also there.

3. ང་ལ་ཡང་བཤད་པ་རེད།
I to even told past c./
nga lä: yä: shäː-pa reː/
I was also told.

4. ཁོང་ལ་ཡང་བཤད་པ་རེད།
he to even told past c./
k'o;ng lä: yä: shäː-pa reː/
He was also told.

5. ངས་ལས་ཀ་ཧུར་ཐག་བྱས་པ་ཡིན་ནའང་ཁོང་ངར་དགའ་གི་མ་རེད།
I-by work hard-did past c. if-even he I-to like neg. fut. c./
ngäː lä:-ka hur-t'aː ch'äː-pa yi;n-nä: k'o;ng nga: ga-k'i ma-reː/
Even if I worked hard, he wouldn't like me.

21. དྲི་ཚིག་ཁག

Interrogative Pronouns

པས་ is not necessary with interrogative pronouns.

21.1. ག་རེ།   གང་།   ཅི། = what

ག་རེ་ is used in colloquial and
གང་ in literary forms.

Examples:

1. འདི་ག་རེ་རེད།
   this what is/
   di k'a-re re:/
   What is this?

2. ཁོང་ག་རེ་རེད།
   he what is/
   k'o;ng k'a-re re:/
   What is he?

3. ངར་ག་རེ་འདུག
   I-to what exist./
   nga: k'a-re du/
   What do I have?

4. ཁྱེད་རང་ལ་ག་རེ་ཡོད།
   you to what exist./
   ky'e-ra;ng la k'a-re yö:/
   What do you have?

5. མི་ཕ་ཚོ་ག་རེ་རེད།
   people those what is/
   mi p'a-ts'o k'a-re re:/
   What are those people?

6. འདི་ག་རེ་བྱེད་ཡག་རེད།
   this what to do is/
   di k'a-re ch'e-ya re:/
   What is this for?

7. ཁྱེད་རང་གི་མཚན་ལ་ག་རེ་ཞུ་གི་ཡོད།
   your name (H.) to what call pres. c./

ky'e-ra;ng-k'i ts'ä;n-la k'a-re shu-k'i yö/

What is your name?

8. ཁོང་གི་མིང་ལ་ག་རེ་ཟེར་གྱི་ཡོག་རེད།

his name to what call pres. c./

k'o;ng-k'i mi;ng-la k'a-re se-ki yò-reː/

What is his name?

9. བོད་ལ་ཐོན་ཁུངས་ག་རེ་ཡོག་རེད།

Tibet to resource what exist./

p'öː-la t'ö;n-k'u;ng k'a-re yò-reː/

What resources does Tibet have?

10. ཁྱེད་རང་ལ་ཚོང་ག་རེ་ཡོད།

you to article-for-sale what exist./

ky'e-ra;ng-la ts'o;ng k'a-re yö/

What do you have for sale?

11. ཁྱེད་རང་འདིར་ག་རེ་གནང་གི་ཡོད།

you here what do (H.) pres. c./

ky'e-ra;ng dä: k'a-re ña;ng-k'i yö/

What are you doing here?

21.1.1. Structure of "whatever"

ག་རེ་ + past stem of verb + ཀྱང་, ཡང་, འང་ or ན་ཡང་ & ནའང་

Examples:

1. ངས་ག་རེ་བྱས་ཀྱང་ཁོང་གིས་བྱེད་ཀྱི་རེད།

I-by what did even he by do fut. c./

ngäː k'a-re ch'äː-kya;ng k'o;ng-k'i ch'e-ki reː/

Whatever I do he will do (too).

2. ཁྱེད་རང་གིས་ག་རེ་གསུངས་ནའང་ཁོང་གིས་ཉན་གྱི་རེད།
you by what say(H.) if even he by listen fut.c./
ky'e-ra;ng k'iˋ: k'a-re su;ng-nä: k'o;ng k'iˋ: nyä;n-k'i reˋ:/
Whatever you say he will listen.

3. ཁོང་ཚོར་ག་རེ་དགོས་ནའང་སྤྲད་ཀྱི་ཡིན།
they-to what need if-even give fut c./
k'o;ng-ts'ò: k'a-re go-nä: ṭä:-ki yi;n/
Whatever they need (I) will give.

4. ཁོང་ལ་ག་རེ་བསླབས་ནའང་སེམས་ལ་ཉར་གྱི་འདུག
he to what taught if-even mind to keep pres. c./
k'o;ng-la k'a-re lab-nä: sem-la nya:-ki du/
Whatever he is taught (he) keeps in (his) mind.

5. ཁྱེད་རང་ལ་ག་རེ་དགོས་ཀྱང་ངས་ཉོ་གི་ཡིན།
you to what need even I-by buy fut. c./
ky'e-ra;ng-la k'a-re göˋ:-kya;ng ngäˋ: nyo-k'i yi;n/
Whatever you need I will buy.

6. ཁྱེད་རང་གིས་ག་རེ་མཆོད་ནའང་ཁོས་བཟའ་གི་རེད།
you by what eat(H.) if-even he by eat fut. c./
ky'e-ra;ng-k'iˋ: k'a-re ch'öˋ:-nä: k'öˋ: sa-k'i reˋ:/
Whatever you eat he will eat (too).

In the past tense, constructive particle པ་ is used in the place of ཀྱང་ e.g.

7. ང་ཚོས་ག་རེ་བྱས་པ་ཁོང་ཚོས་བྱས་པ་རེད།
we by what did they by did past c./
nga;n-ts'öˋ: k'a-re ch'äˋ:-pa k'o;ng-ts'öˋ: ch'äˋ:-pa reˋ:/
Whatever we did, they did (too).

8. ཁོང་ཚོས་ག་རེ་བྱས་པ་ང་ཚོས་ཀྱང་བྱས་པ་ཡིན།
they by what did we-by also did past c./
k'o;ng-ts'ö: k'a-re ch'ä:-pa nga;n-ts'ö: kya;ng ch'ä:-pa yi;n/
Whatever they did, we did too.

9. ངས་ག་རེ་ལབ་པ་ཁོང་ལ་གསུངས་རོགས་གནང་།
I-by what said he to tell(H.) imp.(H.)/
ngä: k'a-re lab-pa k'o;ng-la su;ng-rò: ña;ng/
Please tell him whatever I said.

21.1.2. ག་རེ་ཡང་། = "anything", "any kind of" & "ever".

ག་རེ་ཡང་། is used in colloquial and
གང་ཡང་། in literary forms.

Examples:

1. བོད་ལ་ག་རེ་ཡང་ཉོ་རྒྱུ་*ཡོག་རེད།
Tibet to what even buy to exist./
p'ö:-la k'a-re ya;ng nyo-gyu yò:-re:/
Anything can be bought in Tibet. or
(You) can buy anything in Tibet.

2. བོད་ལ་ག་རེ་ཡང་ཉོ་ཡག་*ཡོག་རེད།
Tibet to what even buy to exist./
p'ö:-la k'a-re ya;ng nyo-ya: yò:-re:/
same as (1)

3. ངས་དུག་སློག་ག་རེ་ཡང་གོན་གྱི་ཡོད།
I-by dress what even wear pres. c./
ngä: t'ug-lò: k'a-re-yä: k'ö;n-k'i-yö:/
I wear any (kind of) dress.

* Both infinitive forms རྒྱུ། & ཡག་ are valid.

4. ཁོང་གིས་ན་བཟའ་ག་རེ་ཡང་མཆོད་ཀྱི་འདུག
he by dress(H.) what even wear(H.) pres. c./
k'o;ng k'i nam-sa k'a-re-ya;ng ch'ö:-ki du/
He wears any (kind of) dress.

5. ཁྲོམ་ལ་ག་རེ་ཡང་འདུག
market to what even exist./
ṭ'om-la k'a-re-yä: du`:/
Everything is there in the market.

21.1.3. ག་རེས། = by what

ག་རེས། is used in colloquial and
གང་གིས། in literary forms.

Examples:

1. སྨན་འདི་ག་རེས་བཟོ་གི་རེད།
medicine this what-by make fut. c./
m̄ä;n di k'a-re`: so-k'i rä/
What will this medicine be made of?

2. བོད་པའི་ཆང་*ག་རེས་བཟོ་གི་ཡོག་རེད།
Tibetan-of beer what by make pres. c/
p'ö-pä: ch'a;ng k'a-re`: so-k'i yò-rä/
What is Tibetan beer made of?

3. བོད་པའི་སྨན་ག་རེས་བཟོས་པ་རེད།
Tibetan-of medicine what by made past c./
p'ö-pä: m̄ä;n k'a-re`: sö`:-pa rä/
What was Tibetan medicine made of?

---

* Beer is the nearest and the most accepted word for Tibetan ཆང་.

4. ན་ཚ་འདི་ལ་སྨན་ག་རེས་ཕན་གྱི་རེད།
illness this to medicine what-by benefit fut. c./
na-ts'a di-la m̄ä;n k'a-rè: p'ä;n-ki-rä/
What medicine will be good for this illness?

5. སྙུང་གཞི་འདིར་ཞལ་ལག་ག་རེས་གནོད་ཀྱི་རེད།
illness (H.) this to food (H.) what by harm fut. c./
n̄yu;ng-shi dä: shä:-là: k'a-rè: n̄ö:-ki rä/
What food will be harmful to this illness?

6. ན་ཚ་དེ་སྨན་ག་རེས་དྲག་པ་རེད།
illness that medicine what-by cured past c./
na-ts'a t'e m̄ä;n k'a-rè: t'à:-pa rä/
What medicine cured that illness?

7. འདི་ག་རེས་བཟོས་པ་རེད།
this what-by made past c./
di k'a-rè: sö̀:-pa rä/
What was this made of?

8. བྱེ་མ་ཀ་ར་ག་རེས་བཟོས་པ་རེད།
sugar what-by made past c./
ch'e-ma-ka-ra k'a-rè: sö̀:-pa rä/
What was sugar made of?

9. བོད་ཤོག་ག་རེས་བཟོ་གི་ཡོག་རེད།
Tibetan-paper what-by make pres. c./
p'ö̀:-shò: k'a-rè: so-k'i yò-rä/
What is Tibetan paper made of?

10. ཤེལ་སྒོ་ག་རེས་བཟོ་གི་ཡོག་རེད།
glass what-by make pres. c./
she:-go k'a-rè: so-k'i yò-rä/
What is glass made of?

21.1.4. ག་རེས་ཀྱང་། = "by whatever" and "by any kind of"

ག་རེས་ཀྱང་། is used in colloquial and
གང་གིས་ཀྱང་། in literary forms.

Examples:

1. ཆང་ག་རེས་བཟོ་གི་ཡོག་རེད།
   Tibetan-beer what-by pres. c.
   ch'a;ng k'a-re: so-k'i yò-rä/
   What is Tibetan beer made of?

2. ཆང་འབྲུ་ག་རེས་ཀྱང་བཟོ་ཐུབ་ཀྱི་རེད།
   Tibetan-beer grain what-by even make able fut. c./
   ch'a;ng ḍu k'a-re:-kya;ng so t'ub-ki re:/
   Tibetan beer can be made out of any grain.

3. སྣག་ཚ་ག་རེས་ཀྱང་བྲིས་ཆོག་གི་རེད།
   ink what-by even write allow fut. c./
   n̄ag-ts'a k'a-re:-kya;ng ṭ'i: ch'ò:-k'i-re:/
   It may be written with any ink.

21.1.5. ག་རེའི། = of what

ག་རེའི། is used in colloquial and
གང་གི་ in literary forms.

1. འདི་སེམས་ཅན་ག་རེའི་པགས་པ་རེད།
   this animal what-of skin is/
   di sem-chä;n k'a-re: pag-pa rä/
   What animal's skin is this?

2. འདི་ལུང་པ་ག་རེའི་སྐད་རེད།
   this country what-of language is/

di lu;ng-pa <u>k</u>'a-re: kä꞉ rä/
*Which country's language is this?

3. འདི་ག་རེའི་སྣུམ་རེད།
this what-of oil is/
di <u>k</u>'a-re: n̄um rä/
What is this oil (made) of?

4. ཕ་གི་སེམས་ཅན་ག་རེའི་རྭ་ཅོ་རེད།
that animal what-of horn is/
p'a-<u>k</u>'i sem-chä;n <u>k</u>'a-re: ra-cho rä/
What animal's horn is that?

5. འདི་ལུང་པ་ག་རེའི་ཆས་རེད།
this country what-of dress is/
di lu;ng-pa <u>k</u>'a-re: ch'ä꞉ rä/
What country's dress is this?

6. འདི་ཤིང་ཏོག་ག་རེའི་ཁུ་བ་རེད།
this fruit what-of juice is/
di shi;ng-tò꞉ <u>k</u>'a-re: k'u-wa rä/
What fruit juice is this?

21.1.6. Exercise II

(a) Make complete sentences with the following terms.

verb + ཀྱང་/ ན་ཡང་/ ནའང་

1.	ག་རེ་དགོས་ཀྱང་	=	whatever (one) needs
2.	ག་རེ་བྱས་ཀྱང་	=	,, ,, does
3.	ག་རེ་ཟས་ཀྱང་	=	,, ,, eats

* In Tibetan the corresponding word is <u>what</u> : ག་རེ།

4.	ག་རེ་ལབ་ཀྱུང་	=	”	”	says
5.	ག་རེ་བྲིས་ཀྱུང་	=	”	”	writes
6.	ག་རེ་སྤྲད་ཀྱུང་	=	”	”	gives
7.	ག་རེ་མཐོང་ཡང་	=	”	”	sees
8.	ག་རེ་བསྟན་ནའང་	=	”	”	shows
9.	ག་རེ་གོ་ན་ཡང་	=	”	”	hears
10.	ག་རེ་དྲན་ན་ཡང་	=	”	”	thinks, remembers

(b) Translate the following into Tibetan

1. What is your name?
2. What is her name?
3. What are you doing?
4. What will she do?
5. What does she have?
6. What do you have?
7. What is this man?
8. What is his work?
9. What do they have?
10. What did you do?
11. What is she doing now?
12. What do you eat?
13. What are you eating?
14. What is this for?
15. What do you need?

21.2. ག་དུས། ནམ། = when

ག་དུས། is used in colloquial and
ནམ། in literary forms.

Examples:

1. ཁྱེད་རང་ག་དུས་ཕེབས་ཀྱི་ཡིན། = ཁྱེད་རང་ག་དུས་ཕེབས་ག
   you when come(H.) fut. c./
   ky'e-ra;ng k̲'a-t̲'ü: p'e-ki yi;n/
   When will you come?

2. ཁྱེད་རང་ག་དུས་ཕེབས་ཀྱི་ཡོད།
   you when come pres. c./
   ky'e-ra;ng k̲'a-t̲'ü: p'e-ki yö:/
   When are you coming?

3. ཁྱེད་རང་ག་དུས་ཕེབས་པ་ཡིན། = ཁྱེད་རང་ག་དུས་ཕེབས་པ།
   you when come past c./
   ky'e-ra;ng k̲'a-t̲'ü: p'e-pa yi;n/
   When did you come?

4. ཁོང་ག་དུས་ཐེགས་གི་རེད།
   she when go (H.) fut. c./
   k'o;ng k̲'a-t̲'ü: t'ä:-ki rä/
   When will she go?

5. ཁོང་ག་དུས་ཐེག་གི་འདུག
   she when go (H.) pres. c./
   k'o;ng k̲'a-t̲'ü: t'ä:-ki du/
   When does she go?

6. ཁོང་ག་དུས་ཐེག་པ་རེད།
   she when go past c./
   k'o;ng k̲'a-t̲'ü: t'ä:-pa rä/
   When did she go?

7. འཛིན་གྲྭ་ག་དུས་འགོ་ཚུགས་ཀྱི་རེད།
class when start fut. c./
zin-ṭ'a k'a-t'ü: go-ts'u:-ki rä/
When will the class start?

8. ཆར་ཞོད་ག་དུས་ཚུགས་ཀྱི་འདུག
monsoon when start pres. c./
ch'a:-shö: k'a-t'ü: ts'u:-ki du/
When does the monsoon start?

9. ཆར་ཞོད་ག་དུས་ཆད་པ་རེད།
monsoon when stop past c./
ch'a:-shö: k'a-t'ü: ch'ä:-pa rä/
When did the monsoon end?

21.2.1. Structure of "whenever", "every time" and "at whatever time".

ག་དུས་ + past stem of verb + ཀྱང་, ཡང་, འང་ or ན་ཡང་ / ནའང་

Examples:

1. ཁྱེད་རང་ག་དུས་ཐེག་ཀྱང་ངར་གསུངས་རོགས་གནང་།
you when go(H.) even I-to tell imp. (H.)/
ky'e-ra;ng k'a-t'ü: t'ä:-kya;ng nga: su;ng-rò:-n̄a;ng/
Please tell me whenever you are going.

2. ཁྱེད་རང་ག་དུས་ཐེག་ན་ཡང་ང་འཁྲིད་རོགས་གནང་།
you when go if-even I take imp./
ky'e-ra;ng k'a-t'ü: t'ä:-na-ya;ng nga ṭ'i:-rò:-n̄a;ng/
Please take me whenever you are going.

3. ཁྱེད་རང་ག་དུས་ཐེག་ནའང་ང་ལྷན་རྒྱས་བཅར་གྱི་ཡིན།
you when go if-even I with come fut. c./

ky'e-ra;ng k̲'a-t̲'ü: t'ä:-nä: nga l̄ä;n-gyä: cha:-k̲'i-yi;n/
Whenever you go I will come along (with you).

4. ང་ཀ་དུས་ཡོང་ནའང་ཁྱེད་རང་བཞུགས་ཀྱི་མི་འདུག
I when come if-even you stay (H.) neg. pres. c./
nga k̲'a-t̲'ü: yo;ng-nä: ky'e-ra;ng sh̲u:-ki mi;n-du:/
Whenever I come you are not there.

21.2.2. ཀ་དུས་ཡིན་ན་ཡང་། = "always" or "never" (according to context)

ཀ་དུས་ཡིན་ན་ཡང་།	is used in colloquial and
ཀ་དུས་ཀྱང་།	in literary forms.

Examples:

1. ངས་ཀ་དུས་ཡིན་ནའང་འདི་འདྲས་བྱེད་མ་མྱོང་།
I-by when even this-like do not experienced/
ngä: k̲'a-t̲'ü: yi;n-nä: di;n-ḍä: ch̲'e: ma-nyo;ng/
I have never done such things.

2. ཁོང་གིས་འདི་འདྲས་ཀ་དུས་ཡིན་ནའང་བྱེད་ཀྱི་མ་རེད།
he by this-like when if-even do neg. fut. c./
k'o;ng-k'i din-ḍä: k̲'a-t̲'ü: yi;n-nä: ch̲'e-ki ma-re:/
He will never do such things.

3. ཁོས་ཀ་དུས་ཡིན་ནའང་རྙོག་ཁྲ་བཟོ་གི་ཡོག་རེད།
he-by when if-even trouble make pres. c./
k'ö: k̲'a-t̲'ü: yi;n-nä: nyòg-ṭ'a s̲o-k̲i yò-re:/
He always causes trouble.

4. ངས་ཀ་དུས་ཡིན་ནའང་ཁོང་ལ་བསླབ་བྱ་རྒྱག་གི་ཡོད།
I-by when if-even he to advise pres. c./
ngä: k̲'a-t̲'ü: yi;n-nä: k'o;ng-la l̄ab-ch̲'a gya:-k̲'i yö:/
I always advise him.

21.2.3. དུས་ / སྐབས་ = "when" or "while" (in connection with a verb)

Examples:

1. ཁྱེད་རང་བོད་ལ་བཞུགས་དུས་ག་རེ་གནང་གི་ཡོད།
you Tibet to live (H.) when what do (H.) pres. c./
ky'e-ra;ng p'ö:-la shu:-t'ü: k'a-re n̄a;ng-k'i yö:/
What were you doing when you were in Tibet?

2. ང་ཚོ་ཞལ་ལག་མཆོད་དུས་ཁོང་འབྱོར་སོང་།
we food(H.) eat(H.) when he arrived past c./
nga;n-ts'o shä:-la: ch'ö:-t'ü: k'o;ng jò:-so/
He arrived while we were having a meal.

3. ཁྱེད་རང་ཕ་གིར་བཞུགས་སྐབས་མི་ག་ཚད་འདུག
you there stay(H.) when people how much exist./
ky'e-ra;ng p'a-k'ä: shu:-kab mi k'a-ts'ä: du/
How many people were there when you were staying there?

4. ང་མ་གིར་སླེབས་དུས་ཆུ་ཚོད་གསུམ་པ་རེད།
I down there arrive when time third is/
nga ma-k'ä: leb-t'ü: ch'u-ts'ö: sum-pa re:/
It was three o'clock when I arrived down there.

5. ང་ཆུང་ཆུང་ཡིན་*དུས་བོད་ཇར་ཞེ་དག་དགའ་པོ་ཡོད།
I small is when Tibetan-tea-to very like exist./
nga ch'u;ng-ch'u;ng yi;n-t'ü: p'ö:-ch'a: she-t'a: ga-po yö:/
When I was small, I was very fond of Tibetan tea.

6. ལས་ཀ་བྱེད་དུས་ལས་ཀ་བྱེད།
work-do while work-do/

---

* In the case of such constructions only ཡིན་ and ཡོད་ are used in the 1st, 2nd & 3rd persons.

lä:-ka ch'e-t'ü:̀ lä:-ka-ch'e:̀/
Work while you work.

7. རྩེད་མོ་རྩེད་དུས་རྩེད་མོ་རྩེད།
game-play while play/
tse:-mo tse-t'ü:̀ tse:-mo-tse:̀/
Play while you play.

8. ཁྱེད་རང་ཆུང་ཆུང་ཡིན་དུས་བོད་ལ་ཐེག་མྱོང་ངས།
you small is when Tibet to go(H.) expr. ?/
ky'e-ra;ng ch'u;ng-ch'u;ng yi;n-t'ü:̀ p'ö:̀-la t'ä:̀ nyò;ng-ngä/
Have you ever been to Tibet when you were small?

9. ཁོང་བོད་ལ་ཡོད་དུས་རྒྱུ་རྫིག་པོ་རེད།
she Tibet to exist. when rich is/
k'o;ng p'ö:̀-la yö:-t'ü:̀ gyu zig-po re:̀/
When she was in Tibet, she was wealthy.

10. ངའི་ཡབ་ཡུམ་གཉིས་ཞལ་བཞུགས་པའི་སྐབས་ལ་ང་སྐྱིད་པོ་ཞེ་དྲག་ཡོད།
my parents(H.) two alive(H.)-of when to I very happy exist./
ngä: yèb-yum nyi: shä:-shu:̀-pä: kèb-la nga kyi-po she-t'a: yö:̀/
I was very happy when my parents were alive.

11. ཁོང་བོད་ལ་ཡོད་དུས་གོ་ས་མཐོ་པོ་རེད།
he Tibet to exist. when rank high is/
k'o;ng p'ö:̀-la yö:-t'ü:̀ k'o-sa t'o-po re:̀/
When he was in Tibet, he was of high rank.

21.2.4. Use of དུས་ / སྐབས་ and also ཚེ་ in combination with པའི་ / བའི་

དུས་ & སྐབས་	are used in colloquial and
ཚེ་	in literary forms.

སྡོད་སྐབས་ / སྡོད་པའི་སྐབས་ལ་ = when (one) stays
འགྲོ་དུས་ / འགྲོ་བའི་དུས་སུ་ = when (one) goes
*འབྱོར་ཚེ་ = if arrives
འབྱོར་བའི་ཚེ་ན་ = when (one)arrives

Examples:

1. ང་བོད་ལ་སྡོད་པའི་སྐབས་ལ་ཁོང་མཇལ་བྱུང་།
I Tibet to stay-of when to he see(H.) p.c./
nga p'ö̀:-la dö̀:-pä: kèb-la k'o;ng jä:-ch'u;ng/
I saw him when I was in Tibet.

2. མེ་འཁོར་འབྱོར་བའི་ཚེ་ན་ = མེ་འཁོར་འབྱོར་བའི་སྐབས་ལ་
train arrive-of when/
me-k'or jor-wä: ts'e-na/
When the train arrives.

3. མེ་འཁོར་དུས་ཐོག་འབྱོར་ཚེ་ = མེ་འཁོར་དུས་ཐོག་འབྱོར་ན་
train time on arrive if/
me-k'or t'ǜ: t'ò: jor-ts'e/
If the train arrives on time.

21.2.5. Exercise 12

(a) Translate the following sentences into Tibetan

1. When will you come here?
2. When does he come?
3. When will the class start?
4. When do you go to work?
5. I told him this when he was here.
6. I saw him when he was in India.
7. I have been to Tibet when I was small.

---

* without བའི་ and ན་ means "if arrives"

(b) Fill in the blanks with the appropriate word:

ཀྱང་   ཡང་   འང་   ན་ཡང་   ནའང་

1. ཁྱེད་རང་ག་དུས་ཕེབས་ ....ངར་གསུངས་རོགས་གནང་།
2. ལས་ཀ་འདི་ག་དུས་བྱས་ ....འགྲིགས་ཀྱི་རེད།
3. ང་ག་དུས་ཕྱིན་ ....ཁོང་སྡོད་ཀྱི་མི་འདུག
4. ཁོང་གིས་ག་དུས་ ....དེ་འདྲས་བྱེད་ཀྱི་མ་རེད།
5. ཁོང་ག་དུས་ ....འདིར་ཕེབས་ཀྱི་མ་རེད།
6. ངས་ག་དུས་ཡིན་ ....འདི་འདྲས་བྱེད་ཀྱི་མེད།

(c) Put the correct interrogative particle:

ག་   པ་/ པས་   སོང་

1. ཁྱེད་རང་ཁྲོམ་ལ་ག་དུས་འགྲོ་ ....། = When will you go?
2. ཁྱེད་རང་ག་དུས་ཕྱིན་ ....། = When did you go?
3. ང་ག་དུས་ཕྱིན་ ....། = When shall I go?
4. ཁོང་ག་དུས་ཕྱིན་ ....། = When did she go?
5. ང་ཚོ་ག་དུས་འགྲོ་ ....། = When shall we go?

(d) Translate the following sentences into English:

1. དེབ་འདི་ང་རྒྱ་གར་ལ་ཡོད་པའི་སྐབས་ལ་བྲིས་པ་ཡིན།
2. མི་འཁོར་འབྱོར་བའི་སྐབས་ལ་ཁོང་འདིར་ཡོག་མ་རེད།
3. མི་འཁོར་དུས་ཐོག་འབྱོར་ན་ང་ཚོ་ཕྱི་པོ་བྱས་ཡོག་མ་རེད།

21.3. ག་གི་ = "which" and related forms

ག་གི་ is used in both colloquial and in literary forms.

Examples:

1. ཁྱེད་རང་གི་གཟིམ་ཤག་ག་གི་རེད།
   your house(H.) which is/

ky'e-ra;ng k'i sim-shaˋ: k'a-k'i rä/
Which is your house?

2. ང་རྣམ་ཚོའི་ཕྱག་སྨྱུག་གསར་པ་དེ་ག་གི་རེད།
your(H.) pen(H.) new that which is/
nga-na-ts'ö: ch'a:-nyuˋ: sa:-pa t'e k'a-k'i rä/
Which is your new pen?

3. ངའི་སྨྱུ་གུ་ག་གི་རེད།
my pen which is/
ngä: nyu-k'u k'a-k'i rä/
Which is my pen?

4. ཁོང་རྣམ་ཚོའི་ཨ་བ་ག་གི་རེད།
their(H.) child(H.) which is/
k'o-na-ts'ö: a-wa: k'a-k'i rä/
Which one is their child?

5. ཁྱེད་རང་གི་སྐུ་ཆས་ག་གི་*ག་གི་རེད།
your things(H.) which-which is/
ky'e-ra;ng k'i ku-ch'äˋ: k'a-k'i-k'a-k'i rä/
Which are your things?

6. ཁྱེད་རང་གི་ཁང་པ་ག་ཚོ་རེད།
your house which-pl. is/
ky'e-ra;ng k'i k'a;ng-pa k'a;n-ts'o rä/
Which are your houses?

7. ཁང་པ་ག་གི་ཚོང་ཡག་རེད།
house which sale to is/
k'a;ng-pa k'a-k'i ts'o;ng yaˋ: rä/
Which house is for sale?

---

* Use of ག་གི་ in repetition denotes plural.

8. ཁྱེད་རང་སྣུམ་འཁོར་ག་གི་གཟིགས་ག
you car which buy(H.) fut. c./
ky'e-ra;ng n̄um-k'or k'a-k'i si: k'a/
Which car will you buy?

9. ཁྱེད་རང་ཆིབས་པ་ག་གི་ཆིབས་ག
you horse(H.) which ride(H.) fut. c./
ky'e-ra;ng ch'ib-pa k'a-k'i ch'ib k'a/
Which horse are you going to ride?

21.3.1. ག་གིས། = by which

Examples:

1. ཁོང་ལ་ཁྱི་ག་གིས་སོ་བརྒྱབ་པ་རེད།
he to dog which-by bite past c./
k'o;ng-la ky'i k'a-k'i: so-gyèb-pa rä/
Which dog bit him?

2. ཁྱི་ག་གིས་ཕལ་གྱི་རེད།
dog which-by bite fut. c./
ky'i k'a-k'i: p'ä:-k'i rä/
Which dog will bite?

3. རྟ་ག་གིས་གཡུག་གི་རེད།
horse which-by throw fut. c./
ta k'a-k'i: ȳu:-k'i rä/
Which horse will throw?

4. གཡག་ག་གིས་བརྡུང་གི་རེད།
yak which-by gore fut. c./
ya: k'a-k'i: du;ng-k'i rä/
Which yak will gore?

5. མི་ག་གིས་གཤེ་གཤེ་གཏང་གི་རེད།
man which-by scold fut. c./
mi k'a-k'i: shä:-shä: ta;ng-k'i rä/
Which man will scold?

6. རྒན་ལགས་ག་གིས་བོད་སྐད་སློབ་གནང་གི་ཡོག་རེད།
teacher(H.) which-by Tibetan language teach(H.) pres. c./
gä;n-la: k'a-k'i: p'ö:-kä: lèb-na;ng-ki yò-rä/
Which teacher is teaching Tibetan language?

7. བཟོ་གྲྭ་ག་གིས་རླུང་འཕྲིན་ཡག་ཤོས་བཟོ་གི་ཡོག་རེད།
factory which-by radio best make pres. c./
so-t'a k'a-k'i: lu;ng-t'i;n yag-shö: so-k'i yò-rä/
Which factory makes the best radio?

8. ཚོས་གཞི་ག་གིས་ག་གི་གསོད་ཀྱི་ཡོག་རེད།
colour which-by which kill pres. c./
ts'ö:-shi k'a-k'i: k'a-k'i sä:-ki yò-rä/
Which colour kills which colour?

9. ཚོས་གཞི་ག་གིས་ག་གི་བཀྱག་གི་ཡོག་རེད།
colour which-by which lift pres. c./
ts'ö:-shi k'a-k'i: k'a-k'i kya:-k'i yò rä/
Which colour brings out which colour?

10. རྐང་པ་ག་གིས་པོ་ལོར་གདོང་རྒྱག་ཞུས་པ་རེད།
foot which-by ball-to kick past c./
ka;ng-pa k'a-k'i: po-lò: do;ng-gya: shü:-pa rä/
Which foot kicked the ball?

21.3.2. ག་གིར། = in which

ག་གིར། is used in colloquial and
གང་དུ། in literary forms

Examples:

1. ཁྱེད་རང་སློབ་གྲྭ་ག་གིར་སློབ་སྦྱོང་གནང་པ།
   you school which to study-do(H.) past c./
   ky'e-ra;ng l̄ab-ṭ'a k'a-k'ä: l̄ob-jo;ng n̄a;ng-pa/
   In which school did you study?

2. ཁྱེད་རང་བོད་ལ་དགོན་པ་ག་གིར་བཞུགས་པ།
   you Tibet to monastery which-to stay(H.) p.c./
   ky'e-ra;ng p'ö̀:-la gö;n-pa k'a-k'ä: shù:-pa/
   In which monastery did you stay in Tibet?

3. བོད་པ་ཚོ་བཙོན་ཁང་ག་གིར་བཅུག་པ་རེད།
   Tibetans prison which-to put past c./
   p'ö̀:-pa-ts'o tsö;n-k'a;ng k'a-k'ä: chù:-pa rä/
   In which prison were the Tibetans kept?

4. ང་རྣམ་ཚོ་ལས་ཁུངས་ག་གིར་ཕྱག་ལས་གནང་གི་ཡོད།
   you(H.) office which-to work-do(H.) pres. c./
   nga-na-ts'o lä:-k'u;ng k'a-k'ä: ch'a:-lä̀: n̄a;ng-k'i yö/
   In which office do you work?

5. ཡིག་ཆ་ག་གིའི་ནང་ལ་གསལ་ཡོག་རེད།
   document which-of into shown pres. c./
   yig-ch'a k'a-k'i: na;ng-la sä: yò-rä/
   In which document is it shown?

6. དེབ་ཀ་གིའི་ནང་ལ་བཀོད་ཡོག་རེད།

book which-of into written pres. c./

t̲'eb k̲'a-k̲'i: na;ng-la kö: yò-rä/

In which book is it written?

7. ཅ་ལག་འདི་ཚོ་སྒམ་ཀ་གིར་འཇུག་དགོས་རེད།

thing these box which-to put have fut. c./

cha-la: di-ts'o gam k̲'a-k̲'ä: chu-gö rä/

In which box are these things to be packed?

8. དེབ་ཀ་གིར་འབྲི་དགོས་རེད།

book which-to write have fut. c./

t̲'eb k̲'a-k̲'ä: t̲'i-go rä/

In which book shall (I) write?

9. ཁང་མིག་ཀ་གིར་ཚོན་གཏང་དགོས་རེད།

room which-to paint have fut. c./

k'a;ng-mi: k̲'a-k̲'ä: ts'ö;n ta;ng-go rä/

Which room is to be painted?

21.3.3. ཀ་གིའི། = of which

ཀ་གིའི་ is used in colloquial and

གང་གི་ in literary forms

Examples:

1. འདི་ཁང་མིག་ཀ་གིའི་ལྡེ་མིག་རེད།

this room which-of key is/

di k'a;ng-mi: k̲'a-k̲'i: de-mi: rä/

Which room is this the key to?

2. འདི་ཆུ་ཚོད་ཀ་གིའི་ཤུབ་རེད།
this watch which-of case is/
di ch'u-ts'ö̀: k'a-k'i: shub rä/
Which watch is the case from?

3. འདི་མཛུ་གུ་ཀ་གིའི་དཔར་རྗེས་རེད།
this finger which-of print is/
di zu-k'u k'a-k'i: par-jè: rä/
Which finger is this print from?

4. འདི་ལྡུམ་ར་ཀ་གིའི་མེ་ཏོག་རེད།
this garden which-of flower is/
di dum-ra k'a-k'i: me-tò: rä/
Which garden is this flower from?

21.3.4. "which" joining a subordinate clause

In affirmative sentences, the demonstrative pronoun དེ་ is used in place of ག་གི་.

Pay attention to the inversions of object and verb.

<table>
<tr><td colspan="6">Structure of the principal clause and the subordinate one joint by "which"</td></tr>
<tr><td>Past:</td><td rowspan="3">pronoun
or
subject</td><td rowspan="3">verb</td><td>པའི་</td><td rowspan="3">object</td><td rowspan="3">དེ་</td></tr>
<tr><td>Present:</td><td>བཞིན་པའི་</td></tr>
<tr><td>Future:</td><td>ཡག་གི་/ རྒྱུའི་</td></tr>
</table>

Examples:

1. ངས་བྲིས་པའི་ཡི་གེ་དེ་ག་པར་ཡོད།
I-by wrote-of letter which where exist./

ngä:̀ t'i:̀-pä: yi-k'e t'e k'a-pa: yö/
Where is the letter which I wrote?

2. ངས་སྤྲད་པའི་དེབ་དེ་བརླག་པ་རེད།
I-by gave-of book which lost past c./
ngä:̀ ṭä:̀-pä: t'eb-t'e l̄a:̀-pa re:̀/
The book which I gave is lost.

Present:

1. ཁྱེད་རང་གིས་བྱེད་བཞིན་པའི་ལས་ཀ་དེ་·······
you by do-continue-of work which/
ky'e-ra;ng k'i:̀ ch'e:̀-shi;n-pä: lä:-ka t'e/
The work which you are doing.......

2. ཁྱེད་རང་གིས་ཉོ་བཞིན་པའི་ས་ཆ་དེ་·······
you by buy-continue-of land which/
ky'e-ra;ng k'i:̀ nyo-shi;n-pä: sa-ch'a t'e/
The land which you are buying.......

3. ཁྱེད་རང་གིས་མཆོད་བཞིན་པའི་ན་བཟའ་དེ་·······
you by wear(H.)-continue-of dress(H.) which/
ky'e-ra;ng k'i:̀ ch'ö:̀-shi;n-pä: nam-sa t'e/
The dress which you are wearing.......

4. ཁྱེད་རང་གིས་ཀློག་བཞིན་པའི་དེབ་དེ་·······
you by read-continue-of book which/
ky'e-ra;ng k'i:̀ l̄ò:̀-shi;n-pä: t'eb t'e/
The book which you are reading.......

5. ཁྱེད་རང་གིས་སློབ་སྦྱོང་བྱེད་བཞིན་པའི་སློབ་ཚན་དེ་·······
you by study-continue-of lesson which/

ky'e-ra;ng k'i: l̄ob-jo;ng ch'e:-shi;n-pä: l̄ob-ts'ä;n t'e/
The lesson which you are studying.......

The infinitive particle ཡག་ or རྒྱུ་ in combination with the genitive གི་/འི་ is used after the main verb to indicate future tense.

Future:

1. ཁོང་གིས་བསྣམ་ཡག་གི་སྐུ་ཆས་དེ་ཚོ·········
he by take(H.) inf. of thing(H.) which-pl./
k'o;ng k'i: n̄am-ya: k'i ku-ch'ä: t'e-ts'o/
The things which he will take.......

2. ཁོང་གིས་བཞོན་ཡག་གི་རྟ་དེ··········
he by ride inf. of horse which/
k'o;ng k'i: shö;n-ya: k'i ta t'e/
The horse which he will ride.......

3. ཁོང་གིས་བེད་སྤྱོད་བྱ་རྒྱུའི་མཛུབ་གནོན་ཡིག་དཔར་དེ·········
he by use inf.-of typewriter which/
k'o;ng k'i: p'e-chö:-ch'a gyü: zub-nö;n-yig-par t'e/
The typewriter which he will use.......

4. ཁོང་ཚོས་བཟོ་ཡག་གི་ཤོག་གུ་དེ་ཚོ·········
they-by make inf. of paper which pl./
k'o;ng-ts'ö: so-ya: k'i shu-k'u t'e-ts'o/
The papers which they will make....... or
The papers which they make.......

21.3.5. Exercise 13

(a) Translate the following sentences into English

1. ཁྱེད་རང་གི་ཕྱག་དེབ་ག་གི་རེད།
2. ཕྱག་དེབ་ག་གི་ཁྱེད་རང་གི་རེད།

3. ག་གི་ཁྱེད་རང་གི་གཟིམ་ཤག་རེད།
4. དཔར་ཆས་ག་གི་ཁོང་གི་འཕྲོ་བརླག་བཏང་པ་རེད།
5. ཡི་གེ་འདི་སྨྱུ་གུ་ག་གིས་བྲིས་པ་རེད།
6. ངས་ཉོས་པའི་ཆུ་ཚོད་དེ་འགྲོ་གི་མི་འདུག
7. ཁོང་ཁང་མིག་ག་གིར་བཞུགས་ཀྱི་རེད།
8. ང་ཚོ་ཁང་མིག་ག་གིའི་ནང་ལ་སྡོད་དགོས་རེད།
9. མི་ག་གིས་རྟོག་ཁྲ་བསྒྲངས་པ་རེད།

(b) Translate the following sentences into Tibetan

1. Which horse threw you?
2. Which dog bit you?
3. Which foot kicked the ball?
4. Which boy made the trouble?
5. In which school did you study?
6. Which class is this?
7. Which one is your class teacher?
8. The watch which you brought for me is very good.

21.4. ག་པར། = "where" and related forms

ག་པར། is used in colloquial and
གང་དུ། in literary forms.

Examples:

1. ཁྱེད་རང་ག་པར་ཐེག་གི་ཡིན། = ཁྱེད་རང་ག་པར་ཐེག་ག
you where go(H.) fut. c./
ky'e-ra;ng k'a-pa: t'ä:-k'i yi;n/
Where will you go?

2. ཁྱེད་རང་ག་པར་ཐེག་གི་ཡོད།
you where go pres. c./

ky'e-ra;ng k̲'a-pa: t'ä:-k̲'i yö̀:/
Where are you going?

3. ཁྱེད་རང་ག་པར་ཐེག་པ་ཡིན། = ཁྱེད་རང་ག་པར་ཐེག་པ།
you where go past c./
ky'e-ra;ng k̲'a-pa: t'ä̀:-pa yi;n/
Where did you go?

4. ང་ག་པར་འགྲོ་གི་རེད།
I where go fut. c./
nga k̲'a-pa: ḍo-k̲'i rä/
Where am I going?

5. ང་ག་པར་འགྲོ་གི་འདུག
I where go pres. c./
nga k̲'a-pa: ḍo-k̲'i du/
Where am I going?

6. ང་ག་པར་ཕྱིན་པ་རེད།
I where went past c./
nga k̲'a-pa: ch'i;n-pa rä/
Where did I go?

7. ཁོང་ག་པར་ཐེག་གི་རེད།
he where go(H.) fut. c./
k'o;ng k̲'a-pa: t'ä:-k̲'i rä/
Where will he go?

8. ཁོང་ག་པར་ཐེག་གི་འདུག
he where go pres. c./
k'o;ng k̲'a-pa: t'ä:-k̲'i du/
Where is he going?

9. ཁོང་ག་པར་ཐེག་པ་རེད།
he where go past c./
k'o;ng k̲'a-pa: t'ä:-pa rä/
Where did he go?

10. ཁྱེད་རང་གི་ཕེབས་འཁོར་ག་པར་ཡོད།
your car(H.) where exist./
ky'e-ra;ng k̲'i p'eb-k'or k̲'a-pa: yö/
Where is your car?

11. ང་ཚོའི་སྣུམ་འཁོར་ག་པར་འདུག
our car where exist./
nga;n-ts'ö: n̄um-k'or k̲'a-pa: du/
Where is our car?

12. ཁོང་གི་ཞབས་ཕྱི་ག་པར་ཡོག་རེད།
his servant(H.) where exist./
k'o;ng k̲'i s̲hèb-ch'i k̲'a-pa: yò-rä/
Where is his servant?

13. སློབ་ཕྲུག་ཚོ་ག་པར་འདུག
students where exist./
l̄ob-ṭ'u:-ts'o k̲'a-pa: du/
Where are the students?

14. བོད་པའི་ཟ་ཁང་ག་པར་ག་པར་*ཡོག་རེད།
Tibetan-of restaurant where where exist./
p̲'ö-pä: s̲a-k'a;ng k̲'a-pa: k̲'a-pa: yò-rä/
Where are the Tibetan restaurants?

15. བོད་ཀྱི་དཔེ་མཛོད་ཁང་ག་པར་ཡོག་རེད།
Tibet of library where exist./

* The double appearance of ག་པར་ (literally: where, where) indicates that there are many restaurants.

p'ö:-ki pen-zö:-k'a;ng k'a-pa: yò-rä/
Where is the Tibetan Library?

16. ཁྱེད་རང་བོད་ལ་བཞུགས་ས་ག་པར་ཡིན་པ།
you Tibet to stay-place(H.) where is/
ky'e-ra;ng p'ö:-la shu:-sa k'a-pa: yi;n-pa/
Where is your home in Tibet?

17. ང་རྣམ་ཚོ་བོད་ལ་བཞུགས་གདན་འཛགས་ས་ག་པར་ཡིན་འགྲོ།
you pl.(H.) Tibet to stay-place where is/
nga-na-ts'o p'ö:-la shu-dä;n-ja:-sa k'a-pa: yi;n-ḍo/
same as (16) but very polite

18. ང་རྣམ་ཚོ་བོད་ལ་བཞུགས་གདན་འཛགས་ས་ག་པར་ཡིན་པ་ནོ།
same as (17)

19. ཁྱེད་རང་བོད་ལ་ག་པར་བཞུགས་ཀྱི་ཡོད།
you Tibet to where stay pres. c./
ky'e-ra;ng p'ö:-la k'a-pa: shu:-ki yö/
Where do you stay in Tibet?

20. ང་རྣམ་ཚོ་བོད་ལ་ག་པར་བཞུགས་གདན་འཛགས་ཀྱི་ཡོད་པ་ནོ།
you pl.(H.) Tibet to where stay-place is/
nga-na-ts'o p'ö:-la k'a-pa: shu-dä;n ja:-ki yö-pa-no/
same as (19) but very polite

21.4.1. ག་པར་ཡང་། "everywhere" & "anywhere"

ག་པར་ཡང་། is used in colloquial and
གང་དུ་ཡང་། in literary forms

Examples:

1. བོད་པའི་ཚོང་ཁང་ག་པར་ཡང་ཡོག་རེད།
Tibetan-of shop where-even exist./

p'ö-pä: ts'o;ng-k'a;ng k'a-pa: ya;ng yò-re:/

Tibetan shops are everywhere.

2. བོད་པའི་མི་ག་པར་ལའང་ཡོག་རེད།

Tibetan-of people where-to-even exist./

p'ö-pä: mi k'a-pa: lä: yò-re:/

Tibetan people are everywhere.

3. ཁོང་ག་པར་ཡང་འགྲོ་གི་རེད། = ཁོང་ག་པར་ལ་ཡང་འགྲོ་གི་རེད།

he where-even go fut.c./

k'o;ng k'a-pa: ya;ng ḍo-k'i-re:/

He will go anywhere.

4. ཁོང་ག་པར་ལ་ཡང་འགྲོ་གི་མི་འདུག

he where-to-even go neg. pres. c./

k'o;ng k'a-pa: lä ḍo-k'i mi;n-du/

He doesn't go anywhere.

5. ང་ཚོ་ཁ་ས་ག་ས་ག་ལ་ཕྱིན་པ་ཡིན།

we yesterday everywhere go past c./

nga;n-ts'o k'ä:-sa k'a-sa-k'a-la ch'i;n-pa yi;n/

Yesterday we went everywhere.

6. གཟའ་ཉི་མའི་ཉིན་སྐང་ང་ཚོ་ག་པར་ལ་ཡང་འགྲོ་ཆོག་གི་རེད།

Sunday-of on we where-to-even go allow/

sa-nyi-mä: nyi;n-ga;ng nga;n-ts'o k'a-pa: lä: ḍo ch'ò:-k'i re:/

We can go anywhere on Sunday.

7. དེའི་ཉིན་སྐང་ཁོང་ག་པར་ལ་ཡང་འགྲོ་བ་རེད།

that-of on he where-to-even go pres. c./

t'e:-nyi;n-ga;ng k'o;ng k'a-pa: lä: ḍo-wa re:/

He goes everywhere on that day (usually).

8. ཁོང་ག་པར་ལ་ཡང་འགྲོ་བ་མ་རེད།
she where-to-even go neg. pres. c./
k'o;ng k'a-pa: lä: ḍo-wa ma-reː/
She doesn't go anywhere (usually).

9. ངས་ལུང་པ་འདི་ནང་བཞིན་གྱི་སྐྱིད་པོ་འདི་འདྲས་ག་པར་ལ་ཡང་མཐོང་མ་བྱུང་།
I-by country this like-of pleasant such where-to-even see neg. past. c./
ngäː lu;ng-pa di na;ng-shi;n-ki kyi-po di;n-ḍäː k'a-pa: lä: t'o;ng ma-ch'u;ng/
I haven't seen such a nice country like this anywhere.

21.4.2. Structure of "wherever"

ག་པར། + past stem of verb + ཀྱང་, ཡང་, འང་, ནའང་ & ན་ཡང་

Examples:

1. ང་ག་པར་ཕྱིན་ཀྱང་ངའི་བུ་མཉམ་དུ་ཡོང་གི་རེད།
I where went even my son with come fut. c./
nga k'a-pa: ch'i;n-kya;ng ngä: p'u nyam-t'u yo;ng-k'i reː/
Wherever I go, my son will come along (with me).

2. ཁྱེད་རང་ག་པར་ཐེག་ནའང་ཁོང་ཡོང་གི་རེད།
you where go(H.) if-even he come fut. c./
ky'e-ra;ng k'a-pa: t'ä:-nä: k'o;ng yo;ng-k'i reː/
Wherever you go, he will come (with you).

3. ཁྱེད་རང་ག་པར་ཐེག་པ་ཡིན་ནའང་ཁོང་ཡོང་གི་རེད།
you where go(H.) if-even he come fut. c./
ky'e-ra;ng k'a-pa: t'ä:-pa-yi;n-nä: k'o;ng yo;ng-k'i reː/
same as (2)

4. མི་འདི་ག་པར་བཏང་ནའང་གོ་ཆོད་པོ་ཡོད།
man this where sent if-even useful exist./

mi di k'a-pa: ta;ng-nä: k'o-ch'ö:-po yö:/

Wherever this man is sent to, he is useful.

21.4.3. ག་པར། & ག་ནས། = "how could"

Examples:

1. འདི་ཉི་མ་གཅིག་ལ་ག་པར་ཀློག་ཚར་གྱི་རེད།
this day one to where read finish fut. c./
di nyi-ma chig-la k'a-pa: lò: ts'a:-k'i rä/
How can this be read in one day?

2. ཁོང་གིས་འདི་ག་ནས་ཁ་ལོ་འཆུན་ཐུབ་ཀྱི་རེད།
he by this from-where manage able fut. c./
k'o;ng k'i: di k'a-nä: k'a-lo-ch'ü;n t'ub-ki rä/
How can he manage this?

3. བུ་མོ་འདི་གཅིག་པུར་ག་པར་འགྲོ་ནུས་ཀྱི་རེད།
girl this alone-to where go dare fut. c./
p'u-mo di chi-po: k'a-pa: ḍo nü:-ki rä/
How dare this girl go alone?

4. ན་ཚ་འདི་འདྲས་ཕྲུ་གུས་ག་པར་འཁྱོག་གི་རེད།
pain this-like child-by where bear fut. c./
na-ts'a di;n-ḍä: pu-k'ü: k'a-pa: ky'ò:-k'i rä/
How can a child bear such a pain?

5. སྐད་ཆ་འདི་ངས་ག་པར་བཟོད་ཐུབ་ཀྱི་རེད།
talk this I-by where bear able fut. c./
kä-ch'a di ngä: k'a-pa: sä: t'ub-ki rä/
How can I stand this talk?

21.4.4. Exercise 14

(a) Translate the following into Tibetan:

1. Where did you go?
2. Where are you going?
3. Where is he going?
4. Where is your wife?
5. Where did they go?
6. Where is the Tibetan Library?
7. Where are they living?
8. How could she do this?
9. How could a child understand this?
10. Wherever I go, I take this with me.

(a) Translate the following into English

1. ཁོང་ག་པར་ཐེག་ན་ཡང་ཁྱི་འདི་འགྲོ་གི་རེད།
2. ང་ག་པར་ཕྱིན་ན་ཡང་ཁྱེད་རང་ཞེབས་གས།
3. ང་ག་པར་ཡང་ཕྱིན་པ་ཡིན།
4. ཁ་སང་ང་ག་ས་ག་ལ་ཕྱིན་པ་ཡིན།
5. བུ་འདི་ག་པར་བཏང་ན་ཡང་འགྲོ་གི་རེད།
6. ཁོང་ལ་ཡོད་ན་ཡང་མེད་གསུང་གི་འདུག
7. ཁོང་ཕ་གིར་མེད་ན་ཡང་ཡོག་རེད་གསུངས་པ་རེད།

21.5. ག་ནས། = "from where" & related forms

ག་ནས། is used in colloquial and
གང་ནས། in literary forms.

Examples:

1. ཁྱེད་རང་ག་ནས་ཡིན་པ།
you from-where is/

ky'e-ra;ng k'a-nä: yi;n-pa/
Where are you from?

2. ང་རྣམ་ཚོ་ག་ནས་ཡིན་པ་ནོ།
you(H.) from-where is/
nga-na-ts'o k'a-nä: yi;n-pa-no/
same as (1) but very polite

3. ཁོང་ཚོ་ལུང་པ་ག་ནས་རེད།
they country from-where is/
k'o;ng-ts'o lu;ng-pa k'a-nä: rä/
Which country are they from?

4. ཁྱེད་རང་ག་ནས་ཕེབས་ཀྱི་ཡིན། = ཁྱེད་རང་ག་ནས་ཕེབས་ག
you from-where come(H.) fut. c./
ky'e-ra;ng k'a-nä: p'e-ki-yi;n/
From where will you come? or
Which way will you come?

5. ཁྱེད་རང་ག་ནས་ཕེབས་ཀྱི་ཡོད།
you from-where come pres. c./
ky'e-ra;ng k'a-nä: p'e:-ki yö/
Where are you coming from?

6. ཁྱེད་རང་ག་ནས་ཕེབས་པ་ཡིན། = ཁྱེད་རང་ག་ནས་ཕེབས་པ།
you from-where come past c./
ky'e-ra;ng k'a-nä: p'e:-pa yi;n/
Where did you come from? or
Where do you come from? (as a general statement)

7. ཁོང་ཚོ་ག་ནས་ཐེག་གི་འདུག
they from-where go(H.) pres. c./

k'o;ng-ts'o k'a-nä: t'ä:-k'i du/

Which way are they going from?

8. ཁྱེད་རང་ག་ནས་ཐེག་ག

they from-where go fut. c./

ky'e-ra;ng k'a-nä: t'ä-k'a/

Which way will you go?

9. ཁོང་རྣམ་ཚོ་ག་ནས་ཐེག་སོང་།

they(H.) from-where go past c./

k'o-na-ts'o k'a-nä: t'ä:-so;ng/

Which way did they go?

10. འདོད་ཆགས་ག་ནས་སྐྱེ་གི་ཡོག་རེད།

Attachment from-where born pres. c./

dö:-ch'a: k'a-nä: kye-k'i yò-rä/

From where does attachment arise?

11. ཆར་པ་ག་ནས་བྱུང་པ་རེད། = ཆར་པ་གང་ལས་བྱུང་ངམ། (lit.)

rain from-where originate past c./

ch'a:-pa k'a-nä: ch'u;ng-pa rä/

From where did the rain originate?

12. སྒོང་ང་ག་ནས་བྱུང་པ་རེད།

egg from-where originate past c./

go-nga k'a-nä: ch'u;ng-pa rä/

From where did the egg originate? or

Where does egg come from? (as a general question)

13. བྱ་མོ་ག་ནས་ཡོང་གི་ཡོག་རེད།

hen from-where come pres. c./

ch'a-mo k'a-nä: yo;ng-k'i yò-rä/

From where does a hen originate?

14. མི་འདི་ག་ནས་སླེབས་པ་རེད།
man this from-where came past c./
mi di k̲'a-nä̀: l̄eb-pa rä/
Where did this man come from?

21.5.1. ག་ནས་ཀྱང་། = "everywhere" & "anywhere"

Examples:

1. འདི་ག་ནས་ཀྱང་རག་གི་རེད།
this from-where-even get fut. c./
di k̲'a-nä̀:-kya;ng ra:-k̲'i rä/
This is available everywhere.

2. འདི་ག་ནས་ཡིན་ན་ཡང་རག་གི་རེད།
this from-where if-even get fut. c./
di k̲'a-nä̀: yi;n-na-ya;ng ra:-k̲'i rè:/
same as (1)

3. དེང་སང་འདི་ག་ནས་ཀྱང་རག་གི་མ་རེད།
these days this from-where-even get neg. fut. c./
t̲'e;ng-sa;ng di k̲'a-nä̀:-kya;ng ra:-k̲'i ma:-rè:/
This is not available anywhere these days.

4. དེང་སང་འདི་ག་ནས་ཡིན་ན་ཡང་རག་གི་མ་རེད།
these days this from-where-even get neg. fut. c./
t̲'e;ng-sa;ng di k̲'a-nä̀:-yi;n-na-ya;ng ra:-k̲'i ma:-rè:/
This is not available anywhere these days.

5. འདིའི་སྐོར་ལ་ག་ནས་ཡིན་ན་ཡང་གོ་ཐུབ་ཀྱི་རེད།
this-of about from-where if-even hear able fut. c./
di: kor-la k̲'a-nä̀: yi;n-na-ya;ng k̲'o t'ub-ki rè:/
(One) can hear from anywhere about this.

21.5.2. Structure of "wherever", "whichever way" & "In whatever way".

ག་ནས། + past stem of verb + ཀྱང་, ཡང་, འང་ or ནའང་/ན་ཡང་

Examples:

1. འདི་ག་ནས་ཉོས་ཀྱང་གོང་གཅིག་པ་རེད།
this from-where bought even price same is/
di k̲'a-nä`: nyö`:-kya;ng k̲'o;ng chig-pa re`:/
Wherever (you) buy this, the price is the same.

2. འདི་ག་ནས་ཉོས་ན་ཡང་གོང་གཅིག་པ་རེད།
this from-where bought if-even price same is/
di k̲'a-nä`: nyö`:-nä: ya;ng k̲'o;ng chig-pa re`:/
same as (1)

3. འདི་ག་ནས་གཟིགས་ནའང་ལྗགས་གོང་གཅིག་པ་རེད།
di k̲'a-nä`: s̲i:-nä: ja:-k̲'o;ng chig-pa re`:/
same as (2) but honorific

4. ག་ནས་ཕེབས་ནའང་ཐག་རིང་ཐུང་གཅིག་པ་རེད།
from-where come if-even distance-length same is/
k̲'a-nä`: p'e:-nä: t'a`: ri;ng-t'u;ng chig-pa re`:/
Whichever way (you) come it is the same distance.

5. ག་ནས་ཕྱིན་ན་ཡང་དུས་ཚོད་གཅིག་ལ་སླེབས་ཀྱི་འདུག
from-where went if-even time one to reach pres. c./
k̲'a-nä`: ch'i;n-nä: t̲'ü:-ts'ö`: chig-la l̄eb-ki du/
Whichever way (we) go (we) reach there at the same time.

6. ག་ནས་བལྟས་ཀྱང་འདྲེ་འདྲ་བ།
from-where looked even ghost like/
k̲'a-nä`: tä`:-kya;ng ḍe-ḍa-wa/
Whichever way (I) look (at you), (you) look like a ghost.

7. ང་ལ་གནོད་པ་མ་སྐྱེལ་ཨང་།
   I to harm not deliver imp./
   nga la n̄ö-pa ma-kyä: a;ng/
   Do not harm me.

8. ག་ནས་བསམ་བློ་བཏང་ཡང་།
   from-where think even/
   k̲'a-nä: sam-l̄o ta;ng-ya;ng/
   In whatever way (I) think,

9. ཆོས་ལས་ལྷག་པ་མི་འདུག
   dharma than more not exist./
   ch'ö:-lä l̄ag-pa mi;n du/
   There is nothing greater than Dharma.

21.5.3. Exercise 15

(a) Translate the following into Tibetan.

1. Where are they from?
2. I do not know where they are from.
3. Where are you from?
4. I am from Tibet.
5. From which country is he?
6. He is from Tibet too.
7. Where did they come from?
8. They came from America.
9. Where am I from?
10. You are from Tibet.

(b) Translate the following into English.

1. ཆར་པ་ག་ནས་བྱུང་བ་རེད།
2. ཆར་པ་རྒྱ་མཚོ་ནས་བྱུང་བ་རེད།

3. སྒོ་ང་ག་ནས་བྱུང་བ་རེད།
4. སྒོ་ང་བྱ་མོ་ནས་བྱུང་བ་རེད།
5. ཁྱེད་རང་ད་ལྟ་ག་ནས་ཕེབས་པ།
6. ང་ད་ལྟ་ནང་ནས་ཡོང་པ་ཡིན།
7. འདི་ཁོང་ལ་ག་ནས་རག་པ་རེད།

21.6. ག་ཚད། = "how much", "how many" and related forms

ག་ཚད། is used in colloquial and
ཇི་ཙམ། in literary forms.

Examples:

1. འདིར་གོང་ག་ཚད་*རེད།
this-to price how-much is/
dä: k'o;ng k'a-ts'ä: rä/
What is the cost of this ?

2. འདིར་ལྗགས་གོང་ག་ཚད་རེད།
this-to price(H.) how-much is/
dä: ja:-k'o;ng k'a-ts'ä: rä/
same as (1) but honorific

3. ཚིགས་ཁེབས་ཆ་གཅིག་ལ་གོང་ག་ཚད་རེད།
finger-ring pair one to price how-much is/
ts'i-k'ò: ch'a-chig-la k'o;ng k'a-ts'ä: rä/
What is the cost of a pair of finger rings?

4. ཕྱག་རྒྱུད་ཆ་**གཅིག་ལ་ལྗགས་གོང་ག་ཚད་རེད།
ring(H.) pair one to price(H.) how much is/

---

* ག་ཚད་ = 'how much', 'how many' appears in the English translation mostly is 'what'

** In Tibetan ཆ་ (pair) is used to any two identical objects.

ch'a-gyü: ch'a chig-la ja:-k'o;ng k'a-ts'ä: rä/
What is the cost of a pair of finger rings?

5. བཞུགས་གདན་ཆ་གཅིག་ལ་ལྗགས་གོང་ག་ཚད་རེད།
carpet(H.) pair one to price how much is/
shu-dä;n ch'a chig-la ja:-k'o;ng k'a-ts'ä: rä/
What is the cost of a pair of carpets?

6. བྱས་ན། ཡ་གཅིག་ལ་ག་ཚད་རེད།
then/ a piece-to how much is/
ch'ä:-na ya chig-la k'a-ts'ä: rä/
And then, how much is one piece (of the pair)?

7. གསོལ་ཇ་ཞལ་དཀར་གང་ལ་ག་ཚད་རེད།
tea(H.) cup(H.) one to how much is/
sö:-ch'a shä:-ka: k'a;ng-la k'a-ts'ä: rä/
How much is a cup of tea?

8. བཞེས་ཐུག་ཞལ་དཀར་དོ་ལ་ག་ཚད་རེད།
noodle(H.) cup two to how much is/
she-t'u: shä:-ka: t'o-la k'a-ts'ä: rä/
How much is two bowls of noodles?

9. འདི་འདྲས་གཅིག་ལ་ག་ཚད་རེད།
this like one to how much is/
di;n-ḍä: chig-la k'a-ts'ä: rä/
How much is one of these?

10. ཁྱེད་རང་ལ་དེབ་འདི་འདྲས་ག་ཚད་ཡོད།
you to book this like how much exist./
ky'e-ra;ng-la t'eb di;n-ḍä: k'a-ts'ä: yö/
How many such books do you have?

11. ཁོང་ལ་དེབ་འདི་འདྲས་ཀ་ཚད་འདུག
he to book this like how much exist./
k'o;ng-la t'eb di;n-ḍäː k'a-ts'äː du/
How many such books does he have?

12. ཁང་པ་འདིའི་ནང་ལ་མི་ཀ་ཚད་ཆུར་གྱི་རེད།
house this-of into people how much fit fut. c./
k'a;ng-pa di: na;ng-la mi k'a-ts'äː ch'u:-k'i rä/
How many people will fit in this house?

13. ཌ་རམ་ས་ལར་མི་འབོར་ཀ་ཚད་ཡོག་རེད།
Dharamsala-to population how much exist./
da-ram-sa-la: mi;n-bor k'a-ts'äː yò-rä/
What is the population of Dharamsala?

14. དཔེ་མཛོད་ཁང་ལ་ལས་བྱེད་ཀ་ཚད་ཡོག་རེད།
library to staff-member how much exist./
pe;n-zöː-k'a;ng-la lä:-ch'eː k'a-ts'äː yò-rä/
How many staff members are in the Library?

15. ད་ལྟ་ཆུ་ཚོད་ཀ་ཚད་རེད།
just-now time how much is/
t'a;n-ta ch'u-ts'öː k'a-ts'äː rä/
What is the time now?

16. དེ་རིང་ཚེས་པ་ཀ་ཚད་རེད།
today date how much is/
t'e-ri;ng ts'e-pa k'ats'äː rä/
What date is it today?

17. ཁྱེད་རང་ལ་དུས་ཚོད་ཀ་ཚད་ཡོད།
you to time how much exist./

ky'e-ra;ng-la t̲'ü:-ts'öː k̲'a-ts'äː yö/
How much time do you have?

18. ཁྱེད་རང་ཉིན་རེ་ཆུ་ཚོད་ག་ཚད་ལས་ཀ་བྱེད་ཀྱི་ཡོད།
you daily hour how much work pres. c./
ky'e-ra;ng nyi;n-re ch'u-ts'öː k̲'a-ts'äː lä:-ka c̲h̲'e-ki yö/
How many hours do you work daily?

21.6.1. ག་ཚད་ལ། = at what

ག་ཚད་ལ། is used in colloquial and
ཇི་ཙམ་ལ། in literary forms.

Examples:

1. ཁྱེད་རང་འདི་ནས་ཆུ་ཚོད་ག་ཚད་ལ་ཐོན་ག
you here from time how much to depart fut. c./
ky'e-ra;ng di näː ch'u-ts'öː k̲'a-ts'äː la t'ö;n-k̲'a/
At what time will you depart from here ?

2. ཆུ་ཚོད་ག་ཚད་ལ་ཁོང་སླེབས་པ་རེད།
time how much to he arrive past c./
ch'u-ts'öː k̲'a-ts'äː la k'o;ng l̄eb-pa rä/
At what time did he arrive?

3. གནམ་གྲུ་འདི་ཆུ་ཚོད་ག་ཚད་ལ་འཕུར་གྱི་རེད།
aeroplane this time how much to fly fut. c./
n̄am-ṯ'u di ch'u-ts'öː k̲'a-ts'äː la p'ir-k̲'i rä/
At what time will this plane take off?

4. ཁོང་ཚོ་འདིར་ཆུ་ཚོད་ག་ཚད་ལ་ཕེབས་ཀྱི་རེད།
they here time how much to come fut. c./
k'o;ng-ts'o dä: ch'u-ts'öː k̲'a-ts'äː la p'e:-ki rä/
At what time will they come here?

5. ཁྱེད་རང་འདིར་ཆུ་ཚོད་ག་ཚད་ལ་ཕེབས་ཀ
you here time how much to come fut. c./
ky'e-ra;ng dä: ch'u-ts'ö: k̲'a-ts'ä: la p'e:-k̲'a/
At what time will you come here?

6. ང་འདིར་ཆུ་ཚོད་ག་ཚད་ལ་ཡོང་དགོས་རེད།
I here time how much to come have is/
nga dä: ch'u-ts'ö: k̲'a-ts'ä: la yo;ng go rä/
At what time should I come here?

7. ང་ཚོ་འདིར་ཆུ་ཚོད་ག་ཚད་ལ་འཛོམས་དགོས་རེད།
we here time how much to gather have is/
nga;n-ts'o dä: ch'u-ts'ö: k̲'a-ts'ä:-la zom go rä/
At what time should we gather here?

8. ཁྱེད་རང་འདི་ནས་ཚེས་པ་ག་ཚད་ལ་ཐོན་ཀ
you this from date how much to depart fut. c./
ky'e-ra;ng di-nä: ts'e-pa k̲'a-ts'ä: la t'ö;n-k̲'a/
On what date will you depart from here?

9. ཁོང་ཚོ་རྒྱ་གར་ནས་ཚེས་པ་ག་ཚད་ལ་ཐོན་པ་རེད།
they India from date how much to depart past c./
k'o;ng-ts'o gya-k̲'a: nä ts'e-pa k̲'a-ts'ä: la t'ö;n-pa rä/
On what date did they depart from India?

21.6.2. ག་ཚད་ཀྱི་ = "how many of"

1. འདི་སྒོར་མོ་ག་ཚད་ཀྱི་རེད།
this coin how much is/
di gò:-mo k̲'a-ts'ä: ki rä/
How much is this? or (How many coins did (you) pay for this?)

2. སློབ་ཚན་འདི་ཉི་མ་ག་ཚད་ཀྱི་རེད།
lesson this day how much of is/
lob-ts'ä;n di nyi-ma k'a-ts'ä: ki rä/
How many days lesson is this of?

21.6.3. ག་ཚད། = "how much" (in statement)

1. ངས་ཁོང་ལ་རོགས་རམ་ག་ཚད་བྱས་ཡོག་རེད། ཁོང་གིས་དྲན་གི་ཡོག་མ་རེད།
I-by he to help how much did exist./ he by remember pres. neg. c./
ngä: k'o;ng-la rog-ram k'a-ts'ä: ch'ä: yò-rä/ k'o;ng-k'i t'ä;n-k'i yò: ma-re:/
He doesn't remember, how much I helped him.

2. དེ་དུས་མི་ག་ཚད་ཡོད་པ་དྲན་གསོས་ཀྱི་མི་འདུག
that time people how much exist. remember neg. pres. c./
t'e-t'ü: mi k'a-ts'ä: yö-pa t'ä;n sö:-ki mi;n-du/
I cannot remember how many people were there at that time.

21.6.4. Exercise 16

Translate the following into Tibetan

1. How much does this pen cost?
2. How much does this pair of socks cost?
3. How many such rings does she have?
4. How many girls are in that school?
5. What is the time now?
6. What date is it today?
7. How much money do you have?
8. How much will each student get?
9. At what time will you start it?
10. At what time do you come to the class?

11. How many days' work is this?
12. What is the price of this?
13. I don't remember how much I gave him.
14. How much money do you need?

21.7. ག་རེ་བྱས་ནས། = "why" and related forms

ག་རེ་བྱས་ནས། ག་རེ་ཡིན་ནམ། is used in colloquial &
གང་ཡིན་ནམ། in literary forms.

Examples:

1. ག་རེ་ཡིན་ནམ།
   what is/? /
   k'a-re yi;n-na/
   Why?

2. ཁོང་སློབ་གྲྭར་ག་རེ་བྱས་ནས་མ་ཕྱིན་པ་རེད།
   he school-to why not went past c./
   k'o;ng l̄ab-ṭ'a: k'a-re-ch'ä-nä ma-ch'i;n-pa rä/
   Why didn't he go to school?

3. ཁོང་ག་རེ་བྱས་ནས་སློབ་གྲྭར་མ་ཕྱིན་པ་རེད།
   he why school-to not went past c./
   k'o;ng k'a-re-ch'ä-nä l̄ab-ṭ'a: ma-ch'i;n-pa rä/
   same as (2)

4. ཁོང་སློབ་གྲྭར་མ་ཕྱིན་པ་ག་རེ་ཡིན་ནམ།
   he school-to not went why/
   k'o;ng l̄ab-ṭ'a: ma-ch'i;n-pa k'a-re-yi;n-na/
   same as (2)

5. ཁྱེད་རང་ག་རེ་བྱས་ནས་དགོངས་པ་འཚོམས་པ་རེད།
you why get angry past c./
ky'e-ra;ng k'a-re-ch'ä-nä go;ng-pa ts'om-pa rä/
Why did you get angry?

6. ང་ཚོ་ག་རེ་བྱས་ནས་འགྲོ་ཆོག་གི་ཡོག་མ་རེད།
we why go allow neg. pres. c./
nga;n-ts'o k'a-re-ch'ä-nä ḍo ch'ò:-k'i yò: ma-rä/
Why are we not allowed to go?

7. ང་ཚོ་འགྲོ་མ་ཆོག་ག་ག་རེ་རེད།
we go not allow why/
nga;n-ts'o ḍo ma-ch'o-k'a k'a-re rä/
same as (6)

8. ཁྱེད་རང་ག་རེ་བྱས་ནས་འགྲོ་ག
you why go fut. c./
ky'e-ra;ng k'a-re-ch'ä-nä ḍo-k'a/
Why will you go?

9. ཁྱེད་རང་ག་རེ་བྱས་ནས་འགྲོ་གི་ཡོད།
you why go pres. c./
ky'e-ra;ng k'a-re-ch'ä-nä ḍo-k'i yö/
Why are you going?

10. ཁྱེད་རང་ག་རེ་བྱས་ནས་ཐེག་པ།
you why go(H.) past c./
ky'e-ra;ng k'a-re-ch'ä-nä t'ä:-pa/
Why did you go?

21.7.1. ག་རེའི་དོན་དག་ལ། = "for what purpose", "why"

ག་རེའི་དོན་དག་ལ། is used in colloquial and
གང་གི་དོན་དུ། in literary forms

Examples:

1. ཁྱེད་རང་འདིར་ཉིན་རྟར་ག་རེའི་དོན་དག་ལ་ཕེབས་ཀྱི་ཡོད།
you here every-day what-of purpose to come pres. c./
ky'e-ra;ng dä: nyi;n-ta: k̲'a-re-t̲'ö;n t̲'a`: la p'e:-ki yö/
Why do you come here every day?

2. ཚོགས་པ་འདི་ག་རེའི་དོན་དག་ལ་འཛུགས་ཀྱི་ཡོག་རེད།
association this what-of-purpose-to establish pres. c./
ts'og-pa di k̲'a-re:-t̲'ö;n-t̲'a`:-la tsu: k̲'i yò-rä/
Why is this association being set up?

3. ཁྱེད་རང་སྐད་ཆ་འདི་འདྲས་ག་རེའི་དོན་དག་ལ་ཤོད་ཀྱི་ཡོད།
you talk this-like what-of-purpose-to tell pres. c./
ky'e-ra;ng kä-ch'a di;n-ḍä`: k̲'a-re:t̲'ö;n t̲'a`:-la shö:-ki yö/
Why are you talking like this?

4. སྨན་ཁང་འདི་ག་རེའི་དོན་དག་ལ་བཙུགས་པ་རེད།
hospital this what-of-purpose-to establish past c./
mä;n-k'a;ng di k̲'a-re:-t̲'ö;n-t̲'a`:-la tsu:-pa rä/
For what purpose was this hospital established?

5. འདི་ག་རེའི་དོན་དག་ལ་ཉོས་པ།
this what-of-purpose-to bought past c./
di k̲'a-re:-t̲'ö;n-t̲'a`:-la nyö-pa/
Why did (you) buy this?

6. ཁྱེད་ཙག་འདི་ན་གང་གི་དོན་དུ་ཕེབས་སམ། (lit.)
you here what-of-purpose-to come ?/

ky'e-cha꞉ di-na k̲'a;ng-k̲'i-t̲'ö;n-t̲'u p'eb-sa;m/
Why do you come here?

7. ཁྱེད་རང་འདིར་ག་རེ་བྱེད་ག་ཡོང་པ།
you here what-do-to come past c./
ky'e-ra;ng dä k̲'a-re c̲h̲'e-k̲'a yo;ng-pa/
Why did you come here?

8. ཁྱེད་རང་ཕ་གིར་ག་རེ་བྱེད་ག་ཕྱིན་པ།
you there what-do-to went past c./
ky'e-ra;ng p'a-k̲'ä: k̲'a-re c̲h̲'e-k̲'a ch'i;n-pa/
Why did you go there?

9. འདི་འདིར་ག་རེ་བྱས་ནས་འཁྱེར་*ཡོང་པ།
this here what-did-from bring past c./
di dä: k̲'a-re-c̲h̲'ä-nä ky'e:-yo;ng-pa/
Why did you bring it here?

21.8. ག་འདྲས། = "how" and related forms

ག་འདྲས། is used in colloquial and
གང་འདྲ། in literary forms.

They are connected with nouns, adjectives and adverbs

Examples:

1. དེང་སང་ཁྱེད་རང་གི་སྐུ་གཟུགས་ག་འདྲས་འདུག
these-days your health(H.) how exist./
t̲'e;ng-sa;ng ky'e-ra;ng k̲'i ku-su꞉ k̲'a;n-ḍä꞉ du/
How is your health these days?

---

* འཁྱེར་ཡོང་ = to bring = བསྣམས་ཕེབས་ (H.)
འཁྱེར་འགྲོ་ = to take = བསྣམས་ཐེག་ ”

2. ཁོང་ཁ་ལག་བཟོ་ཡག་ལ་ག་འདྲས་ཡོག་རེད།
he food(H.) making to how exist./
k'o;ng k'a-la꞉ so-ya꞉-la k'a;n-ḍä꞉ yò-rä/
How is he in cooking?

3. ཁོང་གིས་བྲིས་པའི་དེབ་དེ་ག་འདྲས་འདུག
he by wrote-of book which how exist./
k'o;ng-k'i ṯ'i꞉-pä: t'eb-t'e k'a;n-ḍä꞉ du/
What is the book which he wrote like?

4. དབྱིན་ཇིའི་སློབ་གྲྭ་དེ་ག་འདྲས་ཡོག་རེད།
English-of school that how exist./
in-chi: l̄ab-ṯ'a ṭ'e k'a;n-ḍä yò-rä/
What is that English school like?

5. དེང་སང་རྒྱ་གར་ལ་གནམ་གཤིས་ག་འདྲས་ཡོག་རེད།
these-days India to weather how exist./
ṭ'e;ng-sa;ng gya-k'a:-la n̄am-shi꞉ k'a;n ḍä꞉ yò-rä/
How is the weather in India these days?

6. ལྟོས་དང་། ཁོང་མགྱོགས་པོ་ག་འདྲས་འགྲོ་གི་འདུག
look imp./ he fast how going/
tö꞉-t'a k'o;ng gyog-po k'a;n-ḍä꞉ ḍo-k'i du/
Look! How fast he is going !

7. གཟིགས་དང་། མེ་ཏོག་པ་གི་སྙིང་རྗེ་པོ་ག་འདྲས་འདུག
look(H.)/ flower that beautiful how exist./
si꞉-t'a me-tò꞉ p'a-k'i n̄yi;ng-je-po k'a;n-ḍä꞉ du/
Look! How beautiful that flower is!

The English expression "How are you?" has its equivalent in the Tibetan:

8. ཁྱེད་རང་སྐུ་གཟུགས་བདེ་པོ་ཡིན་པས།
you body(H.) well is ?/
ky'e-ra;ng ku-<u>s</u>u`: de-po yi;n-pä/
How are you? (Are you fine?) lit.

9. ལགས་ཡིན། ང་གཟུགས་པོ་བདེ་པོ་ཡིན།
yes(H.)/ I body well is/
la-yi;n/ nga <u>s</u>ug-po de-po yi;n/
Yes, I am fine.

21.8.1. ག་འདྲས་སེ། = "how" & "in what way"

ག་འདྲས་སེ། / ག་འདྲས་བྱས་ནས། is used in colloquial and
གང་འདྲ། / གང་འདྲ་བྱས། in literary forms

They are connected with verbs:

1. ཁྱེད་རང་བོད་ནས་ག་འདྲས་སེ་ཕེབས་པ།
you Tibet from how come past c./
ky'e-ra;ng <u>p</u>'ö`: nä <u>k</u>'a;n-ḍäs p'e`:-pa/
How did you come from Tibet?

2. ཁོང་བོད་ནས་ག་འདྲས་བྱས་ནས་ཕེབས་པ་རེད།
he Tibet from how come past c./
k'o;ng <u>p</u>'ö`:-nä <u>k</u>'a;n-ḍä`:-<u>ch</u>'ä-nä p'e-pa rä/
How did he come from Tibet?

3. ཁྱེད་རང་ཐུགས་བསམ་ག་འདྲས་སེ་བཞེས་ཀྱི་ཡོད།
you think(H.) how vr. pres. c./
ky'e-ra;ng t'u-sam <u>k</u>'a;n-ḍäs <u>sh</u>e:-ki yö/
In what way are you thinking?

4. འདི་ག་འདྲས་སོ་བཟོ་གི་རེད།
this how make fut. c./
di k'a;n-ḍäs so-k'i rä/
How will this be made?

21.8.2. ག་འདྲས་ཅི། = "what kind of"

ག་འདྲས་ཅི་ is used in colloquial and
གང་འདྲ་ཞིག་ in literary forms

1. ཁྱེད་རང་ལ་གཟིམ་ཁྱི་ག་འདྲས་ཅི་ཡོད།
you to dog(H.) what kind of exist./
ky'e-ra;ng la sim-ky'i k'a;nḍä:-chi yö/
What kind of dog do you have?

2. ངར་ཕྱག་དེབ་ག་འདྲས་ཅི་གནང་ག
I-to book(H.) what kind of give(H.) fut. c./
nga: ch'a:-t'eb k'a;n-ḍä-chi n̄a;ng-k'a/
What kind of book will (you) give me?

3. མི་འདི་ག་འདྲས་ཅི་ཡིན་ངས་ཤེས་ཀྱི་མེད།
man this what kind of is I-by know neg. pres. c./
mi di k'a;n-ḍä-chi yi;n ngä: she;n-ki mä:/
I don't know what kind of person he is.

4. འཕྲུལ་འཁོར་འདི་ག་འདྲས་ཅི་རེད།
machine this what kind of is/
ṭ'ü:-kor di k'a;n-ḍä:-chi rä/
What kind of a machine is this?

21.8.3. Exercise 17

(a) Translate the following into Tibetan

1. Why did she go there?
2. Why didn't he come?
3. Why are they not allowed to go there?
4. For what purpose did you do it?
5. How did he come?
6. How will she make this?
7. How shall I use this?
8. What type of camera does she have?
9. Do you know what kind of a person he is?
10. How is your baby?

(b) Translate the following into English

1. ཚང་མ་ཁོང་གིས་འཁྱེར་འགྲོ་ཡག་ག་རེ་ཡིན་ནམ།
2. ཁྱེད་རང་གིས་ཁོང་ལ་ག་འདྲས་སེ་གསུངས་པ།
3. མི་དེ་ག་འདྲས་ཅི་རེད།
4. འདི་ཁོང་གི་རྩ་ནས་ག་འདྲས་བྱས་ནས་ལེན་པ།
5. ག་རེ་བྱས་ནས་ཡོང་གི་མ་རེད་པས།
6. འདི་ག་རེའི་དོན་དག་ལ་འཁྱེར་ཕྱིན་པ་རེད།
7. ག་རེའི་དོན་དག་ལ།
8. ཨ་ཅེ་ག་རེ་བྱེད་དགོས་རེད།

21.9. Personal interrogative "who" and related forms

21.9.1. སུ། = "who"

1. ཁོང་སུ་རེད།
   he who is/
   k'o;ng su rä/
   Who is he?

2. ཁྱེད་རང་སུ་ཡིན་པ།
   you who is ?/
   ky'e-ra;ng su yi;n-pa/
   Who are you?

3. ཁོང་སུ་ཞུ་མཁན་དེ་ཡིན་པ་ནོ།
he who call(H.) who that is(H.)/
k'o;ng su s̲h̲u-k'ä;n t̲'e yi;n-pa-no/
Who is he? (very polite)

4. ང་རྣམ་ཚོ་སུ་ཡིན་པ་ནོ།
you(H.) who is/
nga-na-ts'o su yin-pa-no/
Who are you? (very polite)

5. ཨ་ཅག་ལགས་ཕ་ཚོ་སུ་རེད།
ladies(H.) those who is/
a-cha:-la: p'a;n-ts'o su rä/
Who are those ladies?

6. ཁྱེད་རང་ལ་བཀའ་མོལ་གནང་མཁན་དེ་སུ་རེད།
you to talk(H.) person that who is/
ky'e-ra;ng la ka-mö:-n̄a;ng-k'ä;n t̲'e ṣu rä/
Who was that person who talked to you?
(honorific to the subject)

7. ང་རྣམ་ཚོར་བཀའ་མོལ་ཞུ་མཁན་དེ་སུ་ཡིན་པ་ནོ།
you-to(H.) talk(H.) person that who is/
nga-na-ts'ò: ka-mö:-s̲h̲u-k'ä;n t̲'e su yi;n-pa-no/
same as (6) It can be used in plural too.
(honorific to the object)

21.9.2. སུའི། = "whose"

སུའི་ is used in colloquial and
སུ་ཡི་ in literary forms

Examples:

1. ཕྲུ་གུ་འདི་སུའི་རེད།
child this whose is/
pu-k'u di sü: rä/
Whose child is this?

2. ཨ་བ་འདི་སུའི་ཡིན་པ་ནོ།
child(H.) this whose is(H.)/
a-wa: di sü: yi;n-pa-no/
same as (1) but honorific

3. འདི་སུའི་སྣུམ་འཁོར་རེད།
this whose car is/
di sü: n̄um-k'or rä/
Whose car is this?

4. འདི་སུའི་ཕེབས་འཁོར་ཡིན་པ་ནོ།
this whose car(H.) is/
di sü: p'eb-k'òr yi;n-pa-no/
same as (3) but honorific

5. ས་ཆ་འདི་སུའི་ཡིན་ཁོང་གིས་མཁྱེན་གྱི་མི་འདུག
land this whose is he by know(H.) neg. pres. c./
sa-ch'a di sü: yi;n k'o;ng-k'i: ky'en k'i mi;n-du/
He does not know whose land this is.

6. ཡིག་གཟུགས་འདི་སུའི་ཡིན་པ་འདྲ་འདུག
handwriting this whose is think/
yig-su: di sü: yi;n-pa ḍa-du/
Whose writing (do you think) is this?

7. དེབ་འདི་སུའི་རྩ་ནས་ལེན་པ་རེད།
book this whose place-from take past c./
t'eb di sü: tsa:-nä len-pa rä/
From whom was this book taken?

8. ཕྱག་དེབ་འདི་སུའི་རྩ་ནས་བཞེས་པ།
book(H.) this whose place-from take past c./
ch'a:-t'eb di sü: tsa:-nä she:-pa/
same as (7) but honorific

9. ཁོང་སུའི་རྩ་ལ་ཐེག་གི་རེད།
he whose place-to go(H.) fut. c./
k'o;ng sü: tsa:-la t'ä:-k'i rä/
To whose place is he going?

10. ཞྭ་མོ་འདི་སུའི་ཡིན་མིན་མཁྱེན་གྱི་ཡོད་པས།
hat this whose whether-or-not know(H.) pres. c./
sha-mo di sü: yi;n-mä;n ky'e;n-k'i yö-pä/
Do you know whose hat this is?

11. འདི་སུའི་སྐད་ཡིན་སྐད་ངོ་ཆོད་གནང་གི་འདུག་གས།
this whose voice is voice-recognize(H.) pres. c./
di sü: kä: yi;n kä-ngo-ch'ö: ña;ng-k'i du-k'ä/
Do you recognize whose voice this is?

21.9.3. སུས། = "by whom"

སུས་ is used in colloquial and
སུ་ཡིས་ in literary forms

Examples:

1. དེབ་འདི་སུས་བྲིས་པ་རེད།
book this who-by wrote past c./

t̲'eb di süː ṭ'iː-pa rä/
Who wrote this book?

2. ཕྱག་དེབ་འདི་སུས་བྲིས་གནང་པ་རེད།
book(H.) this who-by wrote(H.) past c./
ch'a:-t̲'eb di süː ṭ'iː-ña;ng-pa rä/
same as (1) but honorific

3. ཁོང་སློབ་གྲྭར་སུས་འཁྲིད་པ་རེད།
he school-to who-by take past c./
k'o;ng l̄ab-ṭ'a: süː ṭ'iː-pa rä/
Who took him to school?

4. ལས་ཀ་འདི་འདྲས་སུས་བྱེད་ཐུབ་ཀྱི་རེད།
work this-like who-by do able fut.c./
lä:-ka din-ḍäː süː c̲h̲'eː t'ub-ki rä/
Who will be able to do such work?

5. འདི་སུས་བཀྱག་ཐུབ་ཀྱི་རེད།
this who-by lift able fut. c./
di süː kyaː t'ub-ki rä/
Who will be able to lift it?

6. ཁྱེད་རང་ལ་སུས་གསུང་གི་འདུག
you to who-by tell(H.) pres. c./
ky'e-ra;ng la süː su;ng-k̲'i du/
Who is telling you (that)?

7. ལན་སུས་སྐྱེལ་གྱི་འདུག
message who-by deliver pres. c./
lä;n süː kyä:-k̲'i du/
Who is delivering the message?

8. འདི་སུས་བྱས་པ་ཡིན་ཤེས་ཡོག་མ་རེད།
this who-by did is know neg. pres. c./
di sü:̀ ch'ä:̀-pa-yi;n she:̀ yò-ma-re:̀/
It is not known who did it.

9. འདི་རྟའི་སྒང་ནས་སུས་སྒྲུག་ཐུབ་ནའང་གསོལ་རས་རག་གི་རེད།
this horse-of on-from who-by pick-up able if-even prize get fut. c./
di tä: ga;ng-nä sü:̀ ḍu:̀ t'ub-nä: sö:rä:̀ ra:-ki re:̀/
Whoever picks it up from horse-back will get a prize.

21.9.4. སུས་ཀྱང་། = "by anybody" or "nobody"

སུས་ཀྱང་། is used in colloquial and
སུ་ཡིས་ཀྱང་། in literary forms

སུས་ཀྱང་། expresses the meaning of "by anybody" or "by nobody" according to the positive or negative sentence.

Examples:

1. འདི་སུས་ཀྱང་བྱེད་ཐུབ་ཀྱི་རེད།
this who-by even do able fut. c./
di sü:̀ kya;ng ch'e:̀ t'ub-ki re:̀/
Anybody will be able to do this.

2. འདི་སུས་ཀྱང་བྱེད་ཐུབ་ཀྱི་མ་རེད།
this who-by even do able neg. fut. c./
di sü:̀ kya;ng ch'e:̀ t'ub-ki ma-re:̀/
Nobody will be able to do this.

3. གནས་ཚུལ་འདིའི་སྐོར་ལ་སུས་ཀྱང་ཧ་གོ་གི་ཡོག་མ་རེད།
circumstances this-of about to who-by even know neg. pres. c./
nä:-ts'ü: di: kor-la sü:̀-kya;ng ha-k'o-k'i yò:̀ ma-re:̀/
Nobody knows about this thing.

4. ཁང་པ་འདི་སུས་ཀྱང་བེད་སྤྱོད་གནང་ཆོག་གི་རེད།
house this who-by even use(H.) may fut. c./
k'a;ng-pa di sü` kya;ng p'e-chö:-n̄a;ng ch'ò:-k'i re`/
Anybody can use this house.

5. གནས་ཚུལ་འདི་ཚོའི་ཐོག་ལ་སུས་ཀྱང་དོ་སྣང་བྱེད་ཀྱི་མི་འདུག
circumstance these-of on who-by even notice neg. pres. c./
n̄ä:-ts'ü: di-ts'ö: t'ò`-la sü` kya;ng t'o-n̄a;ng ch'e-ki mi;n-du/
Nobody cares about these things.

6. ལས་ཀ་འདི་འདྲས་སུས་ཀྱང་བྱེད་ཐུབ་ཀྱི་རེད།
work this-like who-by even do able fut. c./
lä:-ka din-ḍä` sü` kya;ng ch'e` t'ub-ki re`/
Anybody will be able to do such work.

7. ལས་ཀ་འདི་འདྲས་སུས་ཀྱང་བྱེད་ཐུབ་ཀྱི་མ་རེད།
work this-like who-by even do able neg. fut. c./
lä:-ka din-ḍä` sü` kya;ng ch'e` t'ub-ki ma-re`/
Nobody will be able to do such work.

8. ལས་ཀ་འདི་འདྲས་སུས་ཀྱང་བྱེད་ཀྱི་མ་རེད།
work this-like who-by even do neg. fut. c./
lä:-ka din-ḍä` sü` kya;ng ch'e-ki ma-re`/
Nobody will do such work.

21.9.5. སུ་གང་། = "nobody"

སུ་གང་།	is used in colloquial with negative only.
སུ་ཡང་།	is used in literary with both negative and positive.

Examples:

1. འདིར་སུ་གང་མི་འདུག
here nobody neg. exist./

dä: su-k'a;ng mi;n-du/
There is nobody here.

2. སྔ་མ་ནས་ཁང་པ་འདིའི་ནང་ལ་སྡོད་མཁན་སུ་གང་ཡོག་མ་རེད།
before since house this-of into dweller nobody neg. exist./
nga-ma-nä k'a;ng-pa di: na;ng-la dö:-k'ä;n su-k'a;ng yòˋ: ma-reˋ:/
Nobody has lived in this house for a long time.

3. ཅ་ལག་སྙིང་རྗེ་པོ་འདི་འདྲས་སུ་གང་ལ་ཡོག་མ་རེད།
things beautiful this-like nobody to neg. exist./
cha-laˋ: n̄ȳi;ng-je-po din-ḍäˋ: su-k'a;ng-la yòˋ: ma-reˋ:/
Nobody has such beautiful things.

4. ས་ཆ་འདི་ང་ཚོ་སུ་གང་ལ་བདག་ཡོག་མ་རེད།
land this we nobody to belong neg. exist./
sa-ch'a di nga;n-ts'o su-k'a;ng-la daˋ: yòˋ: ma-reˋ:/
This land belongs to none of us.

5. མགྲོན་ཁང་འདིའི་ནང་ལ་སུ་ཡང་བསྡད་ཆོག་གི་རེད།
guest-house this-of into anybody stay allow fut. c./
ḍö;n-k'a;ng di: na;ng-la su-ya;ng däˋ: ch'ò:-k'i reˋ:/
Anybody can stay in this guest house.

6. ཁང་པ་འདིའི་ནང་ལ་སུ་ཡང་འགྲོ་ཆོག་གི་མ་རེད།
house this-of into nobody go allow neg. fut. c./
k'a;ng-pa di: na;ng-la su-ya;ng ḍo ch'ò:-k'i ma-reˋ:/
Nobody is allowed to go into this house.

7. དེ་རིང་ངར་ཁོང་ཚོ་སུ་ཡང་མཇལ་མ་བྱུང་།
today I-to they anyone see(H.) neg. past c./
t'e-ri;ng nga: k'o;ng-ts'o su-ya;ng jä: ma-ch'u;ng/
I saw none of them today.

8. ཐུགས་སྟོ་འདིའི་ནང་ལ་སུ་ཡང་ཕེབས་ཆོག་གི་རེད།
party(H.) this-of into anybody come allow fut. c./
t'ò:-ṭo di: na;ng-la su-ya;ng p'e꞉ ch'ò:-k'i re꞉/
Anybody may come to this party.

9. ས་ཁུལ་འདིའི་ནང་ལ་སུ་ཡང་ཡོང་ནུས་ཀྱི་མ་རེད།
area this-of into nobody come dare neg. fut. c./
sa-k'ü: di: na;ng-la su-ya;ng yo;ng nü:-ki ma-re꞉/
Nobody will dare come to this area.

21.9.6. སུར་/ སུ་ལ་ = "to whom" (both are used col. & lit.)

Examples:

1. ཁྱེད་རང་སུར་བཀའ་མོལ་གནང་གི་ཡོད།
you who-to talk(H.) pres. c./
ky'e-ra;ng sò: ka-mö:-ña;ng-k'i yö/
Who are you talking to?

2. ཁོང་གིས་སུར་བཀའ་འདྲི་ཞུས་པ་རེད།
he by who-by ask(H.) past c./
k'o;ng k'i sò: ka;n-ḍi-shü-pa rä/
Who did he ask?

3. སུར་བཀའ་མོལ་ཞུ་དགོས་རེད།
who-to talk(H.) have fut. c./
sò: ka-mö:-shu-go rä/
Who shall (I) speak to?

4. སུ་སུར་*སྐད་ཆ་ཤོད་དགོས་རེད།
who-who-to speak have fut. c./

---

* སུ་སུར་ shows the plural that there are some persons among the many whom one has to speak to.

su-sò: kä-ch'a-shö-go rä/
Who shall (I) speak to?

21.9.7. མཁན་ = "who"

མཁན་	is used in colloquial and
མི་	in literary forms.

མཁན་ or མི་ is generally used with a verb to indicate the meaning of 'er' in English as in writer, singer, dancer etc.

འཚོང་ (to sell) + མཁན་ (er) = འཚོང་མཁན་ = seller

ཤོད་མཁན་	(shö:-k'ä;n)	=	teller
འབྲི་མཁན་	(ḍi-k'ä;n)	=	writer
སྡོད་མཁན་	(dö:-k'ä;n)	=	dweller
ཀློག་མཁན་	(l̄ò:-k'ä;n)	=	reader
ཤེས་མཁན་	(she:-k'ä;n)	=	one who knows
འགྲོ་མཁན་	(ḍo-k'ä;n)	=	one who goes

1. ཁང་པ་འདིའི་ནང་ལ་སྡོད་མཁན་ཡོག་རེད་པས།
house this-of into dweller exist. ?/
k'a;ng-pa di: na;ng-la dö:-k'ä;n yò: re-pä/
Is anyone living in this house?

2. འདིར་སྒྲ་སྙན་བཏང་མཁྱེན་མཁན་སུ་ཡང་ཡོད་པས།
here guitar-sent know who anyone exist.
dä: ḍam-n̄ȳä;n-ta;ng ky'e;n-k'ä;n su-ya;ng yö-pä/
Is there anyone who knows how to play the guitar?

3. ཁྱེད་རང་ལ་བཀའ་མོལ་ཞུ་མཁན་མི་དེ་སུ་རེད།
you to talk who man that who is/

ky'e-ra;ng la ka-mö:-shu-k'ä;n mi t'e su-rä/
Who was that person talking to you?

ཉན་ is also used in place of མཁན་ in spoken language.

4. ཁོང་བོད་ལ་འགྲོ་ཉན་རེད།
he Tibet to go er is/
k'o;ng p'ö: la ḍo-nyä;n re:/
He is going to Tibet.

5. བོད་ལ་འགྲོ་ཉན་ཚོས་ཅ་ལག་མང་པོ་ཉོས་པ་རེད།
Tibet to go-er pl.-by things many bought past c./
p'ö: la ḍo-nyä;n-ts'ö: cha-la: ma;ng-po nyö:-pa re:/
The people going to Tibet bought a lot of things.

21.9.8. Exercise 18

(a) Translate the following into Tibetan.

1. Who are you?
2. Who is he?
3. Who am I?
4. Who is that girl who came with you?
5. Who is that man who talked to you?
6. Who did it?
7. Nobody can do it.
8. Nobody knows about it.
9. Do you know who did that?
10. Who knows?
11. Anybody can use it.
12. Whose pen is this?
13. Whom do you ask?
14. Whom do you want to speak to?
15. Whom shall I speak to?

(b) Translate the following into English

1. སུ་ལ་བཀའ་མོལ་ཞུ་དགོས་རེད།
2. འདི་སུས་གསུངས་པ་རེད།
3. འདི་སུའི་ཆོར་འབྲུལ་རེད།

22. Infinitive Particle "ག" & Related Forms

ག་ is used in colloquial and

པར་/ བར་ in literary forms.

These infinitive particles are used only with verb ཡོང་བ་ (coming) and འགྲོ་བ་ (going).

Examples:

1. ང་ལས་ཀ་བྱེད་ག་འགྲོ་གི་ཡིན།
   I work-do to go fut. c./
   nga lä:-ka-ch'e-k'a ḍo-k'i yi;n/
   I shall go to work.

2. ང་ལས་ཀ་བྱེད་པར་འགྲོ་གི་ཡོད།
   I work-do to go pres. c./
   nga lä:-ka-ch'e:-par ḍo-k'i yö:/
   I am going to work. or I go to work.

The Dative here is also used as a literary infinitive according to the verb. (see Dative rules page 51)

3. ང་ལས་ཀ་བྱེད་དུ་ཕྱིན་པ་ཡིན།
   I work-do to went past c./
   nga lä:-ka-ch'e:-t'u ch'i;n-pa yi;n/
   I went to work.

22.1. Infinitive Particle ཡག་ and རྒྱུ།

ཡག་ is used in colloquial and
རྒྱུ་ in literary forms.

These infinitive particles are used with any other verbs.

1. དེབ་འདི་ཁོང་ལ་སྤྲོད་ཡག་ཡིན།
   book this he to give-inf. is/
   t̲'eb di k'o;ng la ṭö:-ya`: yi;n/
   This book is to be given to him.

2. ཚང་མ་ཤོད་ཡག་མ་རེད།
   all tell-inf. not is/
   ts'a;ng-ma shö:-ya`: ma-re`:/
   Not everything is to be told.

3. སྣུམ་འཁོར་འདི་ཉི་མ་གསུམ་གཡར་ཡག་ཡིན།
   car this day three hire-inf. is/
   n̄um-k'or di nyi-ma sum ȳa:-ya`: yi;n/
   This car is to be hired for three days.

4. ཅ་ལག་དགོས་ཡག་ཚང་མ་ད་ལྟ་ཉོ་ཡག་ཡིན།
   things need-inf. all now buy-inf. is/
   cha-la`: go-ya`: ts'a;ng-ma t̲'a;n-ta nyo-ya`: yi;n/
   All the necessary things are to be purchased now.

In some cases, the infinitive is used as a noun. e.g.

1. ང་ཁ་ལག་བཟོ་ཡག་བསླབ་ཀྱི་ཡིན།
   I **cookery** learn fut. c./
   nga **k'a-la`:-so-ya`:** l̄ab-ki yi;n/
   I will learn cookery.

2. ང་སྣུམ་འཁོར་གཏོང་ཡག་སློབ་ཀྱི་ཡོད།
I **driving** learn pres. c./
nga **n̄um-k'or-ta;ng-ya**ཿ l̄ab-ki yöཿ/
I am learning driving.

3. ང་བོད་སྐད་རྒྱག་ཡག་གཅིག་པུ་སྦྱངས་པ་ཡིན།
I **Tibetan-speaking** only learn past c./
nga **p'ö-käཿ-gya:-ya**ཿ chig-po: ja;ng-pa yi;n/
I learned only spoken Tibetan.

The particle སྟངས་ when used in place of ཡག་ or རྒྱུ་ conveys the meaning of **'how to'** or **'the manner of doing'**

4. ང་བོད་པའི་ཁ་ལག་བཟོ་སྟངས་བསླབ་ཀྱི་ཡིན།
I Tibetan-of food make how-to learn fut. c./
nga p'ö-pä: k'a-laཿ s̲o-ta;ng l̄ab-ki yi;n/
I will learn how to cook Tibetan food.

22.2. Use of Double Infinitive in the Sentence

1. ང་གློག་བརྙན་དཔར་རྒྱག་ཡག་བསླབ་ག་འགྲོ་གི་ཡིན།
I movie shoot-inf. learn-of go fut. c./
nga l̄og-n̄yä;n par-gya:-yaཿ l̄ab-k̲'a ḍo-k̲'i-yi;n/
I am going to learn to make films.

2. ཁོང་ཚོ་ཁ་ཤས་ཆུ་ཚོད་བཟོ་བཅོས་རྒྱག་ཡག་བསླབ་ག་ཕྱིན་པ་རེད།
they few watch repair-inf learn-inf. went past. c./
k'o;ng-ts'o k'a-shä ch'u-ts'öཿ s̲o-chöཿ gya:-yaཿ l̄ab-k̲'a ch'i;n-pa reཿ/
Some of them went to learn how to repair watches.

3. ཁ་ཤས་གློག་འཁྲིད་སྟངས་བསླབ་ག་ཕྱིན་པ་འདྲ།
few electricity-lay how-to learn-inf. went think/
k'a-shä l̄ò: ṭ'ö:-ta;ng l̄ab-k'a ch'i;n-pa ḍa/
I think some of them went to learn how to install electric circuit.

22.3. Mixed Examples of Infinitives

1. སློབ་ཕྲུག་ལ་རོགས་རམ་བྱེད་ཡག་དགེ་རྒན་གྱི་ལས་འགན་རེད།
student to help-inf. teacher of duty is/
l̄ob-ṭ'u: la rò:-ram-ch'e-ya: ge-gä;n-k'i lä;n-gä;n re:/
Helping the students is a teacher's duty.

2. དྲང་པོ་ཤོད་ཡག་དེ་ཡག་པོ་རེད།
truth tell-inf. that good is/
t'a;ng-po-shö:-ya: t'e yag-po re:/
Telling the truth is a good thing.

3. ཁོང་ཕ་གིར་ཐེག་ཡག་ལ་མོས་མཐུན་གནང་གི་འདུག
he there go-inf. to agree(H.) pres. c./
k'o;ng p'a-k'ä: t'ä:-ya: la mö-t'ü;n n̄a;ng-k'i du/
He agrees to go there.

4. ཁོང་མི་མཁས་པ་ཞིག་ཆགས་ཡག་གི་བཟོ་འདུག
he man wise a become-inf. of seems exist./
k'o;ng mi k'ä-pa shig ch'a:-ya: k'i so-du/
He is likely to become a wise man.

5. ལས་ཀ་བྱེད་ཡག་དེ་ལུས་རྩལ་ཡག་པོ་ཞིག་རེད།
work-do-inf. that physical-exercise good a is/
lä-ka-ch'e-ya: t'e lü:-tsä: yag-po chi re:/
Working is a good exercise.

6. ཁོང་རྐང་རྩེད་པོ་ལོ་རྩེད་ཡག་ལ་དགའ་པོ་འདུག
he football play-inf. to love exist./
k'o;ng ka;ng-tse⁝-po-lo tse-ya⁝-la ga-po du/
He likes to play football. or He loves playing football.

7. འདི་ཀློག་ཡག་གི་དུས་ཚོད་རེད།
this read-inf. of time is/
di l̄ò⁝-ya⁝ k'i t'ü:-ts'ö⁝ re⁝/
This is the time to read. or This is reading time.

8. ང་ཐ་མ་ཁ་འཐེན་ཡག་ལ་དགའ་པོ་མེད།
I cigarette smoke-inf. to liking neg. exist./
nga t'a-ma⁝ t'e;n-ya⁝ la ga-po mä⁝/
I do not like to smoke cigarettes.

9. ཁོང་དེབ་དཔར་རྒྱག་སྟངས་སློབ་ཀྱི་ཡོག་རེད།
he book print how-to learn pres. c./
k'o;ng t'eb par-gya:-ta;ng l̄ab-ki yò-re⁝/
He is learning how to print books.

10. ང་ཁྱེད་རང་རྩ་ལ་ད་ཀ་སེ་སྐད་ཆ་ཤོད་ཀ་ཡོང་གི་ཡིན།
I you place-to just talk-inf. come fut. c./
nga ky'e-ra;ng tsa:-la t'a-k'a:-se kä-ch'a-shö-k'a yo;ng-k'i-yi;n/
I will come to your place just to talk (to you).

11. ང་ཁྱེད་རང་རྩ་ལ་སྐད་ཆ་བྱེད་ཀ་ཡོང་གི་ཡིན།
I you place-to talk-inf. come fut. c./
nga ky'e-ra;ng tsa:-la kä-ch'a-ch'e-k'a yo;ng-k'i-yi;n/
I will come to your place to discuss (things with you).

22.4. Exercise 19

(a) Translate the following into Tibetan using the infinitive ག་

1. We are going to read books.
2. I am going to write letters.
3. I am going to talk to him.
4. She is going to fetch water.
5. He came to see me.
6. Are you going to buy vegetables?
7. I am going to cook now.

(b) Fill in the blanks with appropriate particles.

ག་ ཡག་ རྒྱུ་ སྟངས་

1. ང་བོད་པའི་ཁ་ལག་བཟོ་..........་བསླབ་ཀྱི་ཡིན།
2. ང་སྣུམ་འཁོར་གཏོང་..........་བསླབས་ཚར་པ་ཡིན།
3. ཁོང་དེང་སང་གནམ་གྲུ་གཏོང་..........་སྦྱོང་གི་ཡོག་རེད།
4. ངས་འཚེམ་བུ་རྒྱག་..........་ཡག་པོ་ཤེས་ཀྱི་ཡོད།
5. བོད་སྐད་བསླབ་..........་ལས་སླ་པོ་རེད།
6. ཁོང་ཁ་ལག་བཟོ་..........་བསླབ་..........་ཕྱིན་པ་རེད།
7. བོད་པའི་ཞལ་ལག་བཟོ་..........་མཁྱེན་གྱི་ཡོད་པས།
8. ང་ཉིན་ལྟར་བོད་ཡིག་བསླབ་..........་འགྲོ་གི་ཡོད།
9. ཁོང་ཚོ་གཟའ་ཉི་མར་ཉ་ཟིན་..........་ཕྱིན་ཤག

23. Intentional & Unintentional Verbs

In Tibetan the distinction between Intentional and Unintentional Verbs is very important.

23.1. Some Common Verbs

བྱ་བྱེད་ཐ་དད་པ། Intentional		བྱ་བྱེད་ཐ་མི་དད་པ། Unintentional	
ལྟ་བ་	to watch	མཐོང་བ་	to see
ཉན་པ་	to listen	གོ་བ་	to hear
དྲལ་བ་	to tear	རལ་བ་	to get torn
སྐྱོམ་པ་	to shake	འཁྱོམ་པ་	to be shaken
སྲེག་པ་	to burn	འཚིག་པ་	to get burned
གཤག་པ་	to split	གས་པ་	to crack
བཀྲམ་པ་	to spread	གྲམ་པ་	to get scattered
འཛུམས་པ་	to close	ཟུམ་པ་	to be closed
གཏོར་བ་	to scatter	འཐོར་བ་	to get scattered
སྤེལ་བ་	to increase, spread	འཕེལ་བ་	to be increased
སྦང་པ་	to soak	བང་པ་	to get wet, soaked
གཅོད་པ་	to cut off	ཆད་པ་	to be cut off
གཅོག་པ་	to break	ཆག་པ་	to be broken
བསམ་བློ་གཏོང་བ་	to think	བསམ་བློ་འཁོར་བ་	to be thought
ཡར་རྒྱས་གཏོང་བ་	to improve	ཡར་རྒྱས་འགྲོ་བ་	to get improved
གོ་ས་སྤར་བ་	to promote	གོ་ས་འཕར་བ་	to be promoted

23.2. The use of these verbs:

With Unintentional Verbs the **verb-complement of the 3rd person** is used for all persons.

In the past tense, however, the verb-complement བྱུང་ is used for the 1st person.

Examples:

	Intentional Verb	Unintentional Verb
1.	ངས་བལྟ་གི་ཡིན། I will watch (TV).	ངས་ཚང་མ་མཐོང་གི་རེད། I will see everything.
2.	ངས་བལྟ་གི་ཡོད། I am watching (TV).	ངས་ཚང་མ་མཐོང་གི་འདུག I see everything.
3.	ངས་བལྟས་པ་ཡིན། I watched (TV).	ངས་ཚང་མ་མཐོང་བྱུང་། I saw everything.
4.	ཁོང་གིས་བལྟ་གི་རེད། He will watch (TV).	ཁོང་གིས་ཚང་མ་མཐོང་གི་རེད། He will see everything.
5.	ཁོང་གིས་ལྟ་གི་འདུག He is watching (TV).	ཁོང་གིས་ཚང་མ་མཐོང་གི་འདུག He sees everything.
6.	ཁོང་གིས་བལྟས་པ་རེད། He watched (TV).	ཁོང་གིས་ཚང་མ་མཐོང་པ་རེད། He saw everything.

23.3. The Pronoun according to Unintentional Verbs:

23.3.1. With following Unintentional Verbs the **instrumental form of the pronoun** is needed.

ངས་མཐོང་གི་འདུག = I can see

ངས་གོ་གི་འདུག = I am hearing

ངས་བསམ་གྱི་འདུག	=	I am thinking (describing the natural flow of thoughts)
ངས་དྲན་གྱི་འདུག	=	I remember
ངས་ནོར་གྱི་འདུག	=	I am making a mistake
ངས་བོ་གི་འདུག	=	I am spilling (something)
ངས་འཁྱག་གི་འདུག	=	I am able to carry (it)
དེ་ངས་ཆག་སོང་།	=	I broke it.

23.3.2. With following Unintentional Verbs the **simple pronoun** is needed:

ང་དགའ་གི་འདུག	=	I like, love
ང་ན་གི་འདུག	=	I feel/am sick
ང་སེམས་སྐྱོ་གི་འདུག	=	I feel/am sad
ང་ཁ་སྐོམ་གྱི་འདུག	=	I feel/am thirsty
ང་གྲོད་ཁོག་ལྟོག་གི་འདུག	=	I feel/am hungry
ང་གཉིད་ཁུག་གི་འདུག	=	I feel/am sleepy
ང་སེམས་པམ་གྱི་འདུག	=	I feel/am disappointed
ང་དྲག་གི་འདུག	=	I am recovering

23.4. Exercise 20

(a) Fill in the blanks with appropriate verbs and translate the sentences into English.

བཀག་ བགག་ དབྲིལ་ རིལ་ ཉུབ་ བསྐུབས་ གཏོར་ འཁོར་ བཅག་
ཆག་ ཡངས་ བསླངས་ གཤག་ གཞགས་ སྦྲང་ བང་

1. ཁྲིས་ཁོ་སྒོ་འགྲམ་ལ་··········པ་རེད།
2. གངས་བབས་ནས་ལམ་ཁ་··········པ་རེད།
3. ངས་ཁོང་ཐེངས་གཉིས་··········པ་ཡིན།

4. པུ་གུ་འདིས་ངའི་སྨྱུ་གུ་..........ཤག
5. ང་འཁྱག་པ་སྣང་ལ་ཐེངས་གཉིས་..........བྱུང་།
6. རྐུབ་ཀྱག་འདིའི་རྐང་པ་ཡ་གཅིག་..........ཤག
7. ཁོང་ཆོས་སངས་རྒྱས་ཀྱི་བསྟན་པ་..........པ་རེད།
8. ལུགས་སྲོལ་འདི་མགྱོགས་པོ་..........ཀྱི་རེད།
9. མི་འདིས་ང་ཁོང་ཁྲོ་..........བྱུང་།
10. ཁོང་དོན་དག་མེད་པར་ཁོང་ཁྲོ་..........སོང་།
11. ཁོང་གིས་ངར་ཆུ་..........གྱི་འདུག
12. འདིར་བསྡད་ན་ཆུ་..........གྱི་རེད།
13. ཁོང་གིས་ཤིང་..........གི་རེད།
14. ཤིང་འདི་མགྱོགས་པོ་..........ཀྱི་རེད།
15. ཁོང་གིས་དུག་སློག་ཚང་མ་ཆུའི་ནང་ལ་..........ཚར་ཤག
16. ངའི་དུག་སློག་ཆར་པས་ཐད་དེ་..........སོང་།

(b) Write down the following sentences in your exercise book and underline the **Unintentional Verbs**.

1. ངས་གསར་འགྱུར་ཉན་གྱི་ཡོད། = I listen to the news.
2. ངས་གསར་འགྱུར་གོ་གི་འདུག = I hear the news.
3. ངས་འདི་གོ་བྱུང་། = I heard this.
4. པུ་གུ་འདིས་ངའི་དེབ་དྲལ་སོང་། = This child tore my book.
5. ངས་ཤིང་སྡོང་མང་པོ་བཅད་པ་ཡིན། = I cut many trees.
6. ངས་དེའི་སྐོར་ལ་བསམ་བློ་གཏོང་གི་ཡོད། = I am thinking about that.
7. འདིར་མི་མང་པོ་རིལ་གྱི་འདུག = Many people fall here.
8. ང་དེའི་ཐོག་ལ་འགྱོད་པ་ཞེ་དྲག་སྐྱེས་བྱུང་། = I regretted it very much.
9. ང་སྐྱུག་མེར་ལངས་ཀྱི་འདུག = I feel like vomitting/I feel sick.
10. ང་འཁྱག་གི་འདུག = I feel cold.
11. ང་ཚ་དུབ་འཚིག་གི་འདུག = I feel hot.
12. ཁོང་ཐད་དེ་འཐོམས་སོང་། = He got completely confused.
13. དེང་སང་ང་ཞེ་དྲག་ཉོབ་ཀྱི་འདུག = These days I feel very lazy.

14. སྐབས་རེ་ང་མགོ་ཡུར་འཁོར་གྱི་འདུག = Sometimes I feel giddy.

15. མཚོ་འདིའི་ནང་ལ་མི་གཅིག་དིམས་པ་རེད། = A man drowned in this lake.

16. ད་ང་དྲོད་ཡོང་གི་འདུག = I am warming up now.

17. ང་གད་མོ་ཞེ་དྲག་ཤོར་གྱི་འདུག = I feel like laughing very much.

18. ཆུ་འདི་འཁོལ་གྱི་འདུག = This water is boiling.

19. ཁོང་གིས་ངར་ཁོང་ཁྲོ་ཞེ་དྲག་བསླངས་བྱུང་། = He made me very angry.

20. ཁྱེད་རང་གི་བོད་སྐད་ཡར་རྒྱས་འགྲོ་གི་འདུག = Your Tibetan is improving.

24. Use of "བྱུང་" & Related Forms

བྱུང་ is used in the past tense only.

24.1. བྱུང་ as a main verb

24.1.1. བྱུང་ = got

1. ངར་བྱུང་།
   I-to got/
   nga: ch'u;ng/
   I got (it).

2. ཁྱེད་རང་ལ་བྱུང་བ་རེད།
   you to got/
   ky'e-ra;ng la ch'u;ng-pa-re:/
   You got (it). (general statement)

3. ཁོང་ལ་བྱུང་བ་རེད།
   he to got/
   k'o;ng la ch'u;ng-pa-re:/
   He got (it). (general statement)

4. ཁོང་ལ་བྱུང་སོང་།
   he to got/
   k'o;ng la ch'u;ng-so;ng/
   He got (it). (definite statement)

5. ཁོང་ལ་བྱུང་ཤག
   he to got/

k'o;ng la ch'u;ng-shà:/

He got (it). (I heard or I was informed about it)

6. ཁོང་ལ་བྱུང་འདུག

he to got/

k'o;ng la ch'u;ng-dù:/

He got (it). (lit.)

Interrogatives:

7. ཁྱེད་རང་ལ་བྱུང་ངས།

you to got ?/

ky'e-ra;ng la ch'u;ng-ngä/

Did you get (it)?

8. ཁོང་ཚོར་བྱུང་པ་རེད་པས།

they to got ?/

k'o;ng-ts'ò: ch'u;ng-pa re-pä/

Did they get (it)? (general)

9. ཁོང་ཚོར་བྱུང་སོང་ངས། = ཁོང་ཚོར་བྱུང་འདུག་གས།

they got to ?/

k'o;ng-ts'ò: ch'u;ng-so;ng-ngä/

same as (8) but definite

24.1.2. བྱུང་ = happened

1. དེའི་རྗེས་ལ་ག་རེ་བྱུང་བ་རེད།

that-of after what happened/

t'e: jè:-la k'a-re ch'u;ng-pa rä/

What happened after that?

2. དེའི་རྗེས་ལ་ག་རེ་བྱས་པ་རེད།
that-of after what happened/
t'e: jè:-la k'a-re ch'ä̀:-pa rä/
same as (1) *but it is more common in speaking*

3. དེ་ནས་ག་རེ་བྱས་པ་རེད།
and-then what happened/
t'e-nä̀: k'a-re ch'ä-pa rä/
And then what happened?

4. ཡག། ངར་ག་རེ་བྱས་པ་རེད།
Oh! I-to what happened/
yà: nga: k'a-re ch'ä-pa rä/
Oh! What happened to me?

5. ཁྱེད་རང་ལ་ག་རེ་བྱས་བྱུང་། = ཁྱེད་རང་ལ་ག་རེ་གནང་བྱུང་། (H.)
you to what happened/
ky'e-ra;ng la k'a-re ch'ä̀:-ch'u;ng/
What happened to you?

6. ཁོང་ལ་ག་རེ་བྱས་པ་རེད། = ཁོང་ལ་ག་རེ་གནང་པ་རེད། (H.)
he to what happened/
k'o;ng la k'a-re ch'ä̀:-pa rä/
What happened to him?

24.2. བྱུང་། as a past verb-complement

24.2.1. With an Unintentional main verb བྱུང་ is used with the 1st person subject:

1. ངས་ཚང་མ་མཐོང་བྱུང་།
I-by all see past c./

ngä̀: ts'a;ng-ma t'o;ng-ch'u;ng/

I saw everything.

2. ངས་ཁྱེད་རང་འདིར་ཡོག་མ་རེད་བསམ་བྱུང་།

I-by you here not exist. thought past c./

ngä̀: ky'e-ra;ng dä: yò̀:-ma-rè: sèm-ch'u;ng/

I thought you are not here.

3. ངར་ལམ་འགག་ལས་སླ་པོར་རྙེད་བྱུང་།

I-to way easily found past c./

nga: lam-gà: lä̀:-l̄a-pò: n̄yè:-ch'u;ng/

I found the way easily.

4. དེ་རིང་ངར་དངུལ་ཁང་ནས་དངུལ་རག་བྱུང་།

today I-to bank from money got/

ṯ'e-ri;ng nga: n̄gü:-k'a;ng nä ngü: rà: ch'u;ng/

Today I got the money from the bank.

24.2.2. With an Intentional main verb, བྱུང་། is used with the second and third person subject:

1. ཁྱེད་རང་གིས་ངར་ཡག་པོ་གནང་བྱུང་།

you by I-to good do(H.) past c./

ky'e-ra;ng ḵ'i: nga: yag-po n̄a;ng-ch'u/

You were good to me.

2. ཁྱེད་རང་གིས་ང་ཚོར་རོགས་རམ་ཞེ་དྲག་གནང་བྱུང་།

you by we-to help very do(H.) past c./

ky'e-ra;ng ḵ'i: nga:n-ts'ò: rò:-ram she-ṯ'a: n̄a;ng-ch'u/

You helped us so much.

3. ཁོང་གིས་ངར་ལབ་བྱུང་། = ཁོང་གིས་ངར་གསུངས་བྱུང་། (H.)

he by I-to tell past c./

k'o;ng k'ì: nga: lèb-ch'u;ng/
He told me (that).

4. ཁོང་གིས་ངར་སྤྲད་བྱུང་། = ཁོང་གིས་ངར་གནང་བྱུང་། (H.)
he by I-to give past c./
k'o;ng k'ì: nga: ṭä̀: ch'u:ng/
He gave (it) to me.

5. ཁོང་གིས་ངར་ཞེ་དྲག་ཡག་པོ་བསླབས་གནང་བྱུང་།
she by I-to very good teach(H.) past c./
k'o;ng k'ì: nga: she-ṭ'a: yag-po l̄èb n̄a;ng-ch'u;ng/
She taught me very well.

6. ཁོང་གིས་ཚང་མ་ངར་བསྟན་བྱུང་།
she by all I-to show past c./
k'o;ng k'ì: ts'a;ng-ma nga: tä;n-ch'ung/
She showed me everything.

7. ཁོས་ངར་དབང་ཡོད་བཤད་བྱུང་།
he-by I-to bully past c./
k'ö̀: nga: w̄a;ng-yö̀:-shä-ch'u/
He bullied me.

8. ཁོས་ངར་ཐུབ་ཚོད་བཏང་བྱུང་།
he-by I-to bully past c./
k'ö̀: nga: t'ub-ts'ö̀:-ta;ng-ch'u/
same as (7)

9. ཁོས་ངར་འགྲོ་ཚོད་བཏང་བྱུང་།
he-by I-to bully past c./
k'ö̀: nga: ḍob-ts'ö̀:-ta;ng-ch'u/
same as (7)

10. ཁོང་ཚོས་ངར་ཅ་ལག་འཁྱེར་རོགས་བྱས་བྱུང་།
they-by I-to things carry-help did past c./
k'o;ng-ts'ö:̀ nga: cha-la:̀ ky'e:-rò:̀ ch'ä:̀-ch'u;ng/
They helped me to carry (my) things.

Interrogatives:

11. ངས་ཁྱེད་རང་ལ་ཕྱག་སྨྱུག་དེ་ཕུལ་བྱུང་ངས།
I-by you to pen(H.) that give(H.) past c./
ngä:̀ ky'e-ra;ng la ch'a:-nyu:̀ t'e p'ü:-ch'u-ngä/
Did I give to you that pen? (H. to person object)

12. ཁོང་གིས་ཁྱེད་རང་ལ་གནང་བྱུང་ངས།
he by you to give(H.) past ?/
k'o;ng k'i:̀ ky'e-ra;ng la na;g-ch'u;ng-ngä/
Did he give to you (that)? (H. to person subject)

13. ཁྱེད་རང་ལ་དངུལ་ཁང་ནས་དངུལ་རག་བྱུང་ངས།
you to bank from money get past c. ?/
ky'e-ra;ng la ngü:-k'a;ng nä ngü: ra:̀ ch'u;ng-ngä/
Did you get money from the bank?

14. དེའི་སྐོར་ལ་ངས་གང་ཡང་ཞུས་བྱུང་ངས།
that-of about I-by anything tell(H.) past c. ?/
t'e: kor-la ngä:̀ k'a;ng-ya;ng shü:̀ ch'u;ng-ngä/
Did I tell (you) anything about that?

15. དེའི་སྐོར་ལ་ཁོང་གིས་གང་ཡང་གསུངས་བྱུང་ངས།
that-of about he by anything tell(H.) past c. ?/
t'e: kor-la k'o;ng k'i:̀ k'a;ng-ya;ng su;ng ch'u;ng-ngä/
Did he tell (you) anything about that?

24.3. Exercise 21

(a) Translate the following into English

1. ང་ཚོར་ཚང་མ་རག་བྱུང་།
2. ཁྱེད་རང་ལ་བྱུང་ངས།
3. ཁོང་ལ་བྱུང་ཤག
4. དེ་ནས་ག་རེ་བྱས་པ་རེད།
5. ཁོང་ལ་ག་རེ་བྱས་པ་རེད།
6. ཁྱེད་རང་ལ་ག་རེ་བྱས་བྱུང་།
7. ང་ཚོས་ཚང་མ་མཐོང་བྱུང་།
8. གསར་འགྱུར་འདི་ངས་ཁ་ས་གོ་བྱུང་།
9. འདི་ཁོང་ཚོས་ངར་སྤྲད་བྱུང་།
10. འདི་ངར་ཁོང་གིས་བསླབས་བྱུང་།

(b) Translate the following into Tibetan

1. He took me with him.
2. He beat me yesterday.
3. I did not get the money from the bank.
4. Did you get the books?
5. Did you see that man?
6. Did he bully you?
7. Did he scold you?
8. What happened to these men?
9. Did you feel cold last night?
10. No, I did not feel cold at all.

25. གྲངས་ཀ་བརྩི་ཚུལ། = Cardinal Numbers:

༡	གཅིག་	(chig)	=	1
༢	གཉིས་	(nyi:)	=	2
༣	གསུམ་	(sum:)	=	3
༤	བཞི་	(shi)	=	4
༥	ལྔ་	($\overline{\text{ng}}$a)	=	5
༦	དྲུག་	(ṭ' u:)	=	6
༧	བདུན་	(dü;n)	=	7
༨	བརྒྱད་	(gyä:)	=	8
༩	དགུ་	(gu)	=	9
༡༠	བཅུ་/བཅུ་ཐམ་པ་	(chu)/chu-t' am-pa	=	10
༡༡	བཅུ་གཅིག་	(chuk-chi:)	=	11
༡༢	བཅུ་གཉིས་	(chu;ng-$\overline{\text{ny}}$i)	=	12
༡༣	བཅུ་གསུམ་	(chuk-sum)	=	13
༡༤	བཅུ་བཞི་	(chüb-shi)	=	14
༡༥	བཅོ་ལྔ་	(chö:-$\overline{\text{ng}}$a)	=	15
༡༦	བཅུ་དྲུག་	(chu-ṯ' u:)	=	16
༡༧	བཅུ་བདུན་	(chub-dü;n)	=	17
༡༨	བཅོ་བརྒྱད་	(chob-gyä:)	=	18
༡༩	བཅུ་དགུ་	(chu-gu)	=	19
༢༠	ཉི་ཤུ་/ཉི་ཤུ་ཐམ་པ་	(nyi-shu)/(nyi-shu-t' am-pa)	=	20

25.1. Numerical Particles:

These particles are used in tens (20 - 90) respectively.

ཙ་ སོ་ ཞེ་ ང་ རེ་ དོན་ གྱ་ གོ་

ཙ is used in twenties: (21-29)

༢༡	ཉི་ཤུ་ཙ་གཅིག་	(nyi-shu tsag-chi꞉)	=	21
༢༩	ཉི་ཤུ་ཙ་དགུ་	(” ” tsa-gu)	=	29
༣༠	སུམ་ཅུ་/སུམ་ཅུ་ཐམ་པ་	(sum-chu)/(sum-chu t' am-pa)	=	30

སོ་ is used in thirties: (31-39)

༣༡	སུམ་ཅུ་སོ་གཅིག་	(sum-chu sò:-chi꞉)	=	31
༣༩	སུམ་ཅུ་སོ་དགུ་	(” ” sò:-gu)	=	39
༤༠	བཞི་བཅུ་/བཞི་བཅུ་ཐམ་པ་	(shib-chu)/(shib-chu t' am-pa)	=	40

ཞེ་ is used in forties: (41-49)

༤༡	བཞི་བཅུ་ཞེ་གཅིག་	(shib-chu she-chi꞉)	=	41
༤༩	བཞི་བཅུ་ཞེ་དགུ་	(” ” she-gu)	=	49
༥༠	ལྔ་བཅུ་ + ཐམ་པ་	(ngab-chu + t' am-pa)	=	50

ང་ is used in fifties: (51-59)

༥༡	ལྔ་བཅུ་ང་གཅིག་	(ngab-chu nga-chi꞉)	=	51
༥༩	ལྔ་བཅུ་ང་དགུ་	(” ” nga-gu)	=	59
༦༠	དྲུག་ཅུ་/དྲུག་ཅུ་ཐམ་པ་	(ṯug-chu) (ṯug-chu t' am-pa)	=	60

རེ་ is used in sixties: (61-69)

༦༡	དྲུག་ཅུ་རེ་གཅིག་	(ṯug-chu re-chi꞉)	=	61
༦༩	དྲུག་ཅུ་རེ་དགུ་	(” ” re-gu)	=	69
༧༠	བདུན་ཅུ་/བདུན་ཅུ་ཐམ་པ་	(dü;n=chu)/(dü;n-chu t' am-pa)	=	70

དོན་ is used in seventies: (71-79)

༧༡	བདུན་ཅུ་དོན་གཅིག་	(dü;n-chu ṯ' ön-chi꞉)	=	71
༧༩	བདུན་ཅུ་དོན་དགུ་	(” ” ṯ' ön-gu)	=	79
༨༠	བརྒྱད་ཅུ་/བརྒྱད་ཅུ་ཐམ་པ་	(gyä-chu)/(gyä-chu t' am-pa)	=	80

The first word of the number 15 and 18 are written as བཅོ་ with Na-Ro (~) instead of བཅུ།
This is for the sake of pronunciation.

ཀྱ་ is used in eighties: (81-89)

༨༡	བརྒྱད་ཅུ་ཀྱ་གཅིག་	(gyä-chu ky'a-chi:)	=	81
༨༩	བརྒྱད་ཅུ་ཀྱ་དགུ་	(" " ky'a-gu)	=	89
༩༠	དགུ་བཅུ་/དགུ་བཅུ་ཐམ་པ་	(gub-chu)/(gub-chu t'am-pa)	=	90

གོ་ is used in nineties: (91-99)

༩༡	དགུ་བཅུ་གོ་གཅིག་	(gub-chu k'ò-chi:)	=	91
༩༩	དགུ་བཅུ་གོ་དགུ་	(" " k'ò-gu)	=	99
༡༠༠	བརྒྱ་/བརྒྱ་ཐམ་པ་	(gya)/(gya-t'am-pa)	=	90

Counting in hundreds:

༡༠༠	བརྒྱ་	(gya)	=	100
༢༠༠	ཉིས་བརྒྱ་	(nyi-gya)	=	200
༣༠༠	སུམ་བརྒྱ་	(sum-gya)	=	300
༤༠༠	བཞི་བརྒྱ་	(shib-gya)	=	400
༥༠༠	ལྔ་བརྒྱ་	(ngab-gya)	=	500
༦༠༠	དྲུག་བརྒྱ་	(ṭug-gya)	=	600
༧༠༠	བདུན་བརྒྱ་	(dü;n-gya)	=	700
༨༠༠	བརྒྱད་བརྒྱ་	(gyä-gya)	=	800
༩༠༠	དགུ་བརྒྱ་	(gub-gya)	=	900
༡༠༠༠	ཆིག་སྟོང་	(ch'ig-to;ng)	=	1,000

25.2. Two ways of counting in thousands:

Traditional way			General system	
༡༠༠༠	ཆིག་སྟོང་	=	སྟོང་ཕྲག་གཅིག་	(to;ng-ṭ'a: chig)
༢༠༠༠	ཉིས་སྟོང་	=	སྟོང་ཕྲག་གཉིས་	(to;ng-ṭ'a: nyi:)
༣༠༠༠	སུམ་སྟོང་	=	སྟོང་ཕྲག་གསུམ་	(to;ng-ṭ'a: sum)
༩༠༠༠	དགུ་སྟོང་	=	སྟོང་ཕྲག་དགུ་	(to;ng-ṭ'a: gu)
༡༠༠༠༠	ཆིག་ཁྲི་	=	སྟོང་ཕྲག་བཅུ་	(to;ng-ṭ'a: chu)

10 - 100 thousands:

༡༠༠༠༠	ཆིག་ཁྲི་	=	ཁྲི་གཅིག་	(ṭ'i-chig)
༢༠༠༠༠	ཉིས་ཁྲི་	=	ཁྲི་གཉིས་	(ṭ'i-$\overline{\text{ny}}$i:)
༣༠༠༠༠	སུམ་ཁྲི་	=	ཁྲི་གསུམ་	(ṭ'i-sum)
༩༠༠༠༠	དགུ་ཁྲི་	=	ཁྲི་དགུ་	(ṭ'i-gu)
༡༠༠༠༠༠	ཆིག་འབུམ་	=	ཁྲི་བཅུ་	(ṭ'i-chu)

100,000 - 1,000,000 million:

༡༠༠༠༠༠	ཆིག་འབུམ་	=	འབུམ་གཅིག་	(bum-chig)
༢༠༠༠༠༠	ཉིས་འབུམ་	=	འབུམ་གཉིས་	(bum-$\overline{\text{ny}}$i:)
༣༠༠༠༠༠	གསུམ་འབུམ་	=	འབུམ་གསུམ་	(bum-sum)
༤༠༠༠༠༠	བཞི་འབུམ་	=	འབུམ་བཞི་	(bum-shi)
༥༠༠༠༠༠	ལྔ་འབུམ་	=	འབུམ་ལྔ་	(bum-$\overline{\text{ng}}$a)
༦༠༠༠༠༠	དྲུག་འབུམ་	=	འབུམ་དྲུག་	(bum-ṯ'u:)
༧༠༠༠༠༠	བདུན་འབུམ་	=	འབུམ་བདུན་	(bum-dü;n)
༨༠༠༠༠༠	བརྒྱད་འབུམ་	=	འབུམ་བརྒྱད་	(bum-gyä:)
༩༠༠༠༠༠	དགུ་འབུམ་	=	འབུམ་དགུ་	(bum-gu)
༡༠༠༠,༠༠༠	ས་ཡ་གཅིག་	=	འབུམ་བཅུ་	(bum-chu)

1 - 10 millions:

༡༠༠༠༠༠༠	ས་ཡ་གཅིག་	(sa-ya-chig)	= 1 million
༢༠༠༠༠༠༠	ས་ཡ་གཉིས་	(sa-ya-$\overline{\text{ny}}$i:)	= 2 million
༣༠༠༠༠༠༠	ས་ཡ་གསུམ་	(sa-ya-sum)	= 3 million
༩༠༠༠༠༠༠	ས་ཡ་དགུ་	(sa-ya-gu)	= 9 million
༡༠༠༠༠༠༠༠	ས་ཡ་བཅུ་	(sa-ya-chu)	= 10 million

10 - 100 millions:

༡༠༠༠༠༠༠༠	བྱེ་བ་གཅིག་	(ch'e-wa:-chig)	= 10 million
༢༠༠༠༠༠༠༠	བྱེ་བ་གཉིས་	(ch'e-wa:-$\overline{\text{ny}}$i:)	= 20 million
༣༠༠༠༠༠༠༠	བྱེ་བ་གསུམ་	(ch'e-wa:-sum)	= 30 million
༤༠༠༠༠༠༠༠	བྱེ་བ་བཞི་	(ch'e-wa:-shi)	= 40 million

༥༠༠༠༠༠༠༠	བྱེ་བ་ལྔ་	(ch'e-wa:-nga)	= 50 million
༦༠༠༠༠༠༠༠	བྱེ་བ་དྲུག་	(ch'e-wa:-ṯ'u:)	= 60 million
༩༠༠༠༠༠༠༠	བྱེ་བ་དགུ་	(ch'e-wa:-gu)	= 90 million
༡༠༠༠༠༠༠༠༠	བྱེ་བ་བཅུ་	(ch'e-wa:-chu)	= 100 million

100 - 1,000 millions:

༡༠༠༠༠༠༠༠༠	དུང་ཕྱུར་གཅིག་	(ṯ'ung-ch'ur-chig)	= 100 million
༢༠༠༠༠༠༠༠༠	དུང་ཕྱུར་གཉིས་	(ṯ'ung-ch'ur-nyi:)	= 200 million
༣༠༠༠༠༠༠༠༠	དུང་ཕྱུར་གསུམ་	(ṯ'ung-ch'ur-sum)	= 300 million
༩༠༠༠༠༠༠༠༠	དུང་ཕྱུར་དགུ་	(ṯ'ung-ch'ur-gu)	= 900 million
༡༠༠༠༠༠༠༠༠༠	དུང་ཕྱུར་བཅུ་	(ṯ'ung-ch'ur-chu)	= 1,000 million

25.3. Counting of hundred upwards:

Counting after བརྒྱ་ (hundred), དང་ (and) should be added:

101 =	༡༠༡	བརྒྱ་དང་གཅིག་	(gya-ṯ'a;ng-chig)
150 =	༡༥༠	བརྒྱ་དང་ལྔ་བཅུ་	(gya-ṯ'a;ng-ngab-chu)
201 =	༢༠༡	ཉིས་བརྒྱ་གཅིག་	(nyi-gya-chig)

Counting of thousand upwards:

1,550 = ༡༥༥༠ ཆིག་སྟོང་ལྔ་བརྒྱ་ལྔ་བཅུ་
(ch'ig-to;ng ngab-gya nga-chu)

2,775 = ༢༧༧༥ ཉིས་སྟོང་བདུན་བརྒྱ་བདུན་ཅུ་དོན་ལྔ་
(nyi-to;ng dün-gya dün-chu ṯ'ön-nga)

Counting of ten thousand upwards:

15,307 = ༡༥༣༠༧ ཆིག་ཁྲི་ལྔ་སྟོང་སུམ་བརྒྱ་བདུན་
(ch'ig-ṭ'i nga-to;ng sum-gya-dü;n)

95,575 = ༩༥༥༧༥ དགུ་ཁྲི་ལྔ་སྟོང་ལྔ་བརྒྱ་བདུན་ཅུ་དོན་ལྔ་
(gu-ṭ'i nga-to;ng ngab-gya dü;n-chu ṯ'ö;n-nga)

Counting of hundred thousand upwards:

123,456 = ༡༢༣༤༥༦ ཆིག་འབུམ་ཉིས་ཁྲི་སུམ་སྟོང་བཞི་བརྒྱ་ལྔ་བཅུ་ང་དྲུག

(ch'ig-bum nyi-ṭ'i sum-to;ng shib-gya ngab-chu nga-ṭ'u:)

999,999 = ༩༩༩༩༩༩ དགུ་འབུམ་དགུ་ཁྲི་དགུ་སྟོང་དགུ་བརྒྱ་དགུ་བཅུ་གོ་དགུ་

(gu-bum gu-ṭ'i gu-to;ng gub-gya gub-chu k'o-gu)

(Note: Unlike in Western system, no commas are used in the Tibetan numerals.)

25.4. Position of the different counting units:

༡	གཅིག	=	Unit
༡༠	བཅུ་	=	Ten
༡༠༠	བརྒྱ་	=	Hundred
༡༠༠༠	སྟོང་	=	Thousand
༡༠༠༠༠	ཁྲི་	=	Ten thousand
༡༠༠༠༠༠	འབུམ་	=	One hundred thousand
༡༠༠༠༠༠༠	ས་ཡ་	=	One million
༡༠༠༠༠༠༠༠	བྱེ་བ་	=	Ten million
༡༠༠༠༠༠༠༠༠	དུང་ཕྱུར་	=	Hundred million

It is important to memorise these digits according to their numerical values.

According to the example given below, the digital value of **159,853** will be one hundred fifty nine thousand eight hundred fifty three.

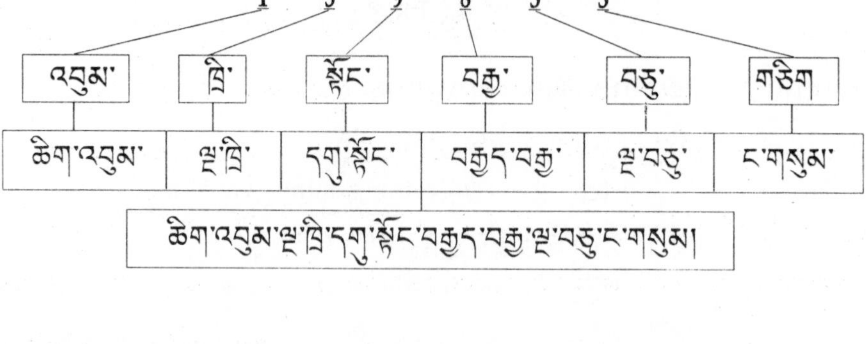

25.5. བརྒྱ་ཆ། = Percentage:

བརྒྱ་ (hundred) + ཆ་ (part) + ལྔ་ (five) = 5 %

བརྒྱ་ཆ་	༢༥	=	25 %	(gya-ch'a nyi-shu tsa-n̄g a)
བརྒྱ་ཆ་	༥༠	=	50 %	(gya-ch'a n̄g ab-chu t'am-pa)
བརྒྱ་ཆ་	༧༥	=	75 %	(gya-ch'a dün-chu ṯ'ön-nga)
བརྒྱ་ཆ་	༡༠༠	=	100 %	(gya-ch'a gya-t'am-pa)

25.6. བཞི་ཆ། = Quarter:

བཞི་ (four) + ཆ་ (part) + གསུམ་ (three) = 3 quarters

བཞི་ཆ་གཅིག་	=	one quarter/fourth	(shi-ch'a chig)
བཞི་ཆ་གཉིས་	=	two quarters	(shi-ch'a n̄y i:)
གསུམ་ཆ་གཉིས་	=	two third	(sum-ch'a n̄y i)
ལྔ་ཆ་གཅིག་	=	one fifth	(nga-ch'a chig)

1. གཞུང་གི་ཚོང་ཁང་ནས་ཅ་ལག་ཉོས་ན་བརྒྱ་ཆ་ ༥ རེ་བཅོག་ཆ་གནང་བ་རེད།
govt. of store from things bought if % 5 each discount give(H.) pres. c./
shu;ng k'i ts'o;ng-k'a;ng nä cha-la: nyö:-na gya-ch'a n̄g a-re chog-ch'a n̄a;ng-wa re:/
If (you) buy things from the government store, (they) give 5% discount.

2. སློབ་ཕྲུག་ཚོར་མེ་འཁོར་གླ་ཆ་བརྒྱ་ཆ་ལྔ་བཅུ་ཆ་ཡང་ཡོག་རེད།
students-to train fare percent 50 concession exist./
l̄ob-ṭ'u:-ts'ò: me-k'or l̄a-ch'a gya-ch'a n̄g a-chu ch'a-ya;ng yò re:/
Students have 50 % concession on train fare.

3. དངུལ་ཁང་ནས་ཉུང་ཤོས་བསྐྱེད་བརྒྱ་ཆ་ལྔ་རེ་སྤྲད་ཀྱི་རེད།
bank from minimum interest percent 5 each give fut. c./
ngü:-k'a;ng nä nyu;ng-shö:̀ kye:̀ gya-ch'a $\overline{ng}$a re ṭä:-ki re:̀/
The bank will give a minimum of 5 % interest.

4. རྒྱན་འདི་ངར་ཐོབ་ཡག་ལ་ཡིད་འཆེས་བརྒྱ་ཆ་བརྒྱ་ཐམ་པ་ཡོད།
bet this I-to win inf. to confidence percent 100 exist./
gyä;n di nga: t'ob-ya-la yi:-ch'e:̀ gya-ch'a gya-t'am-pa yö:̀/
I am hundred percent confident of winning this bet.

5. ས་ཆ་འདིའི་གསུམ་ཆ་གཅིག་ཁོང་ཚོར་བདག་གི་ཡོག་རེད།
land this-of 3 part one they-to belong pres. c./
sa-ch'a di: sum-ch'a chig k'o;ng-ts'ò: da:-ḵ'i yò re:̀/
One third of this land belongs to them.

(Note: ཟུར་ or བཅའ་ is also used in place of ཆ་ without losing the meaning.)

25.7. Exercise 22

(a) Memorise the following numbers (1-20)

༡ ༢ ༣ ༤ ༥ ༦ ༧ ༨ ༩ ༡༠
༡༡ ༡༢ ༡༣ ༡༤ ༡༥ ༡༦ ༡༧ ༡༨ ༡༩ ༢༠

(b) Memorise the following numbers

གཅིག་ བཅུ་ བརྒྱ་ སྟོང་ ཁྲི་ འབུམ་ ས་ཡ་ བྱེ་བ་ དུང་ཕྱུར་

(c) Write the following figures in words

༡༢ ༡༠ ༡༥ ༡༣ ༣༥ ༤༧ ༥༥ ༦༤
༧༧ ༨༥ ༩༩ ༡༠༠ ༡༠༥ ༣༠༥ ༡༠༠༠

(c) Write the following in Tibetan

1. two hundred and fifty six
2. five thousand one hundred and fifty nine
3. fourteen thousand three hundred and thirty four
4. one hundred and fifty six thousand, five hundred and fifty six
5. fifteen thousand five hundred and six
6. two thousand five hundred and eighteen

Answers to the Exercises

Exercise 1 page 25

ra	ka-ta:	ka	=	རྐ་
sa	nga-ta:	n̄ḡa	=	སྔ་
ra	nga-ta:	n̄ḡa	=	རྔ་
sa	na-ta:	n̄a	=	སྣ་
sa	tsa-ta:	tsa	=	སྩ་
ra	t̲s̲'a-ta:	za	=	རྫ་
la	t̲'a-ta:	da	=	ལྡ་
sa	nya-ta:	n̄ȳa	=	སྙ་
ka	ya-ta:	kya	=	ཀྱ་
k̲'a	ya-ta:	k̲y̲'a	=	ཁྱ་
sa	pa-ta:	pa ya-ta: cha	=	སྤྱ་
p'a	ya-ta:	ch'a	=	ཕྱ་
ma	ya-ta:	nya	=	མྱ་
k'a	ra-ta:	ṭ'a	=	ཁྲ་
p̲'a	ra-ta:	ṭ̲'a	=	ཕྲ་
sa	ra-ta:	sa	=	སྲ་
sa	ta-ta:	ta	=	སྟ་
la	cha-ta:	cha	=	ལྕ་
ra	na-ta:	n̄a	=	རྣ་
ka	la-ta:	l̄a	=	ཀླ་
s̲a	la-ta:	da	=	ཟླ་

ka	ya-ta:	kya	s̲h̲ab-kyu	kyu	=	ཀྱུ་
k'a	ya-ta:	ky'a	s̲h̲ab-kyu	ky'u	=	ཁྱུ་
p'a	ya-ta:	ch'a	s̲h̲ab-kyu	ch'u	=	ཕྱུ་
p̲'a	ra-ta:	ṭ'a	na-ro	ṭ'o	=	བྲོ་
k̲'a	ra-ta:	ṭ'a	s̲h̲ab-kyu	ṭ'u	=	གྲུ་
k'a	ra-ta:	ṭ'a	s̲h̲ab-kyu	ṭ'u	=	ཁྲུ་
k̲'a	s̲h̲ab-kyu	k̲'u			=	གུ་
ra	la-ta:	l̄a			=	རླ་
p̲'a	la-ta:	l̄a			=	བླ་
ra	ta-ta:	ta			=	རྟ་
la	ka-ta:	ka	s̲h̲ab-kyu	ku	=	ལྐུ་
la	nga-ta:	n̄ga			=	ལྔ་
la	t̲'a-ta:	da			=	ལྡ་
sa	ka-ta:	ka	deng-po	ke	=	སྐེ་
sa	na-ta:	n̄a	deng-po	n̄e	=	སྣེ་
ma	na-ro	mo			=	མོ་
ra	tsa-ta:	tsa	k̲'i-k̲'u	tsi	=	རྩི་
la	ha-ta:	lha	s̲h̲ab-kyu	l̄hu	=	ལྷུ་
sa	ka-ta:	ka	s̲h̲ab-kyu	ku	=	སྐུ་
ka	la-ta:	l̄a	s̲h̲ab-kyu	l̄u	=	ཀླུ་
ra	na-ta:	n̄a	na-ro	n̄o	=	རྣོ་
sa	pa-ta:	pa	s̲h̲ab-kyu	pu	=	སྤུ་
ma	ya-ta:	nya	s̲h̲ab-kyu	nyu	=	མྱུ་
ra	ma-ta:	m̄a	na-ro	m̄o	=	རྨོ་
la	c̲h̲'a-ta:	ja			=	ལྗ་
sa	ta-ta:	ta			=	སྟ་
ha	ra-ta:	hra	k̲'i-k̲'u	hri	=	ཧྲི་
la	ha-ta:	lha	na-ro	lho	=	ལྷོ་

ra	ka-ta:	ka	shab-kyu	ku	=	རྐུ་
sha	shab-kyu	shu			=	ཤུ་
sa	p'a-ta: ba	ra-ta: ḍa	shab-kyu	du	=	སྦྲུ་
sa	ka-ta: ka	ya-ta: kya	ḍeng-po	kye	=	སྐྱེ་
ra	k'a-ta:	ga	shab-kyu	gu	=	རྒུ་
sa	pa-ta: pa	ya-ta: cha	k'i-k'u	chi	=	སྤྱི་
p'a	ya-ta:	ch'a			=	བྱ་
sa	k'a-ta:	ga	ra-ta:	ḍa	=	སྒྲ་
sa	nya-ta:	n̄ya			=	སྙ་
ra	ka-ta:	ka	ya-ta:	kya	=	རྐྱ་
ra	k'a-ta:	ga			=	རྒ་
ha	ra-ta:	hra	shab-kyu	hru	=	ཧྲུ་
la	ta-ta:	ta			=	ལྟ་
la	pa-ta:	pa			=	ལྤ་
pa	ra-ta:	ṭa	ḍeng-po	ṭe	=	པྲེ་
sa	ma-ta: m̄a	ra-ta: m̄a	k'i-k'u	m̄i	=	སྨྲི་
sa	k'a-ta: ga	ra-ta: ḍa	ḍeng-po	ḍe	=	སྒྲེ་
k'a	ra-ta:	ṭ'a	k'i-k'u	ṭ'i	=	ཁྲི་
sa	na-ta:	n̄a	na-ro	n̄o	=	སྣོ་
sa	la-ta:	da	shab-kyu	du	=	ཟླུ་
p'a	ra-ta:	ṭ'a	na-ro	ṭ'o	=	ཕྲོ་

Exercise 2

page 29

k'ao	sha	ma	sham	= གཤམ་
k'ao	sa	la	säl	= གསལ་
t'ao	ka	ra	kar	= དཀར་
t'ao	w̄a	nga	w̄ang	= དབང་

p'ao	cha	k'a	chag		= བཅག་
p'ao	da	k'a	dag		= བདག་
mao	nga	ra	ngar		= མངར་
mao	t'a	ra	t'ar		= མཐར་

hao	da	k'i-k'u	di ra	dir	= འདིར་
hao	t'a	shab-kyu	t'u nga	t'u;ng	= འཐུང་
ra	k'i-k'u	ri	k'a sa	rig	= རིགས་
k'a	nga	sa	k'a;ng		= གངས་

p'a	na	p'ä;n			= ཕན་
k'a	p'a	k'ab			= ཁབ་
sa	k'a-ta:	ga ma	gam		= སྒམ་
k'ao	sa	ha	sa		= གཟའ་

nya	la	nyä;l			= ཉལ་
nga	sa	ngä:			= ངས་
la	cha-ta:	cha k'a sa cha:			= ལྕགས་
ch'a	k'a	sa	ch'a:		= ཆགས་

p'a	p'a	sa	p'èb		= བབས་
k'a	na-ro	k'o ma sa		k'om	= གོམས་
sa	ta-ta:	ta nga sa		ta;ng	= སྟངས་
p'a	ya-ta:	ch'a k'i-k'u ch'i na		ch'in	= ཕྱིན་

ra	ḍeng-po	re	t'a	re:	= རེད་
hao	da	shab-kyu	du k'a	dug	= འདུག་
ya	k'i-k'u	yi	na	yi;n	= ཡིན་
ya	na-ro	yö	t'a	yö:	= ཡོད་

na	sa	nä:			= ནས་
sa	k'a-ta:	ga	ra-ta:	ḍa	= སྒྲ་

sa	ma-ta꞉	m̄a	ra-ta꞉	m̄a	= སྨྲ་
ra	ta-ta꞉	ta			= ཏྲ་
sa	ka-ta꞉	ka	t̲'a	kä꞉	= སྐད་
ya	k̲'i-k̲'u	yi	k̲'a	yig	= ཡིག་
sha	ḍeng-po	she	sa	she꞉	= ཤེས་
sa	la-ta꞉	l̄a			= སླ་

Exercise 3 page 31

གང་ ལ་ ཡོན་ ཏན་ མཆོག་ མངའ་ བའི།།
དཀོན་ མཆོག་ དེ་ ལ་ ཕྱག་ འཚལ་ ལོ།།
གང་ གིས་ སྨྲ་ དབྱངས་ གསུངས་ པ་ ཡི།།
འཇམ་ པའི་ དབྱངས་ ལ་ ཕྱག་ འཚལ་ ལོ།།

Exercise 4 page 34

ང་ཚོ་ ཁྱེད་རང་ཚོ་ ཁོང་ཚོ་ ཡ་ཚོ་ མ་ཚོ་ འདི་ཚོ་
སློབ་ཕྲུག་ཚོ་ ཕ་ཚོ་ ཕྲན་ཚོ་ གུས་ཚོ་ ཁོ་པ་ཚོ་
ཁོ་བོ་ཚོ་ དེ་ཚོ་ ཁོ་མོ་ཚོ་ གུས་ཕྲན་ཚོ་

Exercise 5 page 40

(a)
1. དེ་སྨྱུ་གུ་རེད།
2. ཕ་ཚོ་མེ་ཏོག་རེད།
3. ང་གྲྭ་པ་ཡིན།
4. ཁྱེད་རང་ཚོ་སློབ་ཕྲུག་རེད།
5. ང་ཚོ་སློབ་ཕྲུག་ཡིན།
6. ཁོང་མི་སེམས་བཟང་པོ་ཞིག་རེད།
7. ཁྱེད་རང་སྤྱང་པོ་རེད།
8. ང་ཚོ་དགེ་རྒན་ཡིན།
9. ཁོང་ཨེམ་ཆི་རེད།
10. འདི་ཚོ་ངའི་དེབ་ཡིན།
11. དེ་ཚོ་གཙང་མ་རེད།
12. ཕ་གི་བླ་མ་རེད།
13. ཡ་གི་མི་རེད།
14. འདི་ཚོ་ཇུབ་ཀྱུག་རེད།

(b) 1. This seems to be our teacher's pen.

2. That appears to be a lama.

3. Those three may be relatives.

4. Those girls seems to belong to a big family.

(c) 1. འདི་ངའི་ལག་པ་རེད་/ཡིན།

2. འདི་ཚོ་ཁོང་ཚོའི་ཨ་བ་རེད།

3. ཕ་གི་ཁོང་གི་དབུ་ཞྭ་རེད།

4. འདི་ཁོང་གི་ཕྱག་ཕད་རེད།

Exercise 6 page 47

1. ང་སློབ་ཕྲུག་མིན།
2. ཁོང་ཡང་སློབ་ཕྲུག་མ་རེད།
3. ཁོང་ཚོ་ཚང་མ་དགེ་རྒན་མ་རེད།
4. འདི་ཚོ་ཁོང་གི་པུ་གུ་མ་རེད།
5. ཕ་གི་ང་ཚོའི་ཁང་པ་མ་རེད།
6. ཡ་གི་གནམ་གྲུ་མིན་པ་འདྲ།
7. འདི་གསར་པ་ཡིན་གྱི་མ་རེད།
8. འདི་ཁྱེད་རང་གི་མིན་པས།
9. ལགས་མིན། འདི་ངའི་མིན།
10. ཕ་ཚོ་ཁོང་གི་མ་རེད་པས།
11. ལགས་མ་རེད། ཕ་ཚོ་ཁོང་གི་མ་རེད།
12. མ་གི་རྟ་མིན་པ་འདྲ།
13. ལགས་མ་གི་དྲེལ་མ་རེད།
14. ཤིང་ཏོག་འདི་ཚོ་མངར་མོ་མ་རེད།
15. འདི་ཡང་མངར་མོ་མ་རེད།
16. འདི་མངར་མོ་མངར་ཀྱང་མ་རེད།
17. ཕ་ཚོ་སྐྱུར་མོ་མ་རེད།
18. ཕ་ཚོ་སྐྱུར་མོ་སྐྱུར་ཀྱང་མ་རེད།

19. སྤྲིན་དམར་པོ་དམར་ཀྱང་མ་རེད།
20. ལས་ཀ་འདི་ལས་སླ་པོ་ཞེ་དྲག་མ་རེད།

Exercise 7 page 62

(a) ང་སློབ་གྲྭར་ཡོད།
ཁོང་ཚོ་ཕ་གིར་འདུག
བོད་ལ་རི་མཐོ་པོ་མང་པོ་ཡོག་རེད།
ཁྱེད་རང་ཚོ་གསོལ་སྟོན་ལ་འདུག
ཁོང་ཚོ་བོད་ལ་འདུག/ ཡོག་རེད།
བོད་ལ་གཡག་མང་པོ་འདུག/ ཡོག་རེད།
དེ་རིང་ཁྲོམ་ལ་མི་མང་པོ་འདུག
ང་ཚོར་དངུལ་མང་པོ་ཡོད།
འདི་སྙིང་རྗེ་པོ་འདུག/ ཡོག་རེད།
ང་ཚོ་འདིར་ཡོད།
འདི་ཡག་པོ་འདུག/ ཡོག་རེད།
རི་འདི་མཐོ་པོ་འདུག/ ཡོག་རེད།
ཁོང་ཡ་གིར་འདུག/ ཡོག་རེད།
རྒྱ་གར་ལ་ཚ་བ་འདུག/ ཡོག་རེད།
རི་ལ་སེམས་ཅན་ཡོག་རེད།
ཁོང་ལ་བུ་གཉིས་འདུག/ ཡོག་རེད།

(b) ང་ནང་ལ་མི་འདུག་གས།
ཁྱེད་རང་ཕ་གིར་མེད་པས།
ཁོང་ཕྱི་རྒྱལ་ལ་མི་འདུག་གས།
ཁོང་བོད་ལ་ཡོག་མ་རེད་པས།
ངར་ཁྲི་གཉིས་མི་འདུག་གས།
ཁྱེད་རང་ལ་དེབ་ལྗང་ཁུ་མེད་པས།
ཁོང་ལ་ལས་ཀ་མི་འདུག་གས།
ཁོང་ཚོར་ཕྱུག་ལས་མི་འདུག་གས།

(c)
1. ཁོང་ལ་དུག་སློག་འདུག་གས།/ ཡོག་རེད་པས།
2. ཁོང་ཁྲོམ་ལ་འདུག་གས།/ ཡོག་རེད་པས།
3. ཁོང་ཁོང་གི་སྐུ་མཆེད་རེད་པས།
4. ཁོང་ཚོར་ཨ་པ་ཡོག་རེད་པས།
5. ཁོང་ཡ་གིར་འདུག་གས།

Exercise 8 page 67

(a)
1. ང་རྒྱ་གར་ལ་བསྡད་པ་ཡིན།
2. ཁོང་བླ་མ་མཇལ་ལ་ག་འགྲོ་བ་རེད།
3. རས་ལ་བྲིས་དགོས་རེད།
4. འདི་ཁ་ལ་ཆུགས།
5. འདིར་བཞུགས།

6. གནས་བསྐོར་ལ་འགྲོ།
7. ཉན་ག་འགྲོ།
8. སྐད་ཆ་ཤོད་ག་འགྲོ།
9. རྟ་བཞོན་ག་འགྲོ།
10. ཆུ་འཐུང་ག་འགྲོ།

(b) 1. ལག་པ་རུ་ལེན།/ ལག་ཏུ་ལེན།
2. ཕྱག་ཏུ་བཞེས།
3. དཔེ་མཛོད་ཁང་དུ་ཕྱིན།
4. བོད་དུ་ཕྱིན།

Exercise 9 page 76

(a) 1. ཁོང་གི་ཕྲུག
2. ང་ཚོའི་ནང་
3. གཡག་གི་ཤ་
4. གནམ་གྱི་སྐར་མ་
5. དཔར་གྱི་སྒྲིང་ཤོག་
6. དཔར་ཆས་ཀྱི་གོང་ཚད་
7. བོད་ཀྱི་ས་ཆ་
8. མིག་གི་གཟི་མ་
9. ནམ་མཁའི་སྤྲིན་པ་
10. རྒྱལ་ཁབ་ཀྱི་མི་མང་
11. བལ་གྱི་སྟོད་བྱུང་
12. ཆོས་ཀྱི་དོན་དག་

(b) ངའི་ཞྭ་མོ་ ཁོང་གི་ཁང་པ་ ཁོང་ཚོའི་དེབ་ ང་ཚོའི་བུ་
ཁོང་གི་ཨ་བ་ཚོ་ དཔར་གྱི་ཚད་ བལ་གྱི་ཨུ་སུ་
ཁྱེད་རང་གི་ཕྲུག་ ཁྱེད་རང་གི་ཕྲུག་སྒུག་

(c) 1. ཆུའི་སྣ་ཆེན་པོ་གོ་གི་ཡོག་རེད།
2. ཤིང་གི་ཡལ་ག་མང་པོ་སྐྱེས་ཤག
3. ངའི་ལུང་པ་སྐྱིད་པོ་ཡོད།
4. གཞས་ཀྱི་ཚིག་འདི་སྙན་པོ་འདུག
5. ཁྱེད་རང་གི་བུ་འདིར་འདུག
6. སྟག་གི་མཆེ་བ་རྣོ་པོ་ཡོག་རེད།
7. སྒམ་གྱི་ལྡེ་མིག་ངར་ཡོད།

8. བོད་པའི་ཞལ་ལག་སྦྲི་པོ་འདུག་གས།
9. ལུང་པའི་ཁྲིམས་ལ་བརྩི་སྲུང་བྱེད་དགོས་རེད།
10. མིའི་རང་བཞིན་ནི་བརྗོད་དཀའ་བ་ཞིག་རེད།
11. རྒྱ་མཚོའི་ཐ་རླབས་གནམ་ལ་མཆོང་བཞིན་འདུག
12. ཞལ་ལག་གི་བྲོ་བ་གཟིགས་རོགས་གནང་།
13. ང་ཚོའི་སྐད་དེ་སྙན་པོ་འདུག་གས།
14. ཆོས་ཀྱི་དོན་དག་ནི་ཟབ་ཅིང་རྒྱ་ཆེ་བ་ཞིག་རེད།
15. ཁོང་གི་ཕྱག་ལ་ཕྲེང་བ་ཞིག་བསྣམས་ཤག

Exercise 10 page 86

(a) 1. ང་ཚོ་ཁྲོམ་ལ་འགྲོ་གི་ཡིན།
2. ཁོང་སློབ་གྲྭར་ཕྱིན་པ་རེད།
3. ང་ཚོ་ལས་ཁུངས་ལ་ཕྱིན་པ་ཡིན།
4. ཁྱེད་རང་ཞལ་ལག་མཆོད་པས།
5. ང་ཡི་གེ་འབྲི་དགོས་ཡོད།
6. ཁོང་གིས་ཕྱག་བྲིས་གནང་པ་རེད།
7. ཁོང་སློབ་སྦྱོང་བྱེད་ཀྱི་འདུག
8. ཁྱེད་རང་ལས་ཀ་བྱེད་ཀྱི་ཡོད་པས།
9. ངས་སྐད་ཆ་བཤད་པ་ཡིན།
10. ང་ཚོས་སློབ་སྦྱོང་བྱས་པ་ཡིན།
11. ཁོང་གིས་བསམ་བློ་བཏང་པ་རེད།
12. ཁྱེད་རང་གིས་དགོངས་པ་བཞེས་རོགས་གནང་།

(b) 1. ང་འགྲོ་གི་ཡིན།
2. ཁོང་ཕེབས་ཀྱི་འདུག
3. ཁོང་ཚོ་སླེབས་སོང་།
4. ཁྱེད་རང་གིས་བྱས་པ་རེད།
5. ང་ཚོ་ཡོང་གི་ཡིན།
6. ཁོང་ཚོས་དེ་ཁྱེད་རང་ལ་འབུལ་གྱི་རེད།

7. དེ་ཁོང་ཚོས་ངར་སྤྲད་བྱུང་།
8. ངས་དེ་འདྲས་བྱེད་ཀྱི་མ་རེད།
9. འདིར་ཁོང་ཕེབས་ཀྱིས།
10. ཁོང་གསོལ་ཇ་མཆོད་ཀྱི་འདུག
11. ང་ཁ་ལག་ཟ་གི་ཡོད།
12. ཁྱེད་རང་ཕེབས་པས།
13. ཁྱེད་རང་འདིར་ཕྱག་ལས་གནང་གས།
14. ཁོང་ཕེབས་ཀྱི་འདུག་གས།
15. ཁོང་ཚོ་སློབ་གྲྭར་འགྲོ་གི་འདུག་གས།
16. ཁོང་ཚོ་ཡོང་གི་འདུག་གས།
17. ང་ཡོང་ག / ང་བཅར་ག
18. ཁྱེད་རང་འཛིན་གྲྭར་ཐེག་པས། / ཕེབས་པས།
19. ཁོང་འདིར་ཕེབས་ཀྱི་མི་འདུག་གས།

Exercise 11 page 106

(a)
1. ཁྱེད་རང་ལ་ག་རེ་དགོས་ན་ཡང་ངས་སྤྲད་ཀྱི་ཡིན།
2. ངས་ག་རེ་བྱས་ན་ཡང་ཁོང་དགའ་གི་མ་རེད།
3. ང་ཚོས་ག་རེ་ཟས་ན་ཡང་ཁོང་ཚོར་སྤྲོད་ཀྱི་ཡོད།
4. ངས་ག་རེ་ལབ་ན་ཡང་ཁོང་ཚོས་ཉན་གྱི་རེད།
5. འདིར་ག་རེ་བྲིས་ན་ཡང་འགྲིགས་ཀྱི་རེད།
6. ཁོང་ལ་ག་རེ་སྤྲད་ན་ཡང་དགའ་པོ་ཡོང་གི་རེད།
7. ཁོང་གིས་ག་རེ་མཐོང་ན་ཡང་ཉོ་གི་འདུག
8. ལྟད་མོ་ག་རེ་བསྟན་ན་ཡང་ང་ལྟ་གི་མེད།
9. ཁོང་གིས་ག་རེ་གོ་ན་ཡང་ང་ཚོར་བཤད་ཀྱི་རེད།
10. ཁོང་གིས་ག་རེ་དྲན་ན་ཡང་བྱེད་ཀྱི་རེད།

(b)
1. ཁྱེད་རང་གི་མཚན་ལ་ག་རེ་ཞུ་གི་ཡོད།
2. ཁོང་གི་མཚན་ལ་ག་རེ་ཞུ་གི་ཡོག་རེད།
3. ཁྱེད་རང་ག་རེ་གནང་གི་ཡོད།
4. ཁོང་ག་རེ་གནང་གི་རེད།

5. ཁོང་ལ་ག་རེ་ཡོག་རེད།
6. ཁྱེད་རང་ལ་ག་རེ་ཡོད།
7. མི་འདི་ག་རེ་རེད།
8. ཁོང་གི་ལས་ཀ་ག་རེ་རེད།
9. ཁོང་ཚོར་ག་རེ་འདུག
10. ཁྱེད་རང་གིས་ག་རེ་གནང་པས།
11. ད་ལྟ་ཁོང་ག་རེ་གནང་གི་ཡོག་རེད།
12. ཁྱེད་རང་ག་རེ་མཆོད་ག
13. ཁྱེད་རང་ག་རེ་མཆོད་ཀྱི་ཡོད།
14. འདི་ག་རེ་བྱེད་ཡག་རེད།
15. ཁྱེད་རང་ལ་ག་རེ་དགོས་འདུག

Exercise 12 page 113

(a)
1. ཁྱེད་རང་འདིར་ག་དུས་ཕེབས་ག
2. ཁོང་ག་དུས་ཡོང་གི་འདུག
3. འཛོན་གྲྭ་ག་དུས་འགོ་ཚུགས་ཀྱི་རེད།
4. ཁྱེད་རང་ལས་ཀར་ག་དུས་འགྲོ་གི་ཡོད།
5. ཁོང་འདིར་ཡོད་དུས་ངས་འདི་ལབ་པ་ཡིན།
6. ཁོང་རྒྱ་གར་ལ་ཡོད་དུས་ངར་མཇལ་བྱུང་།
7. ང་ཆུང་ཆུང་ཡིན་དུས་བོད་ལ་འགྲོ་མྱོང་།

(b)
1. ཁྱེད་རང་ག་དུས་ཕེབས་ཀྱང་/ ན་ཡང་ངར་གསུངས་རོགས་གནང་།
2. ལས་ཀ་འདི་ག་དུས་བྱས་ཀྱང་/ ན་ཡང་འགྲིགས་ཀྱི་རེད།
3. ང་ག་དུས་ཕྱིན་ཀྱང་/ ན་ཡང་ཁོང་སྡོད་ཀྱི་མི་འདུག
4. ཁོང་གིས་ག་དུས་ཀྱང་/ ཡིན་ན་ཡང་དེ་འདྲས་བྱེད་ཀྱི་མ་རེད།
5. ཁོང་ག་དུས་ཀྱང་/ ཡིན་ན་ཡང་འདིར་ཕེབས་ཀྱི་མ་རེད།
6. ངས་ག་དུས་ཡིན་ཡང་/ ན་ཡང་འདི་འདྲས་བྱེད་ཀྱི་མེད།

(c) 1. ཁྱེད་རང་ཁྲོམ་ལ་ག་དུས་འགྲོ་ག

2. ཁྱེད་རང་ག་དུས་ཕྱིན་པ་ཡིན།

3. ང་ག་དུས་ཕྱིན་ག

4. ཁོང་ག་དུས་ཕྱིན་པ་རེད།

5. ང་ཚོ་ག་དུས་འགྲོ་ག/ འགྲོ་གི་ཡིན་པ།

(d) 1. I wrote this book when I was in India.

2. He was not here when the train arrived.

3. If the train had arrived on time, we would not have been late.

Exercise 13

page 122

(a) 1. Which is your book?

2. Which book is yours?

3. Which is your house?

4. Which camera did he spoil?

5. With which pen was this letter written?

6. The watch I bought is not working.

7. In which room will he stay?

8. In which room shall we stay?

9. Which man caused the trouble?

(b) 1. ཁྱེད་རང་ཧ་ག་གིས་གཡུགས་བྱུང་།

2. ཁྱེད་རང་ལ་ཁྱི་ག་གིས་སོ་བརྒྱབ་བྱུང་།

3. ཀང་པ་ག་གིས་པོ་ལོར་གནོད་རྒྱག་ཞུས་པ་རེད།

4. བུ་ག་གིས་རྟོག་ཁྲ་བཟོས་པ་རེད།

5. ཁྱེད་རང་སློབ་གྲྭ་ག་གིར་སློབ་སྦྱོང་བྱས་པ་ཡིན།

6. འདི་འཛིན་གྲྭ་ག་གི་རེད།

7. ག་གི་ཁྱེད་རང་གི་འཛིན་གྲྭའི་དགེ་རྒན་རེད།

8. ཁྱེད་རང་གིས་ངར་བསྣམས་ཕེབས་པའི་ཆུ་ཚོད་དེ་ཡག་པོ་ཞེ་དྲག་འདུག

Exercise 14 page 130

(a) 1. ཁྱེད་རང་ག་པར་ཕེབས་པ།

2. ཁྱེད་རང་ག་པར་ཐེག་ག / ཐེག་གི་ཡོད།

3. ཁོང་ག་པར་འགྲོ་གི་རེད།/ འགྲོ་གི་འདུག

4. ཁྱེད་རང་གི་སྐུ་ཟླ་ག་པར་ཡོད།

5. ཁོང་ཚོ་ག་པར་ཕྱིན་པ་རེད།

6. བོད་ཀྱི་དཔེ་མཛོད་ཁང་ག་པར་ཡོག་རེད།

7. ཁོང་ཚོ་ག་པར་བཞུགས་ཀྱི་ཡོག་རེད།

8. ཁོང་གིས་འདི་ག་པར་བྱེད་ཐུབ་ཀྱི་རེད།

9. པུ་གུས་འདི་ག་པར་ཤེས་ཐུབ་ཀྱི་རེད།

10. ང་ག་པར་ཕྱིན་ན་ཡང་འདི་མཉམ་དུ་འཁྱེར་འགྲོ་གི་ཡོད།

(b) 1. Wherever he goes, this dog will go.

2. Will you come, wherever I go?

3. I have been everywhere.

4. Yesterday I went everywhere.

5. This boy will go wherever he is sent.

6. Although he has, he says he doesn't.

7. Although he was not there he was said to have been there.

Exercise 15 page 135

(a) 1. ཁོང་ཚོ་ག་ནས་རེད།

2. ཁོང་ཚོ་ག་ནས་ཡིན་ངས་ཤེས་ཀྱི་མེད།

3. ཁྱེད་རང་ག་ནས་ཡིན་པ།

4. ང་བོད་ནས་ཡིན།

5. ཁོང་ལུང་པ་ག་ནས་རེད།

6. ཁོང་ཡང་བོད་ནས་རེད།

7. ཁོང་ཚོ་ག་ནས་ཡོང་བ་རེད།
8. ཁོང་ཚོ་ཨ་མི་རི་ཀ་ནས་ཡོང་པ་རེད།
9. ང་ག་ནས་རེད།
10. ཁྱེད་རང་བོད་ནས་རེད།

(b) 1. Where did the rain originate from?
2. The rain originated from the ocean.
3. Where did the egg come from?
4. The egg came from a hen.
5. Where do you come from now?
6. I came from home just now.
7. Where did he get this from?

Exercise 16

page 141

1. སྨྱུ་གུ་འདིར་གོང་ག་ཚད་རེད།
2. ཨུ་སུ་ཆ་གཅིག་ལ་གོང་ག་ཚད་རེད།
3. ཁོང་ལ་ཚིགས་ཁེབས་འདི་འདྲས་ག་ཚད་འདུག
4. སློབ་གྲྭ་ཕ་གིའི་ནང་ལ་བུ་མོ་ག་ཚད་ཡོག་རེད།
5. ད་ལྟ་ཆུ་ཚོད་ག་ཚད་རེད།
6. དེ་རིང་ཚེས་པ་ག་ཚད་རེད།
7. ཁྱེད་རང་ལ་ཕྱུག་དངུལ་ག་ཚད་ཡོད།
8. སློབ་ཕྲུག་རེ་ལ་ག་ཚད་རག་གི་རེད།
9. ཁྱེད་རང་འདི་ཆུ་ཚོད་ག་ཚད་ལ་འགོ་འཛུགས་ཀྱི་ཡིན།
10. ཁྱེད་རང་ཆུ་ཚོད་ག་ཚད་ལ་འཛིན་གྲྭར་ཕེབས་ཀྱི་ཡོད།
11. འདི་ཉི་མ་ག་ཚད་ཀྱི་ལས་ཀ་རེད།
12. འདིར་གོང་ག་ཚད་རེད།
13. ངས་ཁོང་ལ་ག་ཚད་སྤྲད་པ་ཡིན་དྲན་གྱི་མི་འདུག
14. ཁྱེད་རང་ལ་ཕྱུག་དངུལ་ག་ཚད་དགོས་ཀྱི་འདུག

Exercise 17 — page 149

(a) 1. ཁོང་ཕ་གིར་ག་རེ་བྱས་ནས་ཐེག་པ་རེད།

2. ཁོང་ག་རེ་བྱས་ནས་མ་ཡོང་བ་རེད།

3. ཁོང་ཚོ་ཕ་གིར་ག་རེ་བྱས་ནས་འགྲོ་ཆོག་གི་ཡོག་མ་རེད།

4. ཁྱེད་རང་གིས་འདི་ག་རེའི་དོན་དག་ལ་བྱས་པ་ཡིན།

5. ཁོང་ག་འདྲས་སེ་ཡོང་པ་རེད།

6. ཁོང་གིས་འདི་ག་འདྲས་སེ་བཟོ་གི་རེད།

7. འདི་ག་འདྲས་སེ་བེད་སྤྱོད་བྱེད་དགོས་རེད།

8. ཁོང་ལ་དཔར་ཆས་ག་འདྲས་ཅི་ཡོག་རེད།

9. ཁོང་མི་ག་འདྲས་ཅི་ཡིན་ཁྱེད་རང་གིས་མཁྱེན་གྱི་ཡོད་པས།

10. ཁྱེད་རང་གི་ཨ་བ་ག་འདྲས་ཡོད།

(b) 1. Why is he taking all?

2. How did you tell him?

3. What kind of a person is that man?

4. How did (you) get this from him?

5. Why is it not possible?

6. For what purpose did (he) take this?

7. For what purpose? / Why?

8. Then, what should be done?/ So what?

Exercise 18 — page 159

(a) 1. ཁྱེད་རང་སུ་ཡིན་པ།

2. ཁོང་སུ་རེད།

3. ང་སུ་རེད།

4. ཁྱེད་རང་མཉམ་དུ་ཡོང་མཁན་བུ་མོ་དེ་སུ་རེད།

5. ཁྱེད་རང་ལ་བཀའ་མོལ་ཞུ་མཁན་མི་དེ་སུ་རེད།

6. འདི་སུས་བྱས་པ་རེད།

7. འདི་སུ་གང་གིས་བྱེད་ཐུབ་ཀྱི་མ་རེད།
8. འདིའི་སྐོར་ལ་སུ་གང་གིས་ཤེས་ཀྱི་ཡོག་མ་རེད།
9. དེ་སུས་བྱས་པ་ཡིན་ཁྱེད་རང་གིས་མཁྱེན་གྱི་ཡོད་པས།
10. སུས་ཤེས་ཀྱི་རེད།
11. འདི་སུས་ཀྱང་བེད་སྤྱོད་བྱས་ཚོག་གི་རེད།
12. འདི་སུའི་སྐུ་གུ་རེད།
13. ཁྱེད་རང་གིས་སུར་བཀའ་འདྲི་གནང་པ།
14. ཁྱེད་རང་སུར་བཀའ་མོལ་གནང་དགོས་ཡོད།
15. ངས་སུར་བཀའ་མོལ་ཞུ་དགོས་རེད།

(b) 1. Who shall I speak to?
2. Who said this?
3. Whose mistake is this?

Exercise 19 page 165

(a) 1. ང་ཚོ་དེབ་ཀློག་ག་འགྲོ་གི་ཡིན།
2. ང་ཡི་གེ་འབྲི་ག་འགྲོ་གི་ཡིན།
3. ང་ཁོང་ལ་སྐད་ཆ་ཤོད་ག་འགྲོ་གི་ཡིན།
4. ཁོང་ཆུ་ལེན་ག་འགྲོ་གི་རེད།
5. ཁོང་ང་ཐུག་ག་སླེབས་བྱུང་།
6. ཁྱེད་རང་ཚལ་གཟིགས་ག་ཐེག་གི་ཡིན་པས།
7. ད་ང་ཁ་ལག་བཟོ་ག་འགྲོ་གི་ཡིན།

(b) 1. ང་བོད་པའི་ཁ་ལག་བཟོ་སྟངས་བསླབ་ཀྱི་ཡིན།
2. ང་སྣུམ་འཁོར་གཏོང་སྟངས་བསླབས་ཚར་པ་ཡིན།
3. ཁོང་དེང་སང་གནམ་གྲུ་གཏོང་སྟངས་སྦྱོང་གི་ཡོག་རེད།
4. ངས་འཚེམ་བུ་རྒྱག་སྟངས་ཡག་པོ་ཤེས་ཀྱི་ཡོད།
5. བོད་སྐད་བསླབ་ཡག་ལས་སླ་པོ་རེད།
6. ཁོང་ཁ་ལག་བཟོ་ཡག་བསླབ་ག་ཕྱིན་པ་རེད།
7. བོད་པའི་ཞལ་ལག་བཟོ་སྟངས་མཁྱེན་གྱི་ཡོད་པས།

8. ང་ཉིན་ལྷར་བོད་ཡིག་བསླབ་ག་འགྲོ་གི་ཡོད།
9. ཁོང་ཚོ་གཟའ་ཉི་མར་ཉ་ཟིན་ག་ཕྱིན་ཤག

Exercise 20 page 168

(a) 1. ཁྱིས་ཁོ་སྒོ་འགྲམ་ལ་བཀག་པ་རེད།
2. གངས་བབས་ནས་ལམ་ཁ་བཀག་པ་རེད།
3. ངས་ཁོང་ཐེངས་གཉིས་དབྲུལ་པ་ཡིན།
4. ཕྲུ་གུ་འདིས་ངའི་སྨྱུ་གུ་བཅག་ཤག
5. ང་འཁྱག་པ་སྟེང་ལ་ཐེངས་གཉིས་རིལ་བྱུང་།
6. རྐུབ་ཀྱག་འདིའི་རྐང་པ་ཡ་གཅིག་ཆག་ཤག
7. ཁོང་ཚོས་སངས་རྒྱས་ཀྱི་བསྟན་པ་བསྒྱུབས་པ་རེད།
8. ལུགས་སྲོལ་འདི་མགྱོགས་པོ་ནུབ་ཀྱི་རེད།
9. མི་འདིས་ང་ཁོང་ཁྲོ་བསླངས་བྱུང་།
10. ཁོང་དོན་དག་མེད་པར་ཁོང་ཁྲོ་ལངས་སོང་།
11. ཁོང་གིས་ངར་ཆུ་གཏོར་གྱི་འདུག
12. འདིར་བསྡད་ན་ཆུ་འཁོར་གྱི་རེད།
13. ཁོང་གིས་ཤིང་ག་ཤག་གི་རེད།
14. ཤིང་འདི་མགྱོགས་པོ་གཞག་གི་རེད།
15. ཁོང་གིས་དུག་སློག་ཚང་མ་ཆུའི་ནང་ལ་སྤྲངས་ཚར་ཤག
16. ངའི་དུག་སློག་ཆར་པས་ཐད་དེ་བངས་སོང་།

The translations of above sentences

1. The dog stopped him at the door.
2. After the snowfall the road was blocked.
3. I knocked him twice.
4. This child broke my pen.
5. I fell twice on the ice.
6. One leg of this chair is broken.

7. They destroyed the Buddha doctrine.
8. This custom will degenerate soon.
9. This man made me angry.
10. He got angry without reason.
11. He sprinkles water at me.
12. (You) will get swashed if (you) stay here.
13. He will split the wood.
14. This wood will crack quickly.
15. He has already soaked all the clothes in the water.
16. My clothes are completely soaked by the rain.

(b) 1. ངས་གསར་འགྱུར་ཉན་གྱི་ཡོད།

2. ངས་གསར་འགྱུར་གོ་གི་འདུག

3. ངས་འདི་གོ་བྱུང་།

4. བུ་གུ་རེས་ངའི་དེབ་དབྲལ་སོང་།

5. ངས་ཞིང་སྟོང་མང་པོ་བཅད་པ་ཡིན།

6. ངས་དེའི་སྐོར་ལ་བསམ་བློ་གཏོང་གི་ཡོད།

7. འདིར་མི་མང་པོ་རིལ་གྱི་འདུག

8. ང་དེའི་ཐོག་ལ་འཁྲོད་པ་ཞེ་དྲག་སྐྱེས་བྱུང་།

9. ང་སྐྲུག་མེར་ལངས་ཀྱི་འདུག

10. ང་འཁྲུག་གི་འདུག

11. ང་ཚ་དབུ་འཚིག་གི་འདུག

12. ཁོང་ཐད་དེ་འཐོམས་སོང་།

13. དེང་སང་ང་ཞེ་དྲག་ཉོབ་ཀྱི་འདུག

14. སྐབས་རེ་ང་མགོ་ཡུར་འཁོར་གྱི་འདུག

15. མཚོ་འདིའི་ནང་ལ་མི་གཅིག་ཐིམས་པ་རེད།

16. ད་ང་དྲོད་ཁུག་ཡོང་གི་འདུག

17. ང་གད་མོ་ཞེ་དྲག་ཤོར་གྱི་འདུག

18. ཆུ་འདི་འཁོལ་གྱི་འདུག
19. ཁོང་གིས་ངར་ཁོང་ཁྲོ་ཞེ་དྲག་བསྣངས་བྱུང་།
20. ཁྱེད་རང་གི་བོད་སྐད་ཡར་རྒྱས་འགྲོ་གི་འདུག

Exercise 21 page 176

(a)

1. We got all.
2. Did you get (it)?
3. He got (it).
4. Then, what happened?
5. What happened to him?
6. What happened to you?
7. We saw everything.
8. I heard this news yesterday.
9. They gave this to me.
10. He taught me this.

(b)

1. ཁོང་གིས་ང་མཉམ་དུ་འཁྲིད་བྱུང་།
2. ཁོས་ང་ཁ་ས་ཉེས་བྱུང་།
3. ངར་དངུལ་ཁང་ནས་དངུལ་རག་མ་བྱུང་།
4. ཁྱེད་རང་ལ་དེབ་རག་བྱུང་ངས།
5. ཁྱེད་རང་གིས་མི་དེ་མཐོང་བྱུང་ངས།
6. ཁོས་ཁྱེད་རང་ལ་ཐུབ་ཚོད་བཏང་བྱུང་ངས།
7. ཁོང་གིས་ཁྱེད་རང་ལ་གཤེ་གཤེ་བཏང་བྱུང་ངས།
8. མི་འདི་ཚོར་ག་རེ་བྱས་པ་རེད།
9. ཁྱེད་རང་གནང་དགོང་འཁྱག་བྱུང་ངས།
10. ལགས་མ་བྱུང་། ང་ཁྱོན་ནས་འཁྱག་མ་བྱུང་།

Exercise 22 page 184

(a) Memorise 1 - 20

chig	n̄ȳi	sum	s̲h̲i	n̄ḡa
t̲'u꞉	dü;n	gyä꞉	gu	chu
chug-chi꞉	chu;ng-n̄ȳi꞉	chug-sum	chüb-s̲h̲i	chö:-n̄ḡa
chu-t̲'u꞉	chub-dü;n	chob-gyä꞉	chu-gu	nyi-shu

(b) Memorise

chig	chu	gya	to;ng	ṭ'i
bum	sa-ya	c̲h̲'e-wa:	t̲'u;ng-ch'ur	

(c)

བཅུ་གཉིས།	བཅུ། བཅོ་ལྔ།	ཉི་ཤུ་རྩ་གསུམ།
སུམ་ཅུ་སོ་ལྔ་།	བཞི་བཅུ་ཞེ་བདུན།	ལྔ་བཅུ་ང་ལྔ་།
དྲུག་ཅུ་རེ་བཞི།	བདུན་ཅུ་དོན་བདུན།	བརྒྱད་ཅུ་གྱ་ལྔ་།
དགུ་བཅུ་གོ་དགུ	བརྒྱ་ཐམ་པ།	བརྒྱ་དང་ལྔ་།
ཉིས་བརྒྱ་ལྔ་།	ཆིག་སྟོང་ཐམ་པ།	སྟོང་ཕྲག་གཅིག

(d)

1.	༢༥༦	ཉིས་བརྒྱ་ལྔ་བཅུ་ང་དྲུག
2.	༢༥༥༩	ཉིས་སྟོང་ལྔ་བརྒྱ་ལྔ་བཅུ་ང་དགུ
3.	༡༤༣༣༤	ཆིག་ཁྲི་བཞི་སྟོང་སུམ་བརྒྱ་སུམ་ཅུ་སོ་བཞི།
4.	༡༥༦༥༥༦	ཆིག་འབུམ་ལྔ་ཁྲི་དྲུག་སྟོང་ལྔ་བརྒྱ་ལྔ་བཅུ་ང་དྲུག
5.	༡༥༥༠༦	ཆིག་ཁྲི་ལྔ་སྟོང་ལྔ་བརྒྱ་(བཅུ་མེད་)དྲུག
6.	༢༥༡༨	ཉིས་སྟོང་ལྔ་བརྒྱ་བཅོ་བརྒྱད།

དགེ་ལེགས་འཕེལ།།